D1169315

ARAB-AMERICAN FACES AND VOICES

ARAB-AMERICAN FACES AND VOICES
The Origins of an Immigrant Community

Elizabeth Boosahda

 UNIVERSITY OF TEXAS PRESS, AUSTIN

First edition, 2003

Requests for permission to reproduce material from
this work should be sent to Permissions, University
of Texas Press, Box 7819, Austin, TX 78713-7819.

⊗ The paper used in this book meets the minimum
requirements of ANSI/NISO Z39.48-1992 (R1997)
(Permanence of Paper).

Library of Congress Cataloging-in-Publication-Data

Boosahda, Elizabeth, 1926–
Arab-American faces and voices : the origins of an
immigrant community / Elizabeth Boosahda.—
1st ed.
    p.   cm.
Includes bibliographical references and index.
ISBN 0-292-70919-6 (alk. paper) —
ISBN 0-292-70920-X (pbk. : alk. paper)
1. Arab Americans—Massachusetts—Worcester—
History. 2. Arab Americans—Massachusetts—
Worcester—History—Sources. 3. Arab
Americans—Massachusetts—Worcester—Interviews.
4. Immigrants—Massachusetts—Worcester—
History. 5. Immigrants—Massachusetts—
Worcester—History—Sources. 6. Worcester
(Mass.)—Ethnic relations. 7. Arabs—Migrations—
History. 8. Arab countries—Emigration and
immigration—History. 9. United States—
Emigration and immigration—History. 10. Latin
America—Emigration and immigration—History.
I. Title.
F74.W9 B67   2003
974.4′3—dc21   2002015039

To my father, Kalil, a kind and gentle person who preferred silence to mind-less conversation and characterization; my mother, Nazira, a loving, strong-willed, and in-charge person; and my immigrant aunts and uncles who also favorably influenced my life.

And to my brothers, Michael K. Boosahda and Leo S. Boosahda, who are always there for me.

Kalil A. Boosahda, 1985.
(Deceased 1987, aged 97.)

Marriage, Kalil A. Boosahda to Nazira Mishalanie, 1916.

All of us are born for a reason, but all of us don't discover why. Success in life has nothing to do with what you gain in life or accomplish for yourself. It's what you do for others. Blessed is he who knows why he was born.

DANNY THOMAS, 1989. Founder of American Lebanese Syrian Associated Charities/Aid to Leukemia Stricken American Children (ALSAC) and St. Jude Children's Research Hospital, Memphis, Tennessee.

Our early immigrant history in America could be lost forever if my generation [the first American-born] fails to pass on its treasury of memories. We must write our own history and have the history accurate, in all its complexity.

LILLIAN GEORGE SHOUCAIR, 1988. Humanist, active in the preservation of ethnic heritage and immigrant history, and daughter of Simon George and daughter-in-law of Said Shoucair.

CONTENTS

Preface · xii
Acknowledgments · xv
Methodology: Data Collection · xviii

1. HISTORICAL BACKGROUND · 1

2. MIGRATION · 17

3. MULTICULTURAL AND MULTIRELIGIOUS
   NEIGHBORHOODS · 49

4. WORK · 65

5. TRADITION, EDUCATION, AND CULTURE · 91

6. AMERICANIZATION · 131

7. LEGACY AND LINKAGE · 171

Addendum I. Private-Sector Organizations · 197
   A. Syrian Brotherhood Orthodox Society, 1905 · 197
   B. Young Mahiethett Society, 1916 · 200
Addendum II. The Middle East and the Arab World
      after World War II · 204
Genealogy: Expanded Kinship in One Family · 207
Timeline: Eastern Orthodox Syrian Church · 211
Notes · 222
Bibliography · 244
Illustration Credits · 248
Annotated Suggested Reading · 249
Organizations, Collections, and Exhibits · 260
Author Biography · 267
Index of Arabic Terms · 268
General Index · 270

ILLUSTRATIONS

Kalil A. Boosahda, 1985   v

Marriage, Kalil A. Boosahda to Nazira Mishalanie, 1916   v

2.1   Abdelnour family of Kfarchima (now Lebanon), 1900   41

2.2   Inspection card, 1908   41

2.3   Second migration, 1900   42

2.4   Hand embosser and seal of Rev. Michael M. Husson, Syrian Orthodox Church of Worcester, 1899   42

2.5   Consecration of first Syrian Antiochian Bishop of New York and all North America, Worcester, Mass., 1924   43

2.6   Hand embosser and seal of Syrian Brotherhood Orthodox Society, 1905   43

2.7   Lapel badges of the Orthodox Brotherhood Society, 1905, and Young Mahiethett Society, 1916; lapel medal "1905–19, S.B.O.S." (Syrian Brotherhood Orthodox Society)   44

2.8   Reversible sides of lapel badges, 1905, 1916   44

2.9   Members of Syrian Brotherhood Orthodox Society, 1919   45

2.10 Moslem [Muslim] Brotherhood Association of Worcester, Mass., obelisk-shaped monument, front, 1918   46

2.11 Moslem [Muslim] Brotherhood monument, back   46

2.12 Realia montage of organizations, about 1905–54   47

2.13 Realia montage of institution and organizations, about 1917–36   48

2.14 Seal of the Myrra-Bearing Women Society of St. George Orthodox Church of Worcester, 1919   48

3.1   Union Passenger Railroad Station, Worcester, Mass., about 1893   60

3.2   Residential eight-family double house built about 1896   61

3.3   Rectory and church, built 1891–92   61

3.4   Flashback to a used-to-be neighborhood, the west side of el-saha, about 1880–1905   62

3.5 Flashback to a used-to-be neighborhood, the east side of *el-saha*, about 1880–1905 63

3.6 Grafton Street view of "1901 S. George" commercial-residential double house (5½ stories with basement) 64

3.7 Wall Street view of "1901 S. George" double house 64

4.1 Peddling with *kushee* (a box, trunk, or suitcase to carry dry goods and notions) and burlap shoulder satchel, 1898 88

4.2 Peddling by horse and buggy, 1913 88

4.3 On the road showing merchandise, 1913 89

4.4 Two-horse team and driver, about 1915 89

4.5 Journalists and publishers, about 1918 90

5.1 Rev. Michael M. Husson, about 1900 117

5.2 Certificate of baptism, 1916 117

5.3 "Suitable wife," Sophia, 1913 118

5.4 Photograph postal card from suitor in Lebanon, 1919 118

5.5 Marriage, Simon George and Sooriya, 1897 119

5.6 Wedding gift and recording, about 1916 119

5.7 Marriage, Elias F. Haddad (aged 25 years) and Isabella Ashkar (aged 21), 1901 120

5.8 Contemplative bride, 1917 120

5.9 Marriage by bishop, 1926 121

5.10 In vogue, woman's dress, about 1916 122

5.11 In vogue, man's clothing, about 1916 122

5.12 In vogue, four women and child, about 1918 123

5.13 In vogue, Assafe George and Elias Dahrooge families, 1908 123

5.14 In vogue, woman's encasement—the "wasp" waist, 1909 124

5.15 Abisamra family, 1904 124

5.16 Realia montage, 1883–1922 125

5.17–5.23 Children, about 1915–27 126–128

5.24 Cast of *Salah El-Deen*, 1924 129

5.25 Pages from program booklets of *Salah El-Deen* and *Haroun El-Rashad*, 1924 and 1925 respectively 130

5.26 Cast of *Princess Venus of England*, 1932 130

6.1–6.5 "Love Your Country," U.S. servicemen of World War I, 1917–18 161–163

6.6 Participants at military funeral, World War I, 1919 163

6.7 American cuisine cooking class at Friendly House, 1923 164

6.8 Practicing at Friendly House for the city's snaps tournament, about 1935 164

6.9   American Red Cross class at Friendly House, 1928   165
6.10 Members of Drum and Fife and Bugle Corps, about 1923   166
6.11 Members of Syrian American Drum Corps, 1941   166
6.12 Prize-winning float by Syrian American Association for
      Tercentenary Massachusetts Celebration parade, 1930   167
6.13 Seated on parapet of tower, 1931   167
6.14 Festival of Nationalities, Arab folk line dance (the *dabkah*),
      1958   168
6.15 Arab music played by Arab and non-Arab musicians, 1958   168
6.16 Duo Arab dance by old and young, Arab American and non–Arab
      American, late 1950s   169
6.17 Arab culture portrayed through music and dance, 1973   169
6.18 Worcester woman knighted by church, Brooklyn, N.Y., 1951   170
6.19 Testimonial honored Mrs. Constantine Abou-Adal, wife of
      Archpriest Abou-Adal, about 1955   170
7.1   Arab foods great for nutritious snacks, 1972   192
7.2   Resourceful family, 1917   192
7.3   Celebrated 106th birthday, 1988   193
7.4   Bodybuilding, 1918   193
7.5   All-Girl Orchestra, 1940s   194
7.6   "This great hill," section of *el-tellee* and The Meadows, 1988   194
7.7   "Love Your Church," ecumenism continues, 1975   195
7.8   "Love One Another," first American-born generation, 1994   196
      Timeline.1 Mausoleum, Archbishop Victor Aboassaly, 1934
      (photo taken winter 1945)   217

MAPS

1. Arab Empire at Greatest Expansion, 700–850 C.E.   9
2. Ottoman Empire, Seventeenth Century C.E.   9
3. Lebanon: Where the Journey Began   10
4. Mandate Powers under Auspices of League of Nations, 1922   12
5. Landownership in Section of *El-Tellee*, Worcester, Massachusetts, 1922 and Earlier   13

PREFACE

The time is right for sharing thoughts about "my people"—Americans of Arab ancestry—the Lebanese, a few Syrians, and fewer Palestinians, predominantly Christian, but a few Druze (a sect in Islam named after Ismail al-Darazi, a religious leader who died in 1019) and fewer Muslim. From 1880 to 1915 they emigrated in small numbers from the Ottoman Empire provinces of Syria and Palestine at the eastern Mediterranean Sea area. Many migrated to North and South America, and the majority settled in New England. Nearly 200 immigrants and a few members of immigrant families told their stories to the author in taped, face-to-face interviews; pre-1920 photographs, most of them from the homes of those interviewed, and documents contemporaneous with their stories give a profile of the daily lives of the immigrants.

This research developed into a study of the origins and history of Arab-American communities in North and South America that had roots or links to New England and in particular to Worcester, Massachusetts, a major city in the Northeast where large Arab-American communities were established. Their affinities and patterns of migration and integration into American society usually paralleled those of their counterparts in other Arabic-speaking communities in both North America and South America. Generally, they maintained their Arab culture through food and its presentation, the Arabic language, religion (Christianity and Islam), dance, music, literature, philosophy, poetry, and storytelling. Some enterprising individuals lived and conducted businesses in South America and maintained their New England addresses and businesses that often were operated by the wives.

This book is an effort to document the history of the early immigrants before they die, taking with them firsthand knowledge of their immigrant experience, and to use primary sources before they are lost. The immigrants' anecdotes, told by their eyes as well as their voices, are heartwarming and entertaining and make for enlightened reading. Documenting their history is both a tribute to their resourcefulness, determination, and courage and an attempt to bring into clearer focus the multicultural history of the Americas. Their story provides a long-needed addition to what is known or not known, uncovered themes that have not been addressed in the inadequate material that is available about the Arabs and especially about Arab Americans. It makes an important and significant contribution to a little-understood and underreported subject.

Their experiences as related in this book challenge numerous long-held myths and stereotypes about Arabs, Arab Americans, the economic success of Arab women, and the entrepreneurship of Arab men. While most Arab migrants were males, the adventurous Arab woman—a widow accompanied by a child or children, or a single woman—was often first in the family to emigrate. Her initial occupation was frequently as a cook or door-to-door saleswoman (peddler) of dry goods to different ethnic groups who lived in nearby towns and out of state. Arabs referred to in this text generally emigrated for adventure and wealth.

Additionally, the research points to a support system that came about as a result of the interdependency of ethnic minorities and the advocacy of concerned members of the majority group.

Chapters 1 through 4 describe events in the everyday life of the immigrant who arrived from 1880 to 1915. Chapters 5, 6, and 7 cover the years 1880 to 1989. Included are contributions to their adopted country, a legacy to their descendants, and the achievements of some of these immigrants and their descendants. The customs described generally followed the same traditional pattern for both the Christian Arab American and Muslim Arab American. For example, in chapter 5 the type of cordiality described under "Gracious Living and Hospitality" was still experienced in Arab-American homes as late as the early 1980s. However, one custom that differed was the religious marriage ceremony celebrated by Christian Arab Americans. Historical dramas in Arabic were performed until the mid-1930s, when Arabic films rented from New York replaced them. These films were shown in the downtown Little Theatre adjoining the Worcester Memorial Auditorium (now Worcester AUD) until the early 1950s.

Growing up as an American in a community of immigrants gave me firsthand insight and knowledge of traditions that I might not have gained otherwise. Although I was born and raised in an immigrant Arabic-speaking community, I took for granted the many ways its members integrated into mainstream America. With age and experience, however, I realize how difficult, painful, and awe inspiring the process of integration was. I am amazed at the abundance of resources and survival skills of these vision-aries as they coped with their new environment. I am proud of my birth as an American and of my cultural Arab heritage. The experiences of these immigrants is a reminder to us and those who come after us, of people, places, and events that helped shape this great country of ours at a special time in history. The importance and timeliness of this book is accentuated by the Middle East situation. I would like this study to be an offering to my people, the Arab Americans, to all immigrants, and scholars interested in migration and adaptation to American life. May it serve as a living library of memories and traditions and encourage the reader to study Arab history more deeply.

ACKNOWLEDGMENTS

By telling and retelling our Arab-American story, we reclaim the authorship of our own history. I completed this book with the cooperative and collective help of more people than can be named here. Each of them knows who he or she is and to each of them, many thanks. However, I am particularly indebted to those early immigrants who opened their homes and gave their gifts of living voices, shared primary resource material, in particular their bountiful visual legacy of cherished photographs from which themes emerged, and other realia that enabled me to write my book.

I am eternally grateful to my friend Evelyn Abdalah Menconi, who shares my belief in the importance of historical documentation, for her invaluable ongoing assistance, moral support, and outstanding contribution toward this work from its inception to completion. She helped make it the best it can be. Mrs. Menconi is the recipient of many community service awards.

I should also like to thank Alixa Naff, an important resource person, who in the early planning of this project along with others gave me her time and direction. Additionally I was inspired by the Naff Arab American Collection at the Smithsonian Institution's National Museum of American History.

With gratitude I acknowledge the encouragement given me at the beginning of this project by Kenneth J. Moynihan, Janet K. McCorison of Worcester Heritage Preservation Society (now Preservation Worcester), and Abraham W. Haddad.

I am grateful to Carol A. Lavallee, who typed transcripts of the early taped interviews with devotion and skill.

Special thanks to Walter B. Denny for a meaningful critique and crucial insights regarding the early draft. With appreciation I acknowledge the commentary and critique of parts of an early version by Eleanor Abdella Doumato and Michael W. Suleiman. Appreciation is acknowledged for assistance with constructive comments received at the early stages of this project from Nancy A. McBride, Elaine C. Hagopian, and Naseer H. Aruri; and for ongoing important periodic comments by Barbara C. Aswad, Carolyn Fluehr-Lobban, and Elizabeth Fernea.

In the final stages of preparation for the publication of this manuscript, I would like to thank Carol Johnson Shedd for her valuable assistance.

I would also like to thank the institutions and their staff who provided information and materials I needed, in particular, the Worcester Public Library and its Telephone Reference service, Auburn Public Library, Gale Free Library (Holden, Mass.), Rev. Richard D. McGrail of the Catholic Free Press, Massachusetts Society of Genealogists (MASOG) Worcester Chapter, Stephen Trent Seames for the Massachusetts Military Division, Military Museum and Archives (Worcester, Mass.), Cyrus D. Lipsitt for the Worcester Employment Society (predecessor of Worcester Center for Crafts), Gordon P. Hargrove of Friendly House, and Higgins Armory Museum through its exhibits and lectures.

Over the years, I attended annual conferences that offered presentations on the Near East, Arab culture and history, and immigration; these were a source of inspiration and strength. Organizations that sponsored these conferences included American Research Center of Egypt (ARCE); Middle East Studies Association of North America (MESA); Association of Arab-American University Graduates (AAUG); American-Arab Anti-Discrimination Committee (ADC); Arab American Institute (AAI); Oral History Association (OHA); and Immigration History Research Center (IHRC) at the University of Minnesota.

The front cover is based on a design by Emily S. Boosahda.

Finally, my sincere thanks to all those unnamed others, too many to be named personally, who encouraged me to continue, who supplied ideas, and took the time to carry on useful discussions, thereby helping me through the completion of this book. The many participants, named and unnamed, gave me confidence to soar beyond my expectations.

DISCLAIMER

As author of this book I have the ultimate historical responsibility for its accuracy. It is based on research, primary-source oral interviews, and corroboration with numerous sources. To the best of my knowledge the content of this text is factual and true.

E. B.

METHODOLOGY
Data Collection

This anecdotal, sociohistorical documentation of an ethnic group that migrated to the United States from 1880 to 1915 was compiled from taped interviews by the author with nearly 200 people—usually naturalized Americans of Arab ancestry (Syrian, Lebanese, and Palestinian). Most of them were in their late eighties, many were in their nineties, and one was aged 106. Most of the interviews and the collection of data took place between mid-1987 and 1994. From 1991 to early 1999, I did research to corroborate my material. From 1996 to 1998, I traveled within New England, Michigan, and Canada to research further. My selection of interviewees was based upon their being old enough to remember the early period of immigration. They were living at home, though two were in nursing homes—physically weak but mentally alert. I also interviewed about ten children born between about 1902 and 1917 of immigrant parents and about six neighbors of either Italian, French, or Russian descent who also lived in these multicultural-multireligious neighborhoods. The interviews were conducted in person, and some were conducted over the telephone with people who had roots or links to New England and resided elsewhere, for example, Elizabeth A. F. of Spring Valley, Illinois, and Mary K. of Cornwall, Canada. Correspondence and telephone calls were carried on with various institutions, for example, the Orthodox Church in America, Department of History and Archives, Syosset, New York, and the American Baptist Historical Society, Rochester, New York, for information that related to the early Arab-American citizen.

To support the information in the interviews, I used a variety of materials, for example, archives, public records, official documents, Arabic and English printed matter, family records, memorabilia, and a collection of mostly vintage (pre-1920) illustrations. I preserved—unedited—the unaffected anecdotal styles and attitudes of the people I interviewed. This book is their story. We spoke English interspersed with colorful and meaningful Arabic phrases that are still used by many of their descendants. These social-history anecdotes allowed the voices of the immigrants to speak for themselves. From these I constructed a picture of the character, history, and development of the New England Arab-American community and its affinity to other Arab-American communities in North America and South America. At times, many narrators laughed at the comparison of their past to the present with its conveniences. Because of their humility, many were not forthcoming in discussing the many successful family business enterprises, nor did they dwell on family tragedies. Perhaps I failed as an interviewer in my attempts to draw out information about any negative experience or hardship. Or perhaps, on the other hand, their spirituality helped to give them a positive outlook on life and consequently sift out their misfortunes as expressed in an Arabian proverb titled *"Sadiq"* (Friend). The proverb refers to the gentlest of hands that takes and sifts the chaff from the grain and keeps what is worth keeping, and with a breath of kindness blows the rest away.

The interviews revealed what these early Americans of Arab ancestry thought about, how they spent their time, what mattered to them, what type buildings they lived in and what type they built, and how much they loved their adopted country. Their collective narratives reveal that it took courage and money to migrate. Those who eagerly took the road to the unknown soon discovered it was fraught with hardships and tragedies as well as enjoyment. To protect the privacy of the interviewee within the text, I generally use the person's first name and initial of the surname; however, for clarity I use the full name, as, for example, when initials are similar or when the same name is repeatedly used within the text. The full name is also used within the illustration legends and notes. The way in which a name appears in the book is no reflection of the person's status.

This study does not concentrate on the immigrants' dedication, devotion, hard work, and long hours to maintain the religious institutions or practices of the believers of either Christianity or Islam. Nor does it concentrate on U.S. wars after World War i during which many Arab-American families had as many as four and five sons and daughters who answered the call of duty to the United States.

Chapter One
HISTORICAL BACKGROUND

The Arab heritage encompasses a diversity of nationalities and religions. It is a cultural and linguistic identity deeply rooted in the feeling of many people and countries and expressed through a single language and common customs, traditions, and values. Being Arab is not a racial identity, and to identify an Arab by his or her features or name is difficult. An Arab can trace his or her ancestry to an Arabic-speaking country. Arab surnames are frequently biblical, for example, Abraham, Isaac, Moses, and Joseph.

Arabs belong to the Semitic branch of the Caucasian race and were the indigenous people of the Arabian Peninsula. Arabic is the language of the Quran (the Holy Book of Islam) that was revealed to the Prophet Muhammad in the Arabian city of Makkah in the seventh century of the Common Era, and in its classical, or Quranic form, the Arabic language spread to the Fertile Crescent. This was an agricultural region arching from the Nile in Egypt to Mesopotamia (the Tigris-Euphrates valley in present-day Iraq) and passing through the eastern Mediterranean borderlands (see map 1). The majority of the indigenous people of these lands converted to Islam, and they adopted the Arabic language that was a unifying bond among them. Thus today, in the Fertile Crescent, Christians, Muslims, and Druze all worship Allah, the Arabic word for the one God of the three Abrahamic religions, Christianity, Islam, and Judaism. After 1,400 years the Quran remains in its original Arabic text with very few changes. Because Arabic is the language of the Quran, Arabic is read and chanted by millions of Muslims throughout the world.

From the very beginning of our knowledge of Arabic, the language has existed in two entirely separate forms: the written language and the spoken language. I use the word Arabic to cover both the spoken and written forms of Arabic.[1]

In the modern period (roughly the last two centuries) Arabs and their language, Arabic, have come into contact in a more concentrated fashion with the Western world and its languages. This has led to changes in the

language with introduction of foreign vocabulary words and new technical terms. It is generally called Modern Standard Arabic and is the written
language of contemporary Arabs and their literature throughout the Arab
world. It is also the international spoken language of the Arab world, one of
the official languages of the United Nations, and the language of the Arab
League. It is not the language used by Arabs to communicate with each
other within their own countries.

Arabs speak within their own countries to each other on a daily basis
in a colloquial dialect that differs from one region to the other throughout
the Arab world, which stretches from the Atlantic coast of northern Africa
in the west to beyond the Persian Gulf in the east. All these variances show
some similarities to the written language, but they are also different in their
choices of vocabulary and pronunciation.

Throughout this book the Arabic words and expressions used were generally the colloquial language of people who came from geographic Syria
(Syria, Lebanon, Palestine, and Jordan). The transliterations appear as they
would have in the late nineteenth and early twentieth centuries. However,
this transliteration does not reflect what has become the standard of Arabic
transliteration. For consistency's sake, the definite article is transliterated
throughout the book as "el," although "al" and "il" are commonly used.
For brevity in the index the prefix "el" is omitted, for example, *el-saha,
saha,* and *al-jabr, jabr.* Although many Arabic words, such as *fellahin* and
Jabal Lubnan (Zahbal Libnan), are used in American-English dictionaries
and U.S. government maps, they still appear in the index.

Two sources in particular for spelling and transliterations have been
used:

A. J. Arbeely, M.D. (editor and one of the proprietors and founders of Kawkab
America), *Al-Bakoorat al-Gharbeyat Fee Taleem al-Lughat al-Englezeyat* (The first
Occidental fruit for the teaching of the English language), lessons 6–15, 17–38
(New York: Oriental Publishing House, 1896); and
Karl Baedeker, *Palestine and Syria with Routes through Mesopotamia and Babylonia
and the Island Of Cyprus: Handbook for Travellers,* 5th ed., sec. 2, "Vocabulary"
(Leipzig: Karl Baedeker; London: T. Fisher Unwin; New York: Charles Scrib-
ner's Sons, 1912). Earlier edition, *Palestine and Syria: Handbook for Travellers,* ed.
K. Baedeker (Leipsic: Karl Baedeker, 1876).

From about 1880[2] to 1915, Near East Arab people, mostly Lebanese, a
few Syrians, and fewer Palestinians, came to America from the Ottoman
Empire (see map 2), especially from the province of Syria, which included
the semiautonomous administrative district of Jabal Lubnan, also called

Mount Lebanon (see map 3), and the province of Palestine.[3] These provinces on the eastern Mediterranean region were part of the Ottoman Empire. They included Anatolia (today's Turkey) in the north and Egypt to the south and were centered geographically at one of the oldest crossroads of civilization. After World War I Syria, Lebanon, and Palestine became national entities. Now much of the Near East geographic area is commonly called the Middle East.

Before World War I, Arab Americans who emigrated from geographic Syria were identified as Syro-Arab, Arab, or Syrian. Although some historians claim that the term "Arab" was first used after World War II, there is evidence of its use locally in Worcester, Massachusetts, in the early 1890s by authors Elbridge Kingsley and Frederick Knab in *Picturesque Worcester,* 1891; Board of Trade, *Worcester's Columbian Tribute, 1893;* and "Arabian Boardinghouse" listings in the *Worcester House Directory* of 1894 and 1896.[4] In other instances the Arabs were identified as Syro-Arab.[5] Their place of birth was generally stated as Syria, for example, in the *Fifteenth Census of the United States,* table 19, "1900 or Earlier," World War I draft card registrations, and marriage records.[6] After World War I, they frequently identified themselves as either Syrian, Lebanese, or Palestinian American. The period after World War II saw a growing consciousness of Arab identity, and it was common that more people nationally saw themselves as Arab American, although often others continued to refer to themselves as being of Lebanese, Syrian, or Palestinian ancestry.

Frequently Lebanese, more often the Maronites (who use the Syro-Antiochene rite and are in union with the Bishop of Rome),[7] recognize themselves as descendants of the Phoenicians, ancient seafarers and traders.[8] The Phoenicians flourished in the second and early first millennia B.C.E. (Before the Common Era) from city-states at Tyre (capital of ancient Phoenicia), Sidon, and Byblos—the same cities of today's Lebanon. Nevertheless, they are Arabs since they speak Arabic and are enmeshed in its culture.

The Arab Connection

Arabs also trace their heritage to the golden ages of the Abassids. Throughout the Near East, much was changing in the sixth and early seventh centuries. Along with the rise of Islam the Arab Empire was founded and spanned about six-and-a-half centuries, from around 632 C.E. to about 1258. The empire included the Umayyad caliphate at Damascus (632 to about 750) and the Abbasid caliphate at Baghdad (750 to about 1258). It reached its greatest size from 700 to about 850. With the spread of Islam and the conquest of Syria in about 637, the population of the Arab Empire ceased to be predominantly Christian and became predominantly Muslim.

Arab Muslim rule in Spain lasted eight centuries, from 711 to 1492. During the Inquisition of 1492 King Ferdinand V and Queen Isabella I expelled the Arabs from Spain when they resisted attempts to force them to convert to Christianity.

The Arab role in the development of world civilizations and Arab contributions transmitted to modern civilization, for example, modern chemistry, astronomy, geography, mathematics, medicine, literature, and the arts,[9] were an extension of what was acquired and created by them during the Arab golden ages of culture and reflective thought.

The message in the proclamation by the U.S. president on National Arab-American Day, 1989,[10] paid tribute to Arabs for their many contributions to Western civilization as well as to the many ways Arab Americans continue to use their talents to enrich life in America and add strength to its experience. This proclamation was proposed by the American-Arab Anti-Discrimination Committee (ADC) under the leadership of its president, Abdeen Jabara, and James Abourezk, national chairman.

The Ottoman Empire

The thirteenth century saw the decline of the Arab Empire and the rise of the Ottomans. The Ottoman Empire was founded in the northwest of Anatolia (today Asia Minor) around 1288 by Osman I (also called Othman), of the Osmanli dynasty. The empire reached its greatest size in about 1550 and survived until the 1920 Treaty of Sèvres, which divided up the Ottoman Empire after World War I. Its formal dissolution came under the Treaty of Lausanne, signed by the Republic of Turkey (formerly part of the Ottoman Empire) in 1923.[11] Osman's subjects were identified as Osmanlis or Ottomans, and most were Muslim Ottomans, not Muslim Arabs. Today there are over one billion Muslims in the world, of which only about 6 percent are Arabs. The empire was a multinational Islamic state, and its official language was Arabic—for centuries the world's lingua franca.[12] Arabic was an important vehicle of commerce, culture, diplomacy, and science. Between the ninth and twelfth centuries works in various fields of knowledge—science, the humanities, literature—were written in Arabic. Many of the scientists, philosophers, linguists, and poets who expressed themselves in Arabic were not ethnically Arab.

The Ottomans conquered Arab lands, including Syria and Palestine, and ruled most Arabs for four centuries between 1517 and 1917. During this period of rule, Arabs maintained their Arab cultural heritage through their language, food, music, dance, storytelling, and poetry. The ethnicity and cultural heritage of subjects of the Ottoman Empire is described in *A History of the Arab Peoples* by Albert Hourani.[13]

The Millet System

In the Islamic Ottoman Empire sultans administered non-Muslim subjects by means of the Millet (pronounced mil-LET) system introduced first by Sultan Mehmet. The Millet system recognized the legal existence of non-Muslim religious groups and established Ottoman political-social communities based on religious affiliations. (As a carryover from the Millet system, the Arab immigrants who came to America frequently identified themselves by religion.) The clergy and rabbis were responsible for the collection of taxes levied by the sultans. As long as the Christians and Jews paid their taxes, each self-governing millet pursued its own laws, customs, and religions.

William Yale, author of *The Near East,* states:

> The Ottoman government created the Millet system in order to bring the Christian and Jewish subjects within the framework of the imperial government. In conformity with Arab tradition and Byzantine practice with respect to foreigners, the Ottoman sultans granted their non-Moslem [non-Muslim] subjects a limited autonomy under the chief ecclesiastical leaders of the different religious sects. . . . The Millet system conferred extensive powers upon the clergy, which made it possible for the priesthood to exert a strong influence over their lay communities.[14]

Missionaries from Massachusetts

In the late nineteenth and early twentieth centuries, growing contact with Europeans and Americans—such as archaeologists searching out vestiges of ancient civilizations, visitors to the birthplace of the world's great religions, missionaries, travelers, traders, adventurers, educators, and writers who had been attracted to the Near East provided a motivation for Near Eastern people to migrate to America. Missionaries from Massachusetts had been going to the Near East as early as 1819[15] when Pliny Fisk and Levi Parsons of Salem, Massachusetts, Protestant missionaries, traveled to today's Syria, Lebanon, and the communities surrounding Jerusalem. Leaders such as the educator Daniel Bliss, also from Massachusetts, expanded the missionary role. Bliss helped found the Syrian Protestant College in Lebanon, which opened in 1866 and was renamed the American University of Beirut (AUB) in 1920. Arabic was the language of instruction at AUB until 1882, when English began to be used. The English language was an important tool in spreading the Western way of life throughout the Near East. It was a further motivation to leave the homeland for America.

Participation by Arabs at World Expositions

The impact of Arab culture in the United States became more evident at the turn of the century with the growth of world expositions. World fairs were the greatest showcases for peaceful international competition in the late nineteenth and early twentieth centuries. The major cities of Philadelphia, Chicago, and St. Louis held world expositions in 1876, 1893, and 1904, respectively. Citizens of the Ottoman Empire, mainly from Arab countries, exhibited a variety of products rarely seen in the West, such as Arab-style architecture, arts, furnishings, textiles, gold and silver filigree, Arab foods, and religious goods from Jerusalem. The Centennial Exposition at Philadelphia celebrated the 100th year of the independence of the United States of America. According to Louise Seymour Houghton in "Syrians in the United States," "The Centennial Exposition . . . attracted a few Syrians, chiefly traders from Jerusalem, who brought olive wood articles and other curios. These [Syrians] also went back [to their homeland], but their stories of fabulous profits fired the imagination of their people."[16]

The Columbian Exposition at Chicago was the most popular world's fair held in America and was attended by 28 million people. It was held in observance of the 100th year of the adoption of the United States Constitution, and the 400th anniversary of the discovery of the "New World." Historian Adele L. Younis, in "The Coming of the Arabic-Speaking People to the United States," wrote, "The Columbian Exposition attracted tremendous numbers from the Near East, from artisan to the professional classes. . . . The overseas adventurers came from all segments of society."[17]

Younis also described the popularity of the Arab exhibits:

> The Arab East and North Africa were extensively represented with true reproductions of their social and physical world. Here different Arab cultural groups enacted various aspects of their communal lives. The many groups invited to the United States were abundantly photographed in newspapers, journals, and portfolio collections, more so than representatives of other countries. This was not due only to the artistry displayed but also because of the showmanship

and enthusiasm with which the Arabs displayed their cultures. It is quite evident they enjoyed themselves and loved to play, and this became contagious and attracted visitors by the thousands.[18]

In "The Arabs Who Followed Columbus," Younis referred to contributions made by the women:

> Women of ability arrived, schooled in Arabic, French, and English traditions. Many had graduated from the Beirut Female Seminary, later the Beirut College for Women. . . . Women lecturers toured the country. Some played an important role in the Columbian Exposition of 1893.[19]

Regarding the St. Louis Fair, Younis stated: "[The] St. Louis Fair of 1904 completed the successful trilogy by transporting the magnificent culture of the East to the doorsteps of a nation craving for luxuries of older traditions—later to become so much a part of the American panorama."[20]

Lure of Immigration to America

The "New World" had a seemingly insatiable appetite for labor. Recruiters, brokers, steamship lines, and state immigration bureaus sent agents to towns and villages throughout the world to lure cheap labor and settlers with promises of wealth and independence. As a consequence, Arabs learned more about America.

Emigration from a Peaceful Homeland

Emigration from the geographic area of Jabal Lubnan, Syria, and Palestine was at a time of peace from 1861 to 1914,[21] marked by neither famine nor persecution. However, other provinces of the Ottoman Empire did not share in this peace. Generally, the early Arab immigrants came for adventure and wealth, and after a few years some returned to their homelands financially better off. Many of those who decided to settle permanently in America did so after several return migrations, and subsequent trips to their homelands were for visits.

Destination: Worcester, Massachusetts

A heart-shaped souvenir booklet published by the Worcester Board of Trade (forerunner of the Worcester Chamber of Commerce) provides another example of how many immigrants were lured to this distant land of economic opportunity. Distributed at the Alaska-Yukon-Pacific Exposition at Seattle, 1909, it described Worcester as:

An old New England municipality rendered pre-eminent by inventive genius; where employer and employee, meeting together on a common level, labor together for the common good; where culture in the midst of a commercial civilization is still honored, and where the upbuilding and preservation of the home is still recognized as the supremest duty of the American people. [This is] Just a glimpse of its civic life and an epitome of its educational, insurance and industrial eminence from 1658 to 1909.[22]

Worcester (some forty miles west of Boston) was a homogeneous Yankee community before the construction of the Blackstone Canal in 1826. With the opening of the canal, inland Worcester became a port in 1828, linked to Providence, Rhode Island, and thus to the Atlantic Ocean. The first Union Station opened with the arrival of the Boston and Worcester Railroad on Foster Street near Main Street in 1835. When the Providence and Worcester Railroad began operations in 1847, the Blackstone Canal was abandoned the following year, and Worcester was on its way to becoming an important industrial center. After the U.S. Civil War and the opening of the West, Worcester—like other labor-hungry cities—recruited potential residents from many nations to work in plants and mills to support the industrial development that was taking place. Between 1880 and 1920, these opportunities were additional enticement for many Lebanese, Syrian, and Palestinian Arabs to migrate. Their arrival in Worcester began in 1880, thirty-two years after its incorporation as a city in 1848[23] and nineteen years after the United States was divided by the Civil War in 1861. Worcester's population in 1880 was 58,295,[24] and by 1920 it had grown to 179,754.[25]

The Arabs brought with them enormous energy, resourcefulness, and the desire to accumulate wealth and return to the homelands they loved. They were intelligent, ambitious, and adventurous. Upon their arrival in the United States the immigrants, both men and women, generally started at the bottom of the economic ladder working in the dry goods trade, selling from door to door and town to town. With a strict sense of honesty, morality, and a natural feel for commerce, many gradually opened their own thriving businesses, shops, and stores. Other Arab Americans, particularly in Worcester and other areas in North and South America, while still peddling became real estate developers and owners of rental properties (see map 5). They later invested in the stock market. Some worked as industrial laborers. Many returned to their homelands as originally planned and remained there for a few years. However, because of "reverse culture shock," most returned to settle permanently in North and South America.

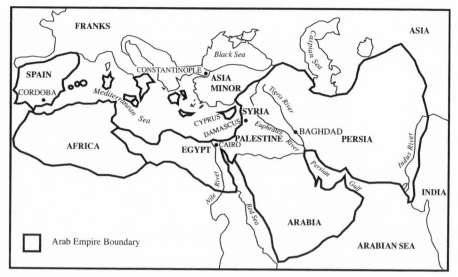

Map 1. Arab Empire at greatest expansion, 700–850 C.E.

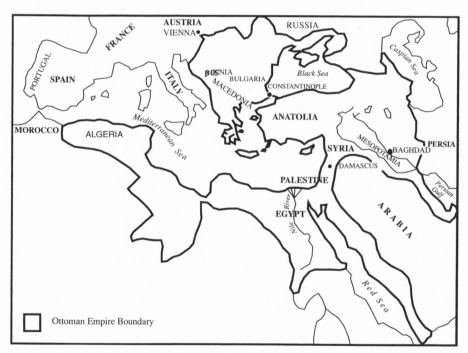

Map 2. Ottoman Empire, seventeenth century C.E.

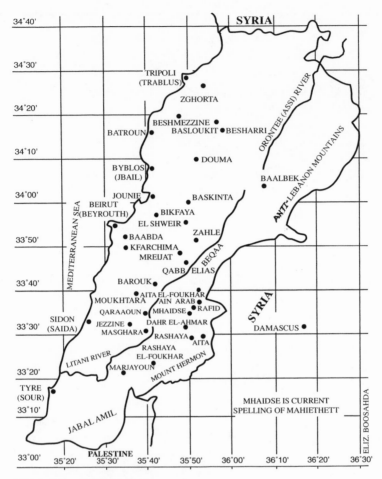

Map 3. Lebanon: Where the journey began

European Mandates—Nationalism Developed

Since religion had been a significant factor in both the administration of the Ottoman Millet system and the European mandates, the religion of the immigrants was their primary identification. After World War I, the political fate of the countries was determined by the mandates formally granted by the League of Nations in 1922, whereby France was responsible for Syria and Lebanon and Britain for Palestine, Transjordan, and Iraq (see map 4). Internal boundaries were arbitrarily drawn based on the religion of the inhabitants. Britain and France introduced the concept of nation-states to the region and it created political boundaries after World War I. Political scientist Leila Meo addresses the issues of mandates and religion,[26] and according to historian Adele L. Younis:

> Until the mandate system was imposed on the Near East, the term Syria implied a unified land and people, at least conceptually. In time, the mandate effectively divided a historically related people into politically distinct groups: the Lebanese, Jordanian, Palestinian, and Syrian nations.[27]

Economic Survival

The paths Americans of Arab ancestry took to pursue economic survival in their adopted country cannot be reduced to a set pattern. Included were a variety of methods used to earn a living while they maintained the unity of the family and integrated into the neighborhood. Their economic survival involved countless risks, sacrifices, hardships, stamina, and frugality. They were industrious and worked hard for long hours. Descendants of other immigrants will recognize parallels in their own backgrounds. Like many others who migrated to the Americas, the Syrians, Lebanese, and Palestinians had a strong drive to be independent entrepreneurs. Most succeeded in their struggles against seemingly impossible odds in an environment where customs, language, and mores were different from those of their homelands.

Lebanon: Where the Journey Began (Map 3)

In ancient times the country now known as Lebanon was almost completely covered by forests. Today most of the famous cedars of Lebanon are near the town of Besharri, the birthplace of Kahlil Gibran. Lebanon is approximately 130 miles long and 20 to 35 miles wide and has a narrow coastal plain with its major cities, Beirut (the capital), Tripoli, and Sidon, along the Mediterranean. The terrain rises swiftly to the mountains, then drops eastward to the Beqaa (a fertile plateau approximately 100 miles long and 6 to 16 miles wide, lying between the Lebanon Mountains and the Anti-Lebanon Mountains), and rises again to the mountains before the Syrian border is reached. Mount Hermon (Jabal Cheikh) is the highest peak in the Anti-Lebanon.

In 1922, under the League of Nations mandate, Britain and France controlled all of what was previously known as the provinces of Syria and Palestine within the Ottoman Empire. In about 1923 modern-day Lebanon was created from the western part of Syria. In 1926 Lebanon became a re-

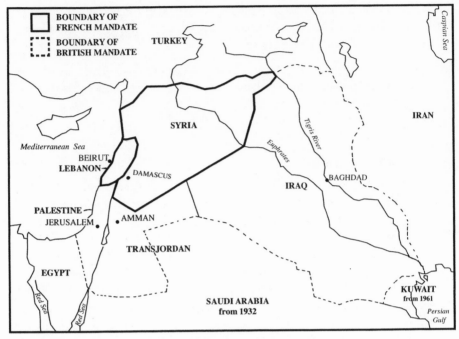

Map 4. Mandate powers under auspices of League of Nations, 1922. Syria and Lebanon under France; Palestine, Transjordan, and Iraq under Britain.

public, a constitution was proclaimed, and its first president was elected. In 1943 Lebanon gained independence from France; in 1946 the French forces evacuated Lebanon and the Republic of Lebanon was established in its first year of complete freedom from foreign occupation. However, Israel invaded Lebanon in March 1978 and again in 1982. For more than two decades Israeli military forces occupied southern Lebanon, from 1978 until its near total withdrawal May 24, 2000.

Lebanon's official language is Arabic, but the majority of the Lebanese are bilingual or trilingual. English and French are widely known because of close financial, tourist, religious, and educational ties with the West.

References Consulted for Map Compilation

Lebanon (map), John Bartholomew & Son, Ltd., Edinburgh EH9 1TA, MCMLX XXIV.

National Council of Tourism in Lebanon (map), Beirut, and printed by the D.A.G. Ministry of Defence, n.d.

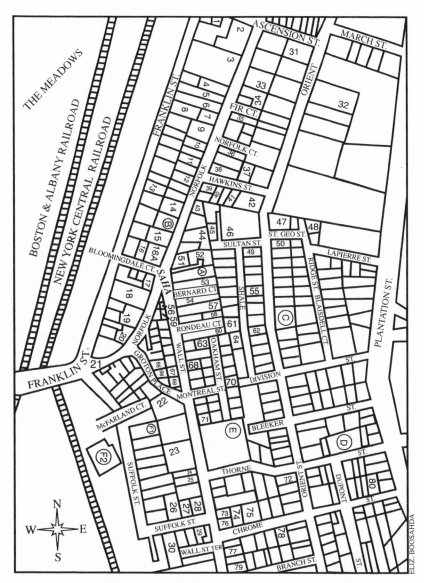

Map 5. Landownership in section of el-Tellee, Worcester, Mass., 1922 and earlier. Area extends from north to south about 3/4 mile from junction of Ascension and Norfolk Streets to Branch and Wall Streets and easterly about 1/2 mile from Franklin and Suffolk Streets to Plantation Street.

Tourist Map of Lebanon. Boulos F. Boulos, former chief of Section of Economy at the Ministry of Agriculture, Beirut, Lebanon, 1966.

Sources for Notations

Haddad, Hassan S., and Basheer K. Nijm, eds. *The Arab World: A Handbook.* AAUG (Association of Arab-American University Graduates) Monograph Series, no. 9. Wilmette, Ill.: Medina Press, 1978, 91.
Hagopian, Elaine, and Samih Farsoun, eds. *South Lebanon,* Special Report no. 2. Detroit: Association of Arab-American University Graduates, Inc. (AAUG), 1978.

Map 3. The Mutassarifiah/Jabal Lubnan (1861 to about 1916)

Civil war broke out in Syria and coincidentally in the United States in 1860 and 1861, respectively. The war in Syria was halted with the landing on its shore of the fleets of England and France. After the landing of these armies, a special committee composed of diplomatic representatives of France, England, Russia, and Austria convened in Beirut in 1861. The outcome was the new entity, Little Lebanon, also called the Mutassarifiah (Governate) during the Ottoman Empire, and also known as Jabal Lubnan, upon which was conferred an internal autonomy guaranteed by these European powers. Jabal Lubnan extended from the outskirts of Tripoli in the north to about the limits of Jezzine in the south. Zahleh and a part of the Beqaa were included in it, but Beirut, Tripoli, and almost the entire southern coastal region remained under Ottoman administration. The capital was Baabda and under one governorship, with a Christian appointed as governor *(mutassarif)* by the sultan and subject to reappointment. The Mutassarifiah lasted over fifty years.

Sources

Phares, Walid. *The Christian People of Lebanon: Thirteen Centuries of Struggle,* 71–72. Beirut, n.d.
Younis, Adele L. *The Coming of the Arabic Speaking People to the United States,* ed. Philip M. Kayal, 58. Staten Island, N.Y.: Center for Migration Studies, 1995.

Landownership in Section of *El-Tellee,* Worcester, Massachusetts, 1922 and Earlier (Map 5)

Code Numbers and Letters

The numbers are consecutive according to location, point to boundaries of lots, and correspond to the following names of Arab-American owners (in-

complete listing). The letters indicate lots owned by institutions, an industry, and private owners, and lot "A" located just above *"SAHA" (el-saha)*
was owned by a parish of Arab Americans.

1. Wood, 2. Debs, 3. Haddad, 4. Salegh (Salih), 5. David, 6. Dowd, 7.
Ezen, 8. Shannazarian (Shannon), 9. AbouRached (Rachid), 10. G. M. Abdow et al., 11. Haddad, 12. Thomas, 13. Geseuse, 14. J. T. Lian, 15. Rayes
(Raize) et al., 16. Penny, 16A. Shannon, 17. K. J. Haddad, 18. Salloom,
19. Esper, 20. Esper, 21. David, 22. Mitchell, 23. Kunib (Kaneb), 24. Farris (Farahart), 25. George, 26. Forzley, 27. Farris, 28. Abodeely, 29. Forzley, 30. Forzley, 31. Abousamra, 32. C. Schuerie (Schwerie), 33. Dowd,
34. Haddad, 35. Himsey et al., 36. Shannazarian (Shannon), 37. A. Gammal, 38. Haffty, 39. Maloof, 40. Heffte (Haffty), 41. Sawyer (Sawayer),
42. Abisamer (Abisamra), 43. Husson, 44. A. Boosahda, 45. Husson, 46.
Husson, 47. Williams, 48. Williams, 49. Samara, 50. Salloom, 51. Abdow,
52. A. Boosahda, 53. Abotaya (Samara) K. S., 54. A. Gliz (Ghiz), 55. A.
Boosahda, 56. Kunib (Kaneb), 57. K. J. Haddad, 58. A. Boosahda, 59. Azar
(Salem), 60. H. George, 61. A. Boosahda, 62. Ghiz, 63. Aboumrad, 64.
A. Boosahda, 65. Hajjar, 66. Rizkalla, 67. Mitchell, 68. Kurkor, 69. Dah-
rooge,, et al., 70. Saber, 71. Debs, 72. Moore, 73. Abodeely, 74. Souda,
75. Swydan, 76. Haddad, 77. Batar (Bitar, or Peters), 78. C. Adams, 79,
Birbara, and 80. K. Assad.

A. St. George Orthodox Church, Wall Street

B. Y. Bianchi, an Italian American, Norfolk Street (also on Richards' 1896
   map as "Italia Bianchi")

C. Worcester Baptist Mission Board, Orient Street (also on Richards' 1886
   map as "Oak Hill Baptist Church, Worcester Baptist City Mission")

D. Little Franciscan Sisters of Mary, French Canadian, Thorne Street (also
   on Richards' 1911 map)

E. St. Joseph's Church (Roman Catholic, French Canadian), Wall Street

F1 and F2. Graton & Knight Manufacturing Company

Generally the sale of property by an Arab American was to another Arab
American, for example, G. Aboumrad was prior owner of property owned
by Rayes et al. (15); E. Bacela et al. prior owner of property owned by
Esper (19); S. George prior owner of property owned by Haffty (38). In
another example A. Boosahda (52) purchased the property in 1904 (*Worcester House Directory,* Real Estate Record, p. 589) and was the same owner
in 1922. Often the same Arab-American names appeared as owners of the

same property on the Richards' maps of 1911 and 1922, and/or names appeared on the 1911 map and not on the 1922 map when they still owned the property. Additionally, by 1911 names were omitted of early developers and/or owners who lived within the above section of *el-tellee* as they had moved out of the area.

A few of the owners were women, for example, C. Schuerie (32) was Catherine/Katerina Schuerie, a widow with three children. In 1914 she purchased the building and lot as Katherina Schuerie (*Grantee Index 1911-1920,* Book 2064, page 100, Registry of Deeds, Worcester County Court House, Worcester, Mass.).

Reference consulted for map compilation: *Richards Standard Atlas of the City of Worcester, Massachusetts* (Springfield, Mass.: Richards Map Co., 1922), plate 18.

Chapter Two
MIGRATION

One of the thousands of immigrants was Bashara K. Forzley, who emigrated from Karhoun (now Qaraaoun, Lebanon). In his autobiography he remembers the words of wisdom spoken by his mother regarding his personal journey:

> On a warm summer day in 1897, Salem Ferris Haddad, Ameen Antoun Forzley, and I, Bashara Kalil Forzley, boarded a ship destined for America, at Beirut, Lebanon. I was the youngest of the three. Before I sailed, mother gave me advice which I have never forgotten. First, "Always associate with people who are your elders." Second, "Do not indulge in liquor, smoking, dating or partying. By this manner of living you will never get into trouble." Third, and last, "Do not forget your folks at home. If you die we will die with you. If you live and succeed we also will succeed by our manifested happiness." She ended by saying, "May God bless and protect you and give you a long healthy life. Our prayer will always be with you." My mother was a wise and practical woman. . . . My family which remained included two brothers, Abraham Saab, Fida Kalil, a sister Rose and my parents.[1]

Arabs from the Near East were not the only people to leave their homeland looking for new opportunities. There was a worldwide movement of people at the turn of the century to the United States, Canada, Argentina, Brazil, Australia, and New Zealand. Author Thomas J. Archdeacon points out,

> Contrary to first impressions, the new immigration was not a phenomenon exclusive to the United States. The dramatic influx that occurred there formed part of a worldwide movement of people in the late decades of the nineteenth century and the early ones of the twentieth century.[2]

Archdeacon further notes that pressure of overpopulation influenced emigration:

In the final decades of the nineteenth century and the first quarter of the twentieth, the countries of Asia and of southern and eastern Europe experienced the population explosions and dislocations that western Europe had earlier undergone. For the first time these countries surrendered hundreds of thousands of their subjects to the United States.[3]

Emigration from the Ottoman Empire

The majority of Arabs who settled or passed through Worcester maintained their specific localized identities as defined by their religious sect and the village from where they emigrated. Predominantly, the Worcester Arab-American community came from Jabal Lubnan (Mount Lebanon), more specifically from the village of Mahiethett (al-Muhayditha; the current spelling is Mhaidse),[4] southeast of Beirut, near Rafid, in the District of Rashaya, and were Eastern Orthodox Christian (Byzantine rite).

In Mahiethett, the Druze comprised the dominant group, and many were feudal landlords. However, the greatest number of *fellahin* (agricultural peasants) were Christian. Other villages and a few cities from where most emigrated are listed in descending order according to where the larger number of emigrants originated from: Masghara, Dahr el-Ahmar, Aita, Zahle, Rashaya, Ain Arab, Zghorta, Aita el-Foukhar, el-Shweir, Marjayoun, Mreijat, Qabb Elias, Jezzine, Jounie, Beshmezzine, Basloukit, Karhoun (Qaraaoun), Barouk, Sidon, Baskinta, Besharri (Bchari), Rashaya el-Foukhar, Batroun, Bikfaya, Douma, and other villages. A few emigrated from Kfarchima, Tripoli, and Moukhtara.

The few people who came from Syria were mainly from Homs, el-Sham (Damascus), Aleppo, Antakya (Antioch), and Hauran. The few from Palestine were predominantly from Jerusalem, Nazareth, Bethlehem, and Safad.

The majority of Muslim and Druze emigrated from Angora (now Ankara, capital of Turkey) and from some of the above-named villages in Lebanon. The few non-Arab Muslims who settled in Worcester were the Tatars from western Russia (now the Republic of Tatarstan, capital Kazan) and White Russians from western Russia (now Belarus, capital Minsk).

Peak immigration years to America were from 1880 to 1924,[5] and the Arabic-speaking immigrants were part of this flow of people. They ranged in age from infancy to thirty-five. Most men and women were single when they emigrated, and many others came with another member of the family, a neighbor, or a friend. A few arrived with their spouse, with or without children. Generally, members of the same family did not emigrate at the same time. They came as traders, merchants, artisans, farmers, writers, cooks, furriers, leather-makers, tanners, and silk weavers with the desire, drive, and confidence to venture away from home. Some were familiar with other languages, the most common being Russian, German, English, and French. Their journey from *el-belaad* (homeland) began on a positive and upbeat note.

One of the narrators, Tekla (Annie) H.A.M., talked about immigrants from Mahiethett:

> Some Mahiethett people went to Brazil, Canada, some of them to another country, I forget, but most Mahiethett people came to Worcester and other places in this country. . . . The ones who went to other countries knew where they were going and that was what they wanted to do, go directly to another country other than America. Habooba [Rose] S. Abufaris's husband had a lot of relatives in Brazil. She used to get a lot of company from Brazil. Francis A. had a lot of cousins in Brazil, too. They came here to visit many times.

Another narrator, Takala H. R., stated that after she and her husband, Salem, settled in Worcester, they decided to live in Brazil where her husband had four brothers. After five years they returned to Worcester as she wanted to be with her family. Subsequently, her return trips to Brazil were for visits and his return trips were for business.

Primary Reasons for Emigration

Most Arabs who settled in Worcester came to America as sojourners and not for permanent residency, and they had the freedom to travel and money to pay for the voyage. In their homeland the *fellahin* who emigrated had tillable land through family inheritance and other property that they had acquired over the years. When the immigrants were asked "Why did you emigrate?" most lifted their shoulders in quiet shrugs with wide-eyed enthusiasm and smiled. They did not dwell on the reasons as they felt initially there was a mystique in being part of the migration to the Americas. However, with a twinkle in their eyes and a pause, many admitted they had too much energy and imagination to accept the time-honored way of life that others, family and neighbors, never questioned. Their lack of motivation, strong emotional attachment to *el-belaad*, and the comfort of familiar routines explained the reluctance of those who chose not to emigrate.

Nazira M. B. explained:

> My father remarried soon after my mother died as he felt his seven children needed a mother. At seventeen, I was the second oldest in my family and did not want to adjust to a stepmother and felt this

was a good opportunity to move on to America. I planned the trip with my younger brother Yusuf; however, Yusuf felt he didn't want to leave just then and planned to join me later. I joined a group from my village who were emigrating, got separated from them accidentally, and ended up in Utica, New York, where I lived with other relatives from my village. Although Yusuf never joined me, as he still felt he was needed at home, I never gave up hope that he would come. We corresponded regularly and I sent cash gifts and outgrown clothes periodically to my sisters and brothers.

Eli S. revealed:

My father wanted to see what was beyond. He was adventurous and curious. He came here because he wanted to see what was going on. He wanted to know. My father came here and then he decided he wanted to make a new life for himself and his family. He had the courage to be free.

From B. K. Forzley's autobiography:

My name and the address of my cousins in Worcester were printed on a tag pinned to my jacket. People directed us to go to our destination, Worcester, by train. Our arrival was a joyous one. Cousins and friends were at the station to greet us. Their hospitality greatly eased my fears of seeing a strange land and people. Once the celebrations were over, my relatives initiated me into the "make a living" group so common among them. Thus, I set forward to earn my own way [as a traveling peddler].[6]

Alice A. E. described her family history:

My parents came to Worcester because there was a Syrian man who was here from Beirut and they followed him. His name was Elias Bacela. He had a wife and two or three children. They moved to New York many years ago and they were Mother and Father's friends.

When my man [husband] asked his father "Would you want me to go to America?" his father said yes, and then he went and borrowed money and sent his son by boat. It took my husband about a month to get here. He came to Worcester from the same town as B. K. [B. K. Forzley], his cousin. My man was seventeen when he came here on his own. He had a brother, but the brother stayed in Lebanon. My man was sending money to him. He said, "Come here, come see how it is." So his brother came to Worcester and then went to Acton, Ohio, got married, and lived there, and raised a family.

Mary K. E. reminisced:

> My two uncles emigrated together before my parents and me. They got separated en route. One ended up in Copenhagen. That's another country, you know, and the other went to Worcester where we had cousins. Later my mother and I emigrated together by way of el-Sham and were there for half a day, then to Zahle, and then to Beirut, arriving at night. Listen to this. I hid our money inside a cummerbund and would wear it, and in the daytime I would take some of that money and we spent some. When my father emigrated from Damascus the only thing he took with him was *el-ud* [a stringed, half-pear-shaped, inlaid wooden musical instrument, played with a plectrum—also called a pick—and a forerunner of the lute and mandolin], no spare clothes, no nothing. He stayed in Marseilles, France, for a year and made money singing. He was like an Elvis Presley of his day. When he arrived in New York he went to see Bishop Hawaweeny. My mother and I met my father in New York at the *matraan*'s [bishop's] home.
>
> Then my mother and I proceeded to Worcester and we stayed with a couple from Syria whom my father knew. The wife was from el-Sham and the husband from Homs. They were just friends who wanted my father to come because he was a singer. Anybody who sees my father wants him because of his music. He was an accomplished musician and a famous vocalist. He became a traveling musician and because of his gifted voice and [because] his romance with music was so great, we rarely saw him.

El-ud was introduced to continental Europe by way of el-Andalus (Andalusia, Iberian Peninsula, Islamic Spain) by strolling minstrels and by European students at the Arab universities of el-Andalus.

Nora A. H. stated:

> My sense of it [migration] is that both my father and mother were great risk takers. My father, Ameen Hannah A., at age twelve and my mother in her early teens both came to this country separately and alone. My father lived with his older sister who had already settled in Worcester, and my mother emigrated to Lawrence to live with her uncle who was working in one of the textile mills there.

Charles H. recalled:

> Masghara, Lebanon, was a major leather center. American recruiters sought them out to come to Worcester to do work at the Graton & Knight tannery[7] as the tannery needed people who could tan

buffalo hide and work in the tannery. Because this was their trade many of our people migrated to Worcester. Others from neighboring towns also came as they figured they had their trades to add to the Arab-American community in Worcester.

Some, according to Tekla H.A.M., migrated because they did not wish to serve in the Ottoman Empire military:

> My husband's mother wanted her son to come to America so he would avoid being drafted [into] the Ottoman Army. She never thought there would be a war over here, and her son was drafted into the U.S. Army during World War i.

Separation from the Group While En Route

The Arab immigrants were willing to take risks for adventure and challenge. For most it was their first trip outside their villages. While en route some immigrants were accidentally separated from their groups, and some unknowingly were directed to other than their intended destination. Emigrating to America meant going to either North or South America. Many whose destination was Worcester found themselves in other places for various reasons. Musa (Moses) H. recalled:

> My brother Esau ended up in South America instead of North America by mistake as he was going to America. After he realized he was going to South America, he returned to North America but couldn't enter as he had inflammation of the eyes, trachoma. So Brazil became Esau's home. My other brother, Hannah [John] Abou Asaly H., and I settled in Worcester, our original destination.

Nicholas A. remembered:

> My father and his two brothers landed in Pittsburgh, Pennsylvania, by mistake. They didn't know anybody there. They were supposed to come to Worcester. They just landed over there and then they found their way around and came to Worcester where they had relatives.

Parenting and the Role of Women

Doris A.S. was astounded when she recalled that mothers emigrated without their children: "How could they do that? I can't leave one child without being worried. I love my children too much to leave them."

The role of parent was a shared responsibility as the family was not considered singly but as part of the whole unit of kinfolk. Extended families were important in the lives of children as well as the elderly. Both knew they would be cared for and loved. Children knew the elders about them were to be respected and obeyed, and this strong bonding was felt through-out the entire clan. Because of this bonding within families, many women were free to emigrate whether unmarried, widowed, wife, or mother, and many were the first in a family to emigrate and the first to start peddling. Some women trained the menfolk who followed in the art of peddling. The father, too, had the same freedom, respect, and trust to travel on extended trips leaving his family behind. Later many children aged thirteen and older emigrated with adults from their village to join their elders.

George (Bob) K. related:

> My mother never knew her father, but she knew her mother was somewhere in the U.S. My mother was left with her uncle, a priest in Mahiethett. She was an orphan when she came here and married my father.

Genevieve M. T. recalled:

> My father's mother left him with his grandfather to care for him while she came to America. The grandfather wanted to send my father to a seminary to become a priest. Whenever my father heard of anyone from America visiting Lebanon, he would hang around near a local area that attracted many tourists. He easily spotted the Western-garbed person and asked, "Do you know where my mother is in America?" My father had a half brother in Cuba.

Miryam (Mary) Debs R. stated, "My grandmother emigrated to Lowell and that is where my husband is from. He emigrated with his mother and father to Lowell, but he had one brother who landed in Australia. I emi-grated later and came directly to Worcester and lived with my aunt."

Castle Garden and Ellis Island

From 1855 until mid-1897, many of the Arab immigrants were processed at the Castle Garden port of entry located at Battery Park on the southern tip of Manhattan Island in New York City. Castle Garden opened under the direction of the state of New York. In mid-1897 the buildings at Castle Garden were destroyed by fire, including the entire wooden station that housed all the records going back to 1855. In the meantime the processing of immigrants took place at the temporary quarters at the Barge office in the Battery. State control of immigration policy shifted to federal jurisdiction when processing began at the newly opened federal immigration port of entry at Ellis Island in 1892.[8]

Health Examinations

Immigration for some became indeed a grim tale of shattered dreams. At the port of entry immigrants were required to pass the health examination, and those who failed were often sent back on the same boat they arrived on. The possibility of failing the examination for trachoma caused much apprehension and concern among the hopeful soon-to-be immigrants, as trachoma was the most common reason for failing the health examination. The examining doctor used a buttonhook to lift up the eyelid to search for the symptoms of trachoma.

Rejection with a Happy Ending

An example of rejection with a happy ending was one in which Joseph John George (more popularly known as Yusuf Hannah), United States Senator George Frisbie Hoar, and President Theodore Roosevelt interceded on behalf of a Syrian family, the Namers. In his *Autobiography of Seventy Years*[9] Senator Hoar described the incident, its sequel, and the visit to his son's office by Yusuf Hannah. The story was retold by author Edward A. Steiner in *On the Trail of the Immigrant*. Steiner dedicated his book to Robert Watchorn, the United States Commissioner of Immigration at the Port of New York, who "has dealt humanely, justly and without prejudice, with men of . . . '[e]very kindred and tongue and people and nation.'" Steiner quoted from Senator Hoar's autobiography:

> During the Christmas holidays of 1901 a very well known Syrian, [Joseph John George] a man of high standing and character, came into my son's office and told him this story:
>
> A neighbour and countryman of his had a few years before emigrated to the United States and established himself in Worcester. Soon afterwards, he formally declared his intention of becoming an American citizen. After a while, he amassed a little money and sent to [for] his wife, whom he had left in Syria, the necessary funds to convey her and their little girl and boy to Worcester. She sold her furniture and whatever other belongings she had, and went across Europe to France, where they sailed from one of the northern ports on a German steamer for New York.
>
> Upon their arrival at New York, it appeared that the children had

contracted a disease of the eyelids, which the doctors of the Immigration Bureau declared to be trachoma, which is contagious, and in adults incurable. It was ordered that the mother might land, but that the children must be sent back in the ship upon which they arrived, on the following Thursday. This would have resulted in sending them back as paupers, as the steamship company, compelled to take them as passengers free of charge, would have given them only such food as was left by the sailors, and would have dumped them out in France to starve, or get back as beggars to Syria.

The suggestion that the mother might land was only a cruel mockery. Joseph J. George, a worthy citizen of Worcester, brought the facts of the case to the attention of my son, who in turn brought them to my attention. My son had meanwhile advised that a bond be offered to the immigration authorities to save them harmless from any trouble on account of the children.

I certified these facts to the authorities and received a statement in reply that the law was peremptory, and that it required that the children be sent home; that trouble had come from making like exceptions theretofore; that the Government hospitals were full of similar cases, and the authorities must enforce the law strictly in the future. Therefore I addressed a telegram to the Immigration Bureau at Washington, but received an answer that nothing could be done for the children.

Then I telegraphed the facts to Senator Lodge, who went in person to the Treasury Department, but could get no more favourable reply. Senator Lodge's telegram announcing their refusal was received in Worcester Tuesday evening, and repeated to me in Boston just as I was about to deliver an address before the Catholic College there. It was too late to do anything that night. Early Wednesday morning, the day before the children were to sail, when they were already on the ship, I sent the following dispatch to President Roosevelt:

To the President,
White House, Washington, D.C.

I appeal to your clear understanding and kind and brave heart to interpose your authority to prevent an outrage which will dishonour the country and create a foul blot on the American flag. A neighbour of mine in Worcester, Mass., a Syrian by birth, made some time ago his public declaration for citizenship. He is an honest, hard-working and every way respectable man. His wife with two small children have reached New York.

He sent out money to pay their passage. The children contracted a disorder of the eyes on the ship. The Treasury authorities say that the mother may land but the children cannot, and they are to be sent back Thursday. Ample bond has been offered and will be furnished to save the Government and everybody from injury or loss. I do not think such a thing ought to happen under your Administration, unless you personally decide that the case is without remedy. I am told the authorities say they have been too easy heretofore, and must draw the line now. That shows they admit the power to make exceptions in proper cases. Surely, an exception should be made in case of little children of a man lawfully here, and who has duly and in good faith declared his intention to become a citizen. The immigration law was never intended to repeal any part of the naturalization laws which provide that the minor children get all the rights of the father as to citizenship. My son knows the friends of this man personally and that they are highly respectable and well off. If our laws require this cruelty, it is time for a revolution, and you are just the man to head it.

[signed by] George F. Hoar.[10]

Steiner continued Senator Hoar's story of the Namers' experience with Immigration at Ellis Island:

Half an hour from the receipt of that dispatch at the White House Wednesday forenoon, Theodore Roosevelt, President of the United States, sent a peremptory order to New York to let the children come in. They have entirely recovered from the disorder of the eyes, which turned out not to be contagious, but only caused by the glare of the water, or the hardships of the voyage. The children are fair-haired, with blue eyes, and of great personal beauty, and would be exhibited with pride by any American mother.

When the President came to Worcester [1902] he expressed a desire to see the children. They came to meet him at my house, dressed up in their best and glorious to behold. The President was very much interested in them . . .

The result of this incident was that I had a good many similar applications for relief in behalf of the immigrants coming in with contagious diseases. Some of them were meritorious, and others untrustworthy. In the December session of 1902 I procured the following amendment to be inserted in the immigration law.

"Whenever an alien shall have taken up permanent residence in this country and shall have filed his preliminary declaration to become a citizen and thereafter shall send his wife and minor children to join him, if said wife or either of said children shall be found to be affected with any contagious disorder, and it seems that said disorder was contracted on board the ship in which they came, such wife or children shall be held under such regulations as the Secretary of the Treasury shall prescribe until it shall be determined whether the disorder will be easily curable or whether they can be permitted to land without danger to other persons; and they shall not be deported until such facts have been ascertained." [11]

Steiner commented on the sequel to Senator Hoar's intervention in *On the Trail of the Immigrant:*

> Senator Hoar had touched however, only one of the many phases of the situation. As the President said, it [Ellis Island] was still "a difficult place." Yet under Commissioner Watchorn changes were soon visible. The place became cleaner; a new and better system of inspection was organized, discipline was maintained and strengthened, the comfort of the immigrants was considered, the money changers were watched, dishonest, discourteous and useless employees were discharged; and above all, the institution in its remotest corner was open to any one who wished to come and inspect the place which is so important in our economic and social life. [12]

Nine months later, on September 2, 1902, when President Roosevelt visited Senator Hoar's home, he was introduced to the Namer (also known as Nemr) children. Excerpted from the Worcester newspaper:

> The Others of the Party Who Had Been waiting his arrival were presented to the president, including the children. And the children played not the least part of the president's reception on Oak avenue.
>
> There were four of them. Two were Senator Hoar's granddaughters, the little daughters of Dist. Atty. [District Attorney] Rockwood Hoar . . . The others were Miss Sophie and Master Azziz Namer, the children of Sasine Namer [also known as Ernest N. Raad] [13] of Worcester, little Syrians whom the president had expressed a desire to meet.
>
> And round them is woven a story of presidential clemency, exercised at the request of Senator Hoar. It may as well be told here as anywhere, to show why the president of the United States took little children in his arms and kissed them, and said nice things to them which they could not understand because they knew no English, and why he otherwise made much of the two former subjects of the Sultan of Turkey [the Ottoman Empire]. And it also tells why the president of the United States posed in a group of which two

were the grandchildren of a great Massachusetts statesman and the other children of humble birth in Asia Minor.[14]

Senator Hoar in response to letters complimenting his efforts to save the children from being deported emphasized the need for President Roosevelt's intervention.[15] Theodore Roosevelt was a familiar traveler in his youth to Syria and had made many friends there.[16]

Rejection Results in Separation from Group

El-Hajj (Abraham B.) emigrated to Worcester for the second time in 1900 and was accompanied by his son Khalil (Charlie, Kalil), his daughter Miryam (Mary), and a neighbor of the same age, Malocke George, who emigrated to join her mother, *Um* (mother of) Embass. (Among Christian Arabs and Muslim Arabs the honorary title of address El-Hajj, male, El-Hajji, female, were given to a Christian or Muslim who had made the pilgrimage, the Hajj. For Christians the Hajj is to the Holy Sepulcher in Jerusalem and for Muslims the Hajj is to the Kabah in Makkah, the birthplace of Islam and the Prophet Muhammad. Some individuals take on the honorary title El-Hajj as a surname.) An immigration doctor rejected Khalil because of his trachoma. The group returned to Marseilles, France, and then on to Worcester by way of Liverpool, England, Canada, and Boston.

Eskandara (Alexandra) F.A.B., wife of El-Hajj B., migrated to join her husband and their son and daughter after the death of her widowed father who died in Mahiethett in 1902. She was accompanied by their children, Elia (Eli), Hilal (Harold), and Assad (Asa). Other members in the group were her half brother Farrah A. and son-in-law Monsour A., and they traveled together from Mahiethett to Naples, Italy, where they boarded a ship. Eli A. B. recalled the incident of his rejection:

> Upon entering the ship the doctor examined the eyes of everyone and found my eyes to have trachoma. My mother, my two brothers, and I were held back due to the fact we had one ticket for four passengers. Farrah and Monsour were ahead of us in line. When they knew the four of us were detained they did not want to leave us alone but we were not allowed to get off—and the group was separated. This was Monsour's return trip to America and he felt responsible for our safety. Monsour's brother Yusuf [Joseph] and my father had planned a party in Boston to celebrate our arrival. However, it was an occasion of mixed emotions as happiness and sadness was shared by all.
>
> Not knowing what happened to his family, my father [Ibrahim]

boarded the ship on its return trip to Naples to find us. He guided our way back to this country by way of Marseilles, France, and Liverpool, England. In Liverpool I was taken to a doctor and the doctor told my father that I would not be admitted to America due to my eye condition. My father managed with the advice of some people there that he should buy me a first-class ticket on the ship, as there are fewer restrictions on this type package. My father bought me a suitcase, which at that time was a box made from straw tied with a strap, in order to give me the appearance that I owned and had my own luggage. I boarded the ship and was conducted by the porter to a private room and for the first time I saw a bathtub. I saw my father, my mother, and brothers on the lower decks while I was on the quarterdeck, where I was walking. A doctor came and spoke to me in English and I was not able to answer him as I did not understand English and the doctor could not understand Arabic. The doctor examined my eyes and saw that I had trachoma and took me off the ship without my parents knowing it. The ship sailed with my parents and brothers, and I was taken to a poolroom where Arabic was spoken, and a man took me to the boardinghouse where I had stayed earlier with my parents and two brothers. A man at the boardinghouse sent an advanced telegram to my parents after the three days that I was forced off in Liverpool. My father corresponded with the manager of the boardinghouse and made arrangements with the man to send me to a doctor to have my eyes treated. After three months I was sent to Canada, arrived in Halifax, and my father met me there. After consulting the doctor about my eyes he found I was able to obtain a certificate from him, and consequently I was admitted into America without any trouble. I boarded the train to Boston, accompanied by my father, and arrived in Worcester, October 5, 1905, having left Mahiethett ten months earlier at age thirteen.

Anglicized Names and Ethnic Confusion

Upon arrival at a port of entry each immigrant was asked his or her name, date, and place of birth, destination, names of relatives, and means of support. Generally, communicating in a strange language caused confusion, and that contributed to some misspelled or arbitrarily anglicized names. Additionally, this same confusion occurred earlier when names were changed or altered on the ship's manifest in Europe by some shipping clerks.

Adding to the general confusion was the problem of how to list the Arab citizens of the Ottoman Empire as to ethnicity. They were referred to on emigration papers as Turk, Arab, Syrian, Armenian, Assyrian, or Asian. Because of cultural similarity among these groups, their ethnic diversity puzzled officials.

Nicholas A. recollected what happened when the immigration official asked him a simple question.

> "What's your name?" The question sounded Arabic to me, *Naasa-nam* (Are you sleeping?). I thought he was speaking in Arabic and in kind I responded in Arabic. *"Una mish naasanam"* (I am not sleeping!). The official sensed the confusion and then asked, "What are you called?" When I responded "El-Win," my name was anglicized to "Alwon." My great-grandfather was nicknamed El-Win after his trade as a calligrapher. He used to write advertisements and addressed envelopes and other stationery in his style of calligraphy. El-Win is like a printer.

Another resident of Worcester, Michael S., stated:

> So, when I came across here they wanted to know how to spell my father's name, I just took a pencil and actually wrote it in French, "Abdow." They wondered how I just came over here and I could write my name in English. So I explained it that there wasn't much difference between the English and French letters and I put on almost the same spelling. Both languages use Latin script.

The Worcester-Link Network of Communication

Business and social networking was a vital part of the immigrant experience, and Worcester was an important link in that system. Its Arab-American community was well developed and adept at providing strong safety nets. Worcester was the intended destination for many immigrants who planned to first seek out a friend, former neighbor, or relative. Some other Massachusetts areas where they settled were Winchendon, Westminster, Gardner, Lawrence, Lowell, Marlboro, and Boston, as well as other communities. Worcester also served as a way station for those who continued their trek to other areas in the Americas. Generally they kept in touch with their Worcester link and resources, the people, institution, and organizations, after settling elsewhere.

Worcester's Arab cultural focus also attracted people from other Arab-American communities. Louise S. recalled:

> My mother was living in Fall River and she longed to go to an Eastern Orthodox church. Because Worcester was known to have

a viable community of Arab Americans, and many out-of-towners attended liturgical services at St. George Orthodox Church, mother convinced father to move to Worcester so she could attend services at an Orthodox Christian church, and that's why we moved to Worcester to live.

Resource Persons

A migrant in need of specific information or assistance found a meeting place for networking at Arab-American-owned coffeehouses, restaurants, stores, boardinghouses, or other establishments located in the areas of Wall and Norfolk Streets, East Central Street, or the lower end of Belmont Street. Mostly the Druze and Muslim frequented the latter area. At these establishments the immigrants spoke with knowledgeable residents who aided them in integrating into a new social system. They exchanged views, experiences, and ideas that usually led to positive results; the immigrant was helped to overcome the feeling of being alone and was provided with the needed support systems to reach his or her anticipated goals. Most residents felt it was their duty, responsibility, and privilege to be in a position to help their country people, whether relatives, acquaintances, or strangers. On occasion when the needed information was not accessible at these establishments, support persons directed the immigrant to families who could provide assistance.

Charitable and civic-minded Arab Americans singly or collectively offered and shared their resources in the support and betterment of the community. For example, an action taken by a civic-minded person was one in which Simon George purchased a burial lot from the city of Worcester in 1904. The lot was divided into several graves—one was used for the burial of a nephew, Michael E. H., who was accidentally killed by a trolley car on Hamilton Street, and another was used for a distant relative, Faris G., who died in the Midwest while merchandising dry goods in 1905. Frank F. G. recalled:

> Simon George shipped back to Worcester the body of the deceased husband of Sayood B. G., who died in Illinois where he was staying while peddling dry goods and linens. Simon George paid the cost of transporting the body and burial of Faris G. as he felt the wife who resided in Worcester would appropriately be buried next to her husband in Worcester.

Immigrant Establishments Serving Multicultural and Multireligious Communities

As the Arab-American community grew so did the need for more assistance and a further sense of connection. An institution for worship was established. Organizations were founded to provide the necessary resources offered previously by individuals and Arab-American-owned establishments.

Religious Institution

A number of Arab Americans founded the Syrian Orthodox Church of Worcester (Eastern Orthodox, Byzantine rite) about 1885 or earlier.[17] It was the forerunner of the still functioning St. George Orthodox Cathedral. Before the founding of the church most Syrian Eastern Orthodox Christians and other Near Eastern people gathered for prayer services on Sundays and religious holidays on Wall or Norfolk Streets in private homes, empty Arab-American-owned storefronts, or outdoors in private yards or open fields. Later they bought and remodeled an existing church building at 100 Wall Street for Orthodox use. They believed in the Bible's words, "For where two or three are gathered together in my name, there am I [Jesus] in the midst of them" (Matthew 18:20).

The Syrian Orthodox Church of Worcester was under the jurisdiction of the Holy Synod of the Russian Church, Moscow, and a member of its multilingual and multinational North American diocese[18] that was canonically united.[19] One of the youngest hierarchs of the Russian Church, Bishop Tikhon, at age thirty-three during his first days in the American diocese in 1898, found that "his flock was not worshiping in proper churches, but was using houses adapted to worship . . . or built in combination with housing and office space."[20] The Syrian Orthodox Church of Worcester was autocephalous, so it had autonomy and independence in matters affecting its internal life and structure.[21]

The parish practiced "brotherhood" as defined by literary writer, poet, philosopher, and artist Kahlil Gibran (1883–1931), an immigrant from Lebanon:

> I love you, my brother, whoever you are—Whether you worship in your church, kneel in your temple, or pray in your mosque. You and I are all children of one faith, for the diverse paths of religion are fingers of the loving hand of one Supreme Being, a hand extended to all, offering completeness of spirit to all, eager to receive all.[22]

Also, the Eastern Orthodox parish was ecumenical as it included Near Eastern people of eight ethnic cultures: Lebanese, Syrian, Palestinian, Albanian, Romanian, Greek, Assyrian, and a few Armenians. The religious sects of the Arab Americans were Eastern Orthodox, Melkite (in union with the Bishop of Rome, Byzantine-Greek rite),[23] a few Maronites, fewer Protestants—mostly Presbyterian, fewer Baptist and Methodist—a few Druze and Muslim. Although they worshipped together, each group maintained its own religious identity.

The non-Arab Christians of Eastern Orthodox faith were Albanian, Romanian, or Greek.[24]

The non-Arab Christians of Apostolic faith were Assyrian or Armenian.

The non-Arab Muslims were Tatar or White Russian.

The interaction between these people included business and marriage.

Shortly before and after World War I, the above-mentioned groups of Arab and non-Arab people established their own places of worship; those places still exist today, except those of the Protestant faith whose churches had already been established.

In 1924 a new era began for the Eastern Orthodox Syrian parishes in North America when the Patriarch of Antioch appointed Archimandrite Victor Aboassaly as the first Antiochian bishop and head of the Syrian Antiochian Church in North America. Although Antioch is part of modern-day Turkey, the Patriarchate of Antioch remains in Syria. The majority of Eastern Orthodox Christian parishes joined the Antiochian archdiocese, although a substantial number of parishes remained faithful to the Orthodox Church of Russia represented by the patriarchate of Moscow and All Russia and in America.[25]

Private-sector Organizations

The purpose of most organizations, as stated in their highly structured by-laws (see Addendum I), was to aid the poor, visit the sick, and promote harmony and cultural activities. According to sociologist and author Elaine C. Hagopian, "Most of the earlier non-church groups were charitable organizations designed to serve the community."[26]

Among the nonchurch charitable and recreational Worcester organizations were the Orthodox Fraternal Association and its affiliate the Orthodox Charitable Association, incorporated in 1905, later incorporated with a name change to the Orthodox Brotherhood Society, and lastly changed to the Syrian Brotherhood Orthodox Society of Worcester in 1932 (see Addendum IA). Consensus is that it is the oldest existing Syrian Eastern Orthodox organization in the Americas.

Although its founding fathers were of the Eastern Orthodox faith, the organization was not affiliated with the church. Its membership was open to "any member of the Syrian [geographic Syria] Race" and included Christian, Druze, and Muslim. Later, when their numbers increased, the Druze, Muslims, and other Christians established their own charitable organizations. The charitable nature of the Brotherhood was expressed on a letterhead dated as late as the 1940s, printed in Arabic and English, and included a statement of dues owed by members to help maintain cemetery plots: "This [amount due] excludes those who are not able to pay; for the motto of our Society is to help others. Those who do not reply are considered unable to pay; and their account is recorded among the charitable activities of this Society."

In 1905 a similar Brotherhood organization was founded in Spring Valley, Illinois, for charitable purposes—another example that this study is representative of Arab-American communities in general.

The Syrian-American Athletic Club was organized sometime before 1908 by young men interested in recreational activities who organized various teams to play baseball in open fields of the neighborhood. In his autobiography, Eli A. Busada talked about the athletic club and a drum corps:

> [T]he boys my age [aged sixteen] organized the Syrian-American Athletic Club. We rented an empty store on the Hill [Oak Hill] and bought athletic equipment for boxing, etc. We had a lot of fun. Later [1909] we [the Syrian American Athletic Club] organized the Fife and Drum Corps. I played the fife.[27]

One of the reasons the Fife and Drum Corps (predecessor of the Drum and Fife and Bugle Corps) was founded was to allow for participation in public celebrations. According to a Grafton, Massachusetts, newspaper report,

> The Drum and Fife and Bugle Corps was organized about 1909 and disbanded in 1919. During its existence, it took part in many parades and competitions in various towns throughout Worcester County and won its share of prizes for playing and drilling.[28]

After World War I, in 1920, the corps reorganized with a name change to Syrian American Drum Corps but disbanded in the mid-1930s. A second reorganization occurred in 1938.

A number of *jebab* (young men) who emigrated from Mahiethett organized the Young Muhaithite Charitable Society, forerunner of the Young Mahiethett Society in 1916 (see Addendum IB). Its constitution was printed in English and Arabic by the *Syrian Daily Eagle* of Brooklyn, New York, and the publisher, Najeeb G. Badran, was a frequent visitor to New England. Summarized in the society's 1962 Annual Installation Banquet brochure were "Important Contributions Made by the Society for the Welfare of Our People." They included "generous" financial contributions to Beatitude Patriarch Gregory of Damascus in 1918 and to Beatitude Patriarch Alexander in 1937; another large contribution aided in a flood disaster in Damascus and the surrounding area in 1925. The Society spearheaded, and aided financially, the successful effort to bring to Worcester the consecration of Archimandrite Victor Aboassaly to Archbishop in 1924.

The final paragraph read, "The many contributions and acts of charity sent to Mahiethey [Mahaithy, Mahiethett] together with assists to our people here in America, are too numerous to mention."

A recent activity of the Society was the planting of a cedar of Lebanon *(Cedrus Libani)* on the lawn at St. George Orthodox Cathedral in 1995. This type of tree is the most famous among the native tree species of Lebanon. As it is not native to the New England climate, the dedication ceremony was delayed until 1997 when the tree had produced good foliage growth. Engraved on the bronze plaque at the foot of the tree are the words:

> THE MAHIETHETT SOCIETY LIVING MEMORIAL
> The roots—our ancestors, laid to rest
> The branches—we, the living
> The new growth—our future generations.

Similar young men's organizations were created in other areas at about the same time, for example, the Lebanon Youth Society, organized in 1916 in Waterville, Maine.

It was common that immigrants from the same villages in the homeland formed charitable organizations to help their villages as well as their local communities. For example, immigrants in Boston who came from Douma (Lebanon) founded the Douma Ladies Charitable Society shortly after World War I, and it still exists, with expanded purposes.

The Muslim and Druze community, too, also organized charitable organizations. Predominant were the Angora Orphan Aid Association, the Moslem [Muslim] Brotherhood Association of Worcester, Massachusetts, founded in 1918, and the Ankara Aide Society. Like people of many religions, a Muslim believes in loving one's brother, the whole human race, as oneself and in helping the needy. The Prophet Muhammad said, "None of you has faith unless he loves for his brother what he loves for himself." The collective responsibility of the Muslim society was not only to ensure that basic survival needs were met, but also those that protected religion and intellect.

The letterhead of the Angora Orphan Aid Association included its name and address, 63 Clayton Street, Worcester, Massachusetts. On the upper left corner of the paper was an oval-shaped illustration of the village of Angora (former name for Ankara, Turkey), and on the upper right an illustration of the crescent that was superimposed on a five-pointed star. The imprint of the association's seal read "Ankara Himayei Etfal Ceniyeti, Worcester Mass., U.S.A., Ankara Orphan Aid Association," and in the center of the seal was the same type crescent and five-pointed star as appeared on its letterhead. The following were some of the founding members of these organizations:

Osman Omar	Abraham Esmaile
John Abraham	Abraham Mohammed
Davis Addren	Ali Ahmed
John Mohammed	Mussan Halil
Mamed Yaza	Abraham Yoosuf
Salah Hassan [Mike Salah]	Isa Muhammed
Mohammed Hassan	Zelpho Zelpho
Mustapha Shurkey	Daish Bocta
John Abdullah	Murad Mustaffa
Mohammed Baker	Omar Mahomet
Abdella Mustapha	Mohammed Salah
Jacob Kalesky	Brayson Romozon

Ms. A. of Northboro, Massachusetts, talked about her parents, Muslims born and married in White Russia, and the Angora Orphan Aid Association:

> My father emigrated first and then my mother followed. They were going to stay here together for a year or so to make a little money and then go back to Europe and buy themselves a piece of land. Somehow they never went back. They settled in New York for a few years and then permanently in the Worcester area at a farm in Northboro, Massachusetts. The Angora Orphan Aid Association used to have picnics at the farm to raise funds for the orphans. The main thing my parents, non-Arab Muslims, had in common with the members was the religion [Islam]—and the wonderful thing about the group was that they cared for each other. They thought of themselves as a brotherhood and that you are one of us. It was that kind of feeling.

Among the services of the Brotherhood was the purchase of a cemetery plot and the administration of the sales of grave lots. The Brotherhood attracted Muslims and Druze from throughout Massachusetts, Rhode Island, and other nearby states. It was fitting that the Muslim cemetery, with more than 200 graves, was adjacent to the Christian Arab-American section.

Ms. A. also remarked:

> You will notice it was mostly men buried at the cemetery and a few women who came over from the other side with their husbands. In those days it was mostly just men who used to come here. These bachelors were young when they came here and they sort of were on their own, but as they got older and they didn't have a family, they sort of clung to relatives or friends that had families and stayed close, and most in their old age went back to their homeland.

The Ankara Aide Society's last identified president was G. Sukrey Bikar in the late 1980s. In his old age he moved back to Turkey and was buried there. However, before he returned, Bikar assigned three Muslim women (Fay B., Minnie K., and Sonya A.) as representatives of the Muslim Brotherhood Association. Only a few are left in this area who have a direct link to the early Muslim and Druze community. Generally the present-day Muslim and Druze emigrated around the period of World War II and were part of the steady increase in the second wave of Muslim and Druze immigrants and represented many Arab and non-Arab countries. The largest group came from Pakistan and then Egypt, India, Iran, Saudi Arabia, Afghanistan, Greece, Turkey, Yugoslavia, and Lebanon. Their native languages include Farsi, Urdu, Arabic, Hindi, Persian, and Greek. They worship at the Islamic Society of Greater Worcester—in the same area at the lower end of Belmont Street where the earlier believers of Islam settled.

Muslims believe that the Prophet Muhammad is the human Messenger of God. The term Muslim means "one who surrenders to the will of God." Allah is the Arabic name for God. Instead of correctly identifying a believer of Islam as "Muslim" and the Prophet as "Muhammad," pre–World War II Western society commonly labeled incorrectly the Prophet as Mahomet and a believer as Mahometan or Mohammedan. Even many American Muslims identified themselves as "Mohammedan"—the label given them. Since post–World War II, most of Western society correctly refers to the believer as "Muslim" and the Prophet as "Muhammad." However, some local public records continue to list the believer as Mahometan, Mohammedan, or Moslem without "Muslim" or "Muhammad" cross-references. Therefore, when you ask for material on "Muslim" or "Islam" at certain public establishments, the response may be "We have none." Once you learn to ask, incorrectly, for "Mahometan," "Mohammedan," or "Moslem," the records are found.

The United Syrian Christian Association of North America was founded around 1920 or earlier and was headquartered in Worcester. It provided networking opportunities for Arab Americans generally in North America. Listed on the left-hand margin of the letterhead were its officers:

Shokri K. Swydan, Worcester, General Secretary

Dr. Solomon David, Houston, Texas

Joseph G. Zakhem, Lincoln, Nebraska, President

Najeeb G. Badran, Editor, *Syrian Daily Eagle*, Brooklyn, New York

Its branches were located in Worcester, New York City, Lincoln and Omaha, Nebraska, Toledo and Akron, Ohio, Detroit, Michigan, Charleston, West Virginia, Wichita, Kansas, Willimantic and Danbury, Connecticut, Montreal, Canada, and Cochrane, Ontario, Canada.

Some of the above institution and organizations are represented in two montages (see 2.12 and 2.13).

Church-related Organizations

An example of a church-related organization was the Myrra (Arabic for myrrh) Bearing Women Society at St. George Orthodox Church of Worcester, forerunner of the Ladies of St. George Orthodox Antioch Society, later named Young Ladies Aid Society, then changed to the Women's Club, which continues to this day. The society changed its name each time to more accurately define its goals. The organization was founded about 1919 or earlier by a number of women.[29]

The original name was inspired by the myrrh-bearing women of the New Testament who were actively involved in Christ's public ministry. The organization has been dedicated to supporting the goals of the church. In 1928 its elected president was Nerzeh (Dadah) Kaneb, a Maronite married to an Eastern Orthodox man. The Women's Club brochure titled "History Of The Women's Club, St. George Orthodox Cathedral," dated May 14, 1978, stated that between 1928 and 1954, more than $25,000 was raised by members of the Women's Club, which helped to pay off the mortgage, build additions, and make improvements to the church hall, kitchen, and rectory. Referring to the founders, it read:

These wonderful and dear ladies were our grandmothers, mothers and aunts. . . . We remember our past members with reverence and gratitude for the foundation which they have established and upon which our present organization has been built.

A similar organization, the Ladies Society of St. George Church (Syrian Ladies Aid Society), Boston, was founded in 1917 and is still in existence. A Ladies Myrrh Bearing Society of St. George Church of Washington, D.C., was established in 1921 and was dedicated to supporting the goals of its church. These examples demonstrate how this study is representative, in general, of the Arab-American community.

Family Ties — Staying in Touch

Many families and individuals who first settled in Worcester and then branched out to other parts of the country kept in touch through visits and correspondence with their families and friends in Worcester. The city had an attraction that drew some to return to it permanently, or to visit from distant places in North and South America where they were earning their livelihood. Their return visits to Worcester were for weeks or even months at a time in Arab-American homes. Hospitality was considered a pleasure and privilege as well as a responsibility and was instilled and practiced early in the lives of family members.

Nora A. H. recalled her mother was the first in her family to emigrate:

> My mother, Sophie — Shafeeka née Ferage — at age sixteen, went to Lawrence from Lebanon. Later her parents and three sisters emigrated to Brazil and I'm not sure how that happened. My mother had already come here, and she always felt sad about that — that the rest of her family was in Brazil. When I was about seven years old my parents took me to Brazil with them to attend the wedding of my mother's nephew, Miguel. For the first time I met my maternal grandparents and my three aunts. Yes, that's right, they kept in touch with one another with this great distance and without all of the media we have now. There was this great sense of connecting then.

Homeland Ties — Return Migrations and Visits

The deeply rooted idea of *el-belaad,* the homeland, was etched in the memory of many Arab-American immigrants. Because of their creative intelligence, hard work, stamina, and frugality, many fulfilled their goal within a couple of years and returned in Western dress to *el-belaad* in an improved financial state. They were recognized as *mohajar* (immigrant) and over-whelmed with attention and honors. Some returned to spouses, relatives, and friends; others renewed ties with their families and remained in their villages for a few years. Some marriages were arranged, and the couple and their families shared their wedding festivities with folks in their villages or urban settlements. Bachelors and the widowed often came back to find a bride or husband and then returned to New England. Many returned several times to *el-belaad,* mostly for four or five years each time before deciding that America would be their permanent home. Others, after putting down roots in America, sent for their families and/or relatives. Tufeek A. related:

> My father came home one day and said to my mother, who was pregnant with me, "Well, I want to go back to Syria. I want to visit my family." My mother said to him, "Why don't you wait until the baby is born? This is no time for us to travel across the ocean." His response was, "No, I want to go now." And off they went. Otherwise, if they had remained a few more months I would have been born here—I was conceived in this country and born across.

Those who did not return to America were the ones who had become homesick for *el-belaad,* for its familiar lifestyle, where the rhythm of life was more agreeable to them. For many, *el-belaad* was a place where people were comfortable with who they were, with what they had, and with the routines that filled their lives.

The majority of illustrations date from around 1870 to 1920 and portray the appearance and social attitude of Arab-American immigrants of that era with its memorabilia, romance, street scenes, and architecture. Frequently portraits were taken at studios located on Front Street in downtown Worcester, and some were made as a postal card with a portrait on one side of the card. It was common to distribute prints to family, relatives, and friends here and in their homelands.

2.1. Abdelnour family of Kfarchima (now Lebanon), 1900. *Clockwise from top left:* Virginia, Aneese, Genevieve, Fuad (Alfred), Abraham (father), Emily Fahardt Abdelnour (mother), and Anyssa. Missing was Milhelm Abdelnour, who emigrated to Jamaica, British West Indies. Aneese emigrated to Jamaica in 1905 at age sixteen, then settled in Worcester in 1910. Alfred Abdelnour emigrated to Worcester and served in the U.S. Army in World War I. After the war he returned to Worcester for a couple of years, then settled in Lebanon.

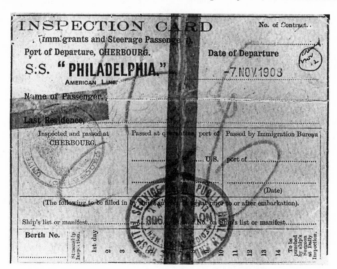

2.2. Inspection Card (Immigrants and Steerage Passengers). Name of Passenger: Hannah, Afoumime [Afoumia]; Last Residence: Mouhaii [Mahiethett, Lebanon]; Date of Departure: 7 Nov. 1908; Arrived at Ellis Island. The card includes a record for fourteen days of daily health inspection punched by ship's surgeon. Reverse side indicates the bearer has been vaccinated, and it contains instructions in eight common languages.

2.3. Second migration by El-Hajj Boosahda (Abraham Boosahda), 1900. *Clockwise from lower right:* Miryam (Mary) (daughter), El-Hajj (father), Khalil (Kalil, "Charlie")(son), and Malocke George (neighbor). The bouquet of artificial flowers, boutonniere, American flag, and gun were props of the studio photographer. Dangling from a chain in El-Hajj's vest pocket was a gold cross. Ages at death were 73, 83, 97, and 96, for Mary Boosahda Haddad, Abraham Boosahda, Kalil A. Boosahda, and Malocke George Dahrooge, respectively. *Top center:* The name Malocke is written in Arabic for future identification, to indicate she was of a different lineage than others in the photograph.

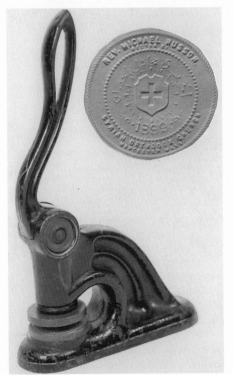

2.4. Hand embosser and seal in English and Arabic. Seal (actual size): "Rev. Michael [M.] Husson—Rector of—Syrian Orthodox Church, Worcester, Mass., 1899." Embosser: height eleven inches, weight six pounds.

2.5. Consecration of first Syrian Antiochian Bishop of New York and all North America, Archbishop Victor Aboassaly, Worcester, Mass., 1924. *Clockwise top row left:* Nassif Mitchell, Bashara K. Forzley, Gamil (James) Nassar, Habeeb Husson, Nicholas Haddad, Shokri K. Swydan, Andrew Habib, Ameen Forzley, Monsour Abdelmaseh. *Front row:* Thomas Ferris George, altar boy unknown, unknown, Archimandrite Thimi Theodos (priest, Church of St. Mary's Assumption, today called St. Mary's Assumption Albanian Orthodox Church), two priests unknown, Rev. Michael Husson, Archbishop Victor, Rev. Samuel David (later Bishop Samuel David), Metropolitan Gerassimos Messarra of Beirut, Archbishop Panteleimon, three priests unknown, two altar boys unknown, Michael Ansara. Each altar boy carried a long-stemmed flower. The banner on the left was of the Syrian American Society, and its motto, written in Arabic, was "Freedom, Brotherhood, Equality." The seal of the State of Massachusetts was on the banner on the right. The consecration was held at St. Mary's Assumption Church as the facilities at St. George Syrian Orthodox Church at 100 Wall Street were too small to accommodate the large attendance.

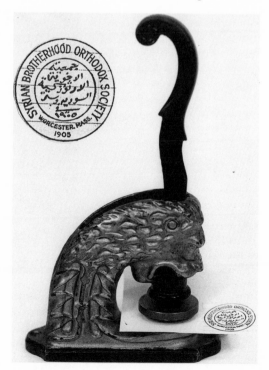

2.6. Hand embosser and seal in English and Arabic. Seal: "Syrian Brotherhood Orthodox Society, Worcester, Mass., about 1905." Embosser: Gold-colored lion's head, with black, elongated handle. Actual size of embossed seal was two inches in diameter.

2.7. Lapel badges. *Left:* worn by members of Syrian Brotherhood Orthodox Society, founded 1905. *Center:* lapel medal "S.B.O.S. 1905–1919." *Right:* worn by members of Young Mahiethett Society, founded 1916. The light blue satin side of the reversible badges was worn at festivities and meetings. Badges were bordered with gold cord and had gold-fringed bottom edges; name of organization was in gold letters in Arabic and English. Both societies used the handclasp emblem that signified brotherhood and charity.

2.8. Reversible sides of lapel badges, 1905 and 1916. Black satin side legend: "In Memoriam." Badges worn at wakes and in funeral processions by members.

SYRIAN BROTHERHOOD ORTHODOX SOCIETY
Worcester. Massachusetts
1919

Seated, left to right: Geo. Peters, Abraham Gammal, Snoor Peters, *Rev.* Michael Husson, *Metropolitan* Germanous, *Publisher* N.Badran, Shokri Swydan, Abraham Booshda, B.K.Fordey, Aneen Forzley
Middle Row, left to right: Nassif Mitchell, Awdy Mitchell, Essa Kalil, Assaf George, Hanna Kaaeb, George Rayis, Elias T Birbara, Samuel M. Kouri, Elias J. Eid, George A. Haddad
Back Row, left to right: George M. Husson, Joseph Jalboot, Nicholas Gesous, Moses Mackoul, Kalil Abou-asaly, Assad Awad, Thomas F.George, Simon George

2.9. Members of Syrian Brotherhood Orthodox Society at the Syrian Orthodox Church, 100 Wall Street, 1919. To identify the individuals, Arabic numeral markings were made on either the left or right of their lapels. Names were written in Arabic and English. Members wore their badges on their left lapel, and the medal was worn by some on their right lapel. *First row center:* Archbishop Germanos (Shehadi); to his left is Najeeb G. Badran, editor and publisher of *Al-Nasr, The Eagle,* and the *Syrian Daily Eagle,* published in Brooklyn, N.Y. Archbishop Germanos and Badran were frequent visitors to New England and traveled nationwide.

2.10. Moslem [Muslim] Brotherhood Association of Worcester,
Mass., obelisk-shaped monument topped with a globe, front.
Left center: founding date of the
brotherhood, 1918. *Right foreground:* tombstone of Rakip Belul
Skrapari 1874–1950. *Center
back:* monument with Christian
cross is in adjoining Christian
Arab-American section.

2.11. Moslem [Muslim] Brotherhood Association of Worcester, Mass., monument, back.
The founding date of the brotherhood was engraved in Arabic as 1334 Hijra according to
the Muslim lunar calendar. Also engraved in
Ottoman Turkish script was a poem of wistful
yearning for a life in the homeland with family
and friends. Many other Muslim monuments
have engraved verses from the Quran in Arabic
or Ottoman Turkish script.

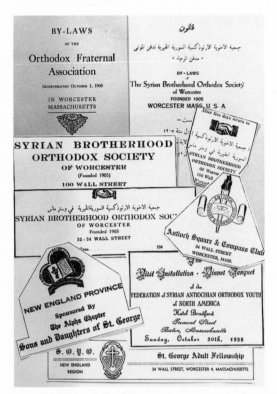

2.12. Realia montage of organizations (local and North America) organized about 1905–54. Cover page of bylaws of the Orthodox Fraternal Association, incorporated 1905; cover page in Arabic and English of bylaws of the Syrian Brotherhood Orthodox Society, 1932; letterhead of Syrian Brotherhood Orthodox Society, 100 Wall Street, pre-1928; envelope address of Syrian Brotherhood Orthodox Society, 100 Wall Street, pre-1928; letterhead of Syrian Brotherhood Orthodox Society, 32-34 Wall Street, 1940s; letterhead of Antioch Square & Compass Club, about 1954. Its membership was open "to any person being a Master Mason of near east extraction by descent or marriage" and a resident of Massachusetts. In 1983 a testimonial dinner was given to honor George A Wood, who earned his 33rd degree, Freemasonry's highest honor, in recognition of his meritorious achievement, selfless charitable hard work, and continuing adherence to high principle. In 1983 there were 119 members and 13 out-of-state members. Disbanded late 1980s; cover page of program book of the New England province of the Orthodox-Catholic Frontier of America (OCF) fifth annual convention, hosted by the Alpha Chapter Sons and Daughters of St. George (Church), Boston, Mass., 1942. OCF's motto was "Hope, Faith and Charity." Guests were the Most Rev. Antony Bashir, Metropolitan of New York and All North America, Exarch of His Holiness Alexander, Patriarch of Antioch the Great and All the East; and His Grace Samuel David, Archbishop of Toledo and Its Dependencies; cover page of program book of First Installation Dinner Banquet of the Federation of Syrian Antiochian Orthodox Youth of North America [S.O.Y.O.]. Guest: His Excellency Antony Bashir, Archbishop, New York and North America. Hosted by St. John of Damascus Young Peoples' Association of Boston, at Hotel Bradford, Boston, 1938; letterhead of St. George Adult Fellowship, 34 Wall Street, Worcester, member of S.O.Y.O. New England Region, about 1938.

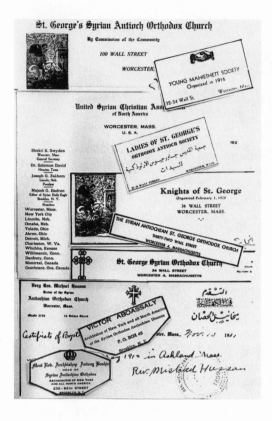

2.13. Realia montage of institution and organizations (local and North America), about 1917–36. Letterhead of St. George's Syrian Antioch Orthodox Church, By Commission of the Community, 100 Wall Street, Worcester, and top left ikon of Saint George slaying dragon and princess standing in entryway to castle, pre–1928; calling card of Young Mahiethett Society, around 1928; letterhead of United Syrian Christian Association of North America, 1920s; calling card of Ladies of St. George's Orthodox Antioch Society at 32-34 Wall Street, Worcester, printed in Arabic and English, about 1928; letterhead of Knights of St. George, 34 Wall Street, Worcester, with ikon of Saint George slaying dragon, organized 1929; letterhead of the Syrian Antiochian St. George Orthodox Church (formerly Syrian Orthodox Church); letterhead of St. George Syrian Orthodox Church, 34 Wall Street, pre-1970; certificate of baptism on letterhead stationery of "Very Rev. Michael [M.] Husson, Rector of the Syrian Antiochian Orthodox Church, Worcester, Mass., 1931 (*top left*, 10 Sultan Street address in English, *top right*, address in Arabic, *bottom right*, rector's 1899 seal); letterhead of Archbishop Victor Aboassaly, first "Archbishop of New York and all North America of the Syrian Orthodox Antiochian Diocese," Brooklyn, N.Y., about 1927; letterhead of Most Rev. Archbishop Antony Bashir, successor to Archbishop Victor Aboassaly, about 1936.

2.14. Seal in English (actual size), reads: "The Myrra Bearing Women Society, Founded 1919, St. George Orthodox Church of Worcester."

Chapter Three
MULTICULTURAL AND
MULTIRELIGIOUS NEIGHBORHOODS

From the hills and valleys of western Syria, the Arab-American immigrants made their journey to the hills and valleys of Worcester. They settled in three vibrant multicultural and multireligious neighborhoods on the east side of the city near the Union Passenger Railroad Station.

The neighborhoods were open and fluid ethnomicrocosms of immigrant America, with successive waves of immigrants. One neighborhood was located in a section of Oak Hill, one of Worcester's fifteen hills,[1] in the area of Norfolk and Wall Streets. The second neighborhood was in the area of East Central and East Worcester Streets at the lower end of Shrewsbury Street, near Old Pine Meadow Road.[2] The third was on Chandler Hill in the lower Belmont Street area. Today these areas are commonly called Grafton Hill, The Meadows, and Bell Hill, respectively.

Albert B. Southwick, in *More Once-Told Tales of Worcester County*, commented on the diversity in Worcester, noting that while most medium-sized cities had two or three main ethnic groups, Worcester was more like New York—a League of Nations. He said that some historians claim that Worcester's population is drawn from more than thirty [ethnic] groups, many of which have lost their identity in the melting pot.[3]

As early as 1893 the Board of Trade (forerunner of the Worcester Chamber of Commerce), in its *Tribute to the Columbian Year,* recognized integrated neighborhoods:

> There are a few streets that do not have both rich and poor living near each other. No one ward can be considered a distinctively poor one, nor any other especially rich.[4]

Cultural Names of Oak Hill

According to when a particular cultural group predominated, the residents called Oak Hill by various cultural names. When the Irish arrived and settled there, it was called Dungarvan Hill;[5] when residents were predominantly French Canadian, it took on an additional ethnic name, French Hill. According to authors Elbridge Kingsley and Frederick Knab, in *Picturesque Worcester: City and Environments,* the Irish and French Canadians arrived around 1826.[6]

Oak Hill was described in *The Dictionary of Worcester,* 1893:

> The rising land southeast of the Union Railroad Station, [is] popu-lated largely with French Canadians. The slope rises abruptly from the railroad, and the houses rise one above the other in full view up the declivity. The Bloomingdale Road runs along the side of the hill.[7]

Italians began to arrive around the 1870s. The majority settled in the Wall Street and Suffolk Street areas and on Shrewsbury Street. According to Dr. John McCoy, pastor of Saint Ann Roman Catholic Church:

> In 1894 an Italian priest, Vincent Migliore, gathered the people of his race into Saint Stephen's Church [an Irish parish] with the in-tention of forming a parish for their benefit. During that time he was unable to make headway to its parish formation beyond the purchase of the piece of property at the junction of Suffolk and Wall Streets . . . and the result was that one of the priests at Saint Stephen's, who spoke Italian because he had studied in Italy, at-tempted to do all what he could for the people in the absence of a native Italian priest.[8]

The majority of Syrians settled in the Oak Hill area around Norfolk and Wall Streets and were a relatively small group until after World War I when they became predominant. Most Arab Americans referred to Oak Hill as *el-tellee* (the hill, feminine form), and frequently today Arab Americans still refer to it as *el-tellee.*

Many of the Maronites from Lebanon settled in The Meadows, which was called *harrate tahta* (the place below—the meadows) by the Arab Americans of *el-tellee.* Among the neighbors of the Maronites were the Irish and Italians, and these three groups worshiped together at Saint Ann Church, founded in 1855.[9] Now the two Roman Catholic parishes, Saint Ann and Our Lady of Mount Carmel are joined. Their present church on Mulberry Street was built in 1929. It was common that Arab Americans, Maronites in particular, attended Saint Ann parochial school.

Most of the Druze and Muslims settled in the lower end of Belmont Street at Lincoln Square, with some in *el-tellee.*

Communication: The Language Barrier

Although the Arab Americans and their neighbors of other cultures spoke in different languages, interaction took place through shared food, music, handicraft, and interplay with the children. Neighbors communicated in pantomime that had a grace and dignity of its own. Some immigrants learned each other's jargon; usually the phrases first learned were curse words—and at times these words were not always used in jest. Neighbors, however, exchanged greetings and spoke mainly in the language of gentleness and kindness. They respected each other as part of America with shared common goals that transcended barriers created by history, diversity, and culture.

Tour: *El-Saha* and a Section of *El-Tellee*

Time: Turn of the Century

The centerfold gives a vivid description not only in the geographical sense but also in the sense of the moment. One gets the feel of a section of *el-tellee* as it was at the turn of the century. It almost invites you to enter *el-saha* (a large, open square) at the junction of Wall and Norfolk Streets. *El-saha* was a dramatic locale where on festive or sad occasions, processions and centuries-old Arab traditions took place. Saturday was a time for music and dancing in the street.

Charles A. George talked about the festivity:

> Every Saturday the *mijwiz* [a musical instrument similar to an end-blown flute] and the *darabukkah* [a vase-shaped hand drum with goatskin across its head] are played right out on the street. People dance in the middle of the street. Every Saturday—it is like in Lebanon. It is the most beautiful sight. People—the Irish, the French, and the Italians—come and watch. The women mix in with the men and dance together the *dabkah* [a folkloric line dance with a leader]. Pete Abdow and Abraham Williams played the *mijwiz* at different times. I watch each play the *mijwiz* and wonder how he is breathing as he keeps playing, and it seems he hardly ever takes the *mijwiz* out of his mouth. The people keep dancing until it gets dark, and then they quit and go home.

Buildings That Bordered El-Saha

The five imposing commercial-residential buildings that bordered *el-saha* were either of three, four, or five stories. Among them were four double-deckers, also called double houses, which provided two three-bedroom apartments on each floor, separated by a staircase and hallway. Generally, stores occupied the lower level of the buildings, although at various times some were used as residences. Most buildings in *el-tellee* were built into the steep hillside, with the lowest story, wholly or partly below ground, called the basement. When fully underground it was called a cellar. Each store had its own entrance, and the residences upstairs had separated front indoor entrances and a back outdoor stairway with porches. Some buildings had front and back porches with fancy carved railings. Often interviewees pointed to a certain building in the photographs and remarked happily, "I was born in that building."

Street signs were posted so a driver seated high in a horse-drawn wagon could see them; pedestrians needed to lift their heads to read them. On the east side of *el-saha* was the sign "WALL STREET" posted high on a utility pole in front of the steep pathway near the stone wall. Directly across the street was the "BLOOMINGDALE CT. PRIVATE STREET DANGEROUS" sign, posted on the right side of the building above the second-floor window at the corner of Bloomingdale Court and Norfolk Street.

On the west side of *el-saha* is Bloomingdale Court, a narrow, steep hill leading to Franklin Street. In 1899 the land at 41-43-45 Norfolk Street adjoining Bloomingdale Court was owned by Akil E. Haddad.[10] In 1902 it was sold to Shaker Saayeke (Syiegh) [later spelled Syiek] and Naahim Saayeke.[11] Shaker Saayeke was the developer of the four-story commercial-residential building. The photograph includes a lone Arab-American gentleman seated on a homemade wooden bench on a wooden slab platform set flush with the double-decker. He wore a black derby, black coat, black high-laced shoes, black suit, necktie, and black vest with a pocket watch gold chain suspended from his vest pocket. His outstretched arms and extended fingers rested on top of the bench. The empty milk can at the far end of the platform was ready for pickup by the milkman, and in exchange for the can the storekeeper received credit.

The first Syrian bakery was located in the above-mentioned building; its entrance was on the basement level, off Bloomingdale Court at the corner of Norfolk Street. Syiek ran the bakery, and later another man called Abou A-jaj ran it. He had four or five sons, and one of his sons, Moxie, was killed in an auto accident. George S., grandson of Shaker Saayeke, mentioned that his parents described Bloomingdale Court many times as picturesque because of its dangerous incline and added:

Bloomingdale Court is rockbound. It was all ledge, and the road was covered with dirt and small rocks. After each storm the ledge was exposed and water rushed down from *el-saha* and the street took on the appearance of a running brook with houses located on each side. Not until after World War II did the city pave the street, and now water just runs right off the asphalt.

One of the many regular occurrences in the daily routine of *el-saha* neighborhood was the arrival of the milk wagon. The photograph shows a two-horse team in the distance at the upper end of Norfolk Street. The sound of the cadence of horse hoofs and the faint squeak of wagon wheels usually signaled its approach. The swirling dust from the unpaved dirt and gravel street was kicked up by the horses and with it sometimes the smell of horse manure. At certain times of the day, to control the dust, a resident poured water on the street.

32-34-36 Norfolk Street

At the east side of *el-saha* at 32-34-36 Norfolk Street was one of its imposing structures with bay windows at each front corner of the five-story double-decker dwelling for eight families. On the front of each floor were ten windows, each with functional wooden louvered shutters. As you can see, some shutters were completely drawn, some were set with the upper half closed, while others were folded out to let the sunlight in. Particularly at sunset the leaded stained-glass top sections of the storefront windows reflected brilliant shades of color. Above these windows were striped awnings with scalloped borders. The architectural trim at the base of the windows was granite slabs surrounded by red brick. One of Simon George's dry goods stores was located at 32 Norfolk Street.

Frequent references were made to the early Arab-American immigrant owners of the building, Nimry (Saba) Husson, a woman dry goods peddler and wife of Makhool Husson, who returned to Aita several times and died there; then Worde "Rose" Abdow, another woman peddler and widowed mother of George Abdow. In 1900 Nasiph M. Abdow was the owner, and a few years later George Abdow owned the double-decker. Interviewees who had lived on the top floor smiled when they recalled that anyone who visited them had to climb at least sixty steps to reach the fifth story.

Visible at the open shutters and open-curtained sunlit window on the second story of the building are three children. Perhaps their mother had asked them to let her know when they saw the milk wagon come down the street as she had no milk and wanted to make *mahallabiyeh* (a delicate milk pudding) for their lunchtime dessert. As the milkman drove his team past the front of their house, he would make a left turn up the pathway of horizontally laid railroad ties that showed ruts and wear and tear from wheels of horse-drawn wagons. The milkman stopped and made deliveries using the back stairways of homes on both sides of the pathway. Instead of using the same way as the milkman to go to and from their homes, children with arms outstretched to balance themselves often walked on top of a stone wall that today still extends from *el-saha* to midway up the hill.

Slightly visible is 76-78 Wall Street and, in the upper right of the illustration, the front corner of a four-story shingled double-decker with two storefronts on the lower level facing Wall Street. At various times the storefronts were used as shops for dry goods, groceries, coffeehouses, restaurants, barbershops, and even a poolroom. These establishments maintained an open-door policy and as such served as gathering places for socializing and as places where strangers could obtain needed information and direction.

At the south side of *el-saha*, at the junction of Wall and Norfolk Streets, was a triangular-shaped four-story double-decker called the flatiron.[12] Its narrowest section pointed to *el-saha*. On the front side (75-77 Wall) and back side (23-30-30½ Norfolk) of each floor were porches with wooden railings. Because of the slope of *el-tellee*, the front of the basement floor facing Wall Street was built into the ground and gave the appearance that the building was residential only. From Norfolk Street, however, the basement floor with its three outside entrances was visible; the center door opened to upstairs residences, and to the right and left were business entrances. One was to the Ducharme Bakery[13] (French American), where French bread, cakes, and cookies were baked; the other entrance was to the Kamel Najemy Bakery (Arab American), where Syrian bread was baked. A few houses down the hill toward the beginning of Norfolk Street was the Gannon Bakery[14] (Irish American), where Irish bread was baked.

The fifth building (33-35-35½-37 Norfolk Street) at the southwest side of *el-saha* at the corner of Bloomingdale Court and Norfolk Street was an oblong-shaped three-story commercial-residential building with three apartments on each of the two floors, and two apartments or businesses on the basement level. Each apartment had two or three bedrooms. Because the shape of the building was similar to the ones at military camps, after World War I, returning servicemen and local residents called it the

Outpost, and after World War II it was called the Barracks.[15] It had two lower-level storefronts, five entrances, and two side entrances. One store was occupied by George Abodeely's retail dry goods business,[16] and at the opposite end of the building Salem Rochette (Salim Rachid) operated the grocery store. He also operated the "Arabian boardinghouse"[17] on the second floor. Louis P. recalled:

> Salim Rachid had a grocery store and the rooming house up above. The immigrants, when they first came to this area, lived in his boardinghouse or one of the others, or else they roomed with other immigrants in their homes.

Down the hill at the corner of Bloomingdale Court and 94-96-98 Bloomingdale Road (today's Franklin Street) was a building with architecture identical to the Barracks. Another "Arabian boardinghouse"[18] was located at the 98 Bloomingdale Road address.

After World War II the five imposing buildings that bordered *el-saha* were destroyed by fires at different times and were demolished. The church at 100 Wall Street was torn down in 1978.

Syrian Orthodox Church

Midway up the pathway was the two-story brick-and-shingle Syrian Orthodox Church at 100 Wall Street,[19] topped with an Oriental-bulbous lantern (see photo 6.1, top right) built on top of the roof with open-window walls, a belfry, and a cross. Now the location is the parking lot directly behind the El Morocco Restaurant. Church services were held on the second floor, which was accessible by a separate outdoor stairway and side entrance. In keeping with the period style of buildings, the ground floor was used by Akil Haddad and his cousin Thomas Haddad for their dressmaking shop and also their other businesses: Haddad Akil, dry goods; A. Haddad & Co.; Akil & Co. (T. Haddad), wrapper mfrs.; and Thomas A. Haddad & Co.).[20] When Akil Haddad, son of Badaway Haddad Abodeely, moved to the lower level of the church, he sold his dry goods store at 94 Bloomingdale Road to Salim Debs.

Thomas Haddad's daughter, Adele H. A., recalled:

> My father and Akil Haddad opened a store and were making ladies' dresses. I don't remember the name of the store but it was located at 100 Wall Street and the building is gone. Our church, the Syrian Orthodox Church, was upstairs and their store was on the ground floor. It was a small church and at times had visiting priests.

The plot of land where the church stood was owned by "Badaway [Haddad] Abudula, widow, . . . otherwise known as Badaway Abodeely" in 1907.[21] Eli A. B. wrote in a letter to his niece Alexandra:

> The Syrian Orthodox Church paid rent to Badaway Abodeely. She was a widow and migrated with her son, Nassar Abodeely. You know Mike Abodeely's father was not the first in his family to emigrate—it was Mike's great-grandmother, Badaway Abodeely.

When the church bell rang from the belfry calling people to prayer on Sundays and church holidays, it was a common sight to see a child going up and down while holding onto the end of the bell rope that rang the bell. Supposedly the jubilant child felt responsible for ringing the bell while the father or grandfather supplied the muscle power on the rope.

From midway up the pathway looking down on the rolling hills of Worcester, one can see next to many homes the gardens of herbs, vegetables, grape arbors, fruit trees, and backyard farms spread out into open fields. On numerous occasions many of the people interviewed recalled how *el-tellee*'s natural beauty with its surrounding hills and valleys was similar to the villages they left behind in *el-belaad*, particularly Mahiethett.

Some street names were changed. For example, Lawn Street became Sultan Street and York Street became St. George Street. Additionally some street numbers represented two buildings with the same address; 100 Wall Street was also a one-story storefront that faced Wall Street and behind it midway up the hill was the Syrian church with the same address. There were two addresses of 32 Norfolk Street, one a five-story commercial-residential double-decker that fronted Norfolk Street and behind it midway up the hill was the four-story residential double-decker.

A few houses north of *el-saha* on the same side of the street was the three-story home of Yacoub Tunous Lian (Jacob Thomas Lian) and his wife, Emeline Lian. As their family grew, L-shaped additions were made on both sides of the cottage with first-floor storefronts, and a center courtyard at 57-59 Norfolk Street.[22] One store was a cobbler shop, the other a grocery store. Later the storefront at 57 Norfolk was the site of the first Melkite mass held in Worcester.[23] At different times mass was offered at other homes, for example, the home of Max Haddad at 8 Montreal Street.[24]

Section of *El-Tellee*—Its Architecture and Landownership

A considerable number of Arab-American developers had built three-deckers with basements or cellars and commercial-residential buildings in *el-tellee* (see map 5); 29 Norfolk Street, a three-decker at the lower end of Norfolk Street near Bloomingdale Road, was built by developer Ameen An-toun; several (mostly commercial-residential buildings) were built by developer Simon George; and a three-decker by his brother, developer Asaffe George. The multifamily three-deckers got their name because the porches resembled the decks of ships. Asaffe's son, Charles A. George, recalled:

> My father didn't build as much as he remodeled the old-fashioned houses on Wall Street. He made them safe with two doors, front and back doors, and other remodeling. In 1898 my father bought that house on 72 Wall Street (still standing) and I was born in that house. Then he bought this three-decker where I live on Hamilton Street. In the meantime he built [developed] at the corner of Wall and Groton Place a three-decker with a store. There was a cottage next to the building, and he had the cottage moved, and that's where my sister [Malocke George Dahrooge] and her family lived. The Abodeelys were the ones that rented my father's store for about five years until they built their own store.

A few houses down from the church, at 80 Wall Street[25] at the corner of Rondeau Court, was the three-story, commercial-residential, one-family house of the French Canadian Rondeau family, subsequently purchased by Abraham Boosahda. Both Rondeau and Boosahda were devout Christians. Boosahda prayed formally five times daily, and before his prayers at dusk he required those in his area, especially the teenagers who were knowledgeable in Arabic and English, to participate in the recitation of prayers. When Boosahda owned all the buildings (five houses) on Rondeau Court, he contemplated changing the name to Boosahda Court but did not, out of respect to Rondeau. The ground-level storefronts at 80 Wall Street housed a Syrian bakery subsequently owned or rented by Boosahda, Najemy, Kalil, and Salloum, in turn.

Across the street from Rondeau Court was a residential eight-family double house, five stories with basement at 65 Wall Street. The developers were Salim Azar (1838–1925) and his wife Helen (Bourisk) Azar (1848–1937). Their three sons dug up the foundation by using horses and shovels.

Charles A. George remembered:

> There were three brothers and they worked hard. Ohhh, did they work hard. They dug the whole foundation with horses and shovel behind the horse. I don't know where all that dirt went. They would hold the horse with the reins and one would hold the plow and then

they would plow out the dirt. Then they hired people to do the foundation, and then they got someone to lay the brick, and then up went the carpenter's work. But the brothers did the dirty and hard work and besides that they had their regular jobs.

Salim and Helen Azar's children had as their surname Salim (Salem), the first name of the father, and that was according to worldwide custom. In later years some of the Salem grandchildren reverted to the family name Azar as their surname.

Located on the hill at the lower end of Wall Street at the corner of Wall and Thorne Streets were four buildings. Not visible is the three-story hall behind the church, which may be seen in photo Timeline.1. The redbrick Saint Joseph Church (Roman Catholic) and rectory were built in 1891–92 for the French Canadian parishioners. In 1928 they were purchased by the Syrian Antiochian St. George Orthodox Church of Worcester (formerly the Syrian Orthodox Church, 100 Wall Street). The three-story rectory with first- and second-floor wraparound porches[26] was connected to the church sanctuary by a first-floor hallway. On an outdoor concrete step of the first landing from the street to the church was chiseled the church's name and date built, "St. Joseph 1892." When in 1928 the four buildings were purchased by the Eastern Orthodox Christians, "St. George E.O. 1928" was chiseled on a step of the second landing. Located at the left foreground of the grounds was the convent of the Sisters of Saint Anne, a three-story shingle-and-brick cottage with first- and second-floor wraparound porches.

At the lower end of Wall Street at the corner of Grafton Street was a 5½-story (a mezzanine floor on ground level), commercial-residential, six-family double house with basement. Simon George, the developer, purchased the land in 1898. Above the second-story corner window was a date-and-name stone with the inscription "1901 S. George." The sidewalk at the front of the building was made of heavy glass blocks that admitted daylight to the high-ceilinged basement. Porches for each floor were at the back of the building. Across the street on the opposite corner is the Grafton Street School, a two-and-a-half-story brick structure built in 1879; the building still stands.[27]

Among the turn-of-the-century multicultural *el-saha*'s architectural links to the past that still stand are the four-story Bianchi (Italian American) home built into the hill between 1882 and 1887 by developers Ytalia Bianchi and her husband, Angelo Bianchi. Later the husband returned to his beloved Italy. In 1912 the Ytalia Macaroni factory was built next to the residence and closed around 1969. Later both buildings were owned by charitable organizations (Pope John XXIII Council 5481, Knights of Columbus, and then by Worcester Aerie 4311, Fraternal Order of Eagles). Across the street from the Bianchi homestead is the two-story O'Connor (Irish American) home, and next to it is a three-story tenement built by developers Ferris Abdow and wife Sooriya El-Hajj Abdow (Arab Americans) in 1920.

Multicultural and Integrated Neighborhoods

The dynamics of the cross-cultural and integrated neighborhoods where most Arab Americans lived, namely *el-tellee,* The Meadows, and the lower end of Bell Hill, were an affirmation of diversity and coexistence. Generally the immigrants of different cultural backgrounds recognized their common values, aspirations, difficult circumstances, and the goal to attain an American identity while maintaining their cultural heritage.

3.1. Union Passenger Railroad Station, Worcester, Mass., about 1893. Second constructed Union Station with 200-foot Norman clock tower, opened in 1874 at the eastern side of Washington Square. The train shed was demolished in 1910 and the clock tower was razed to make way for Interstate 290 in 1958. *Upper left:* Bianchi homestead. *Upper right:* steeple of former St. George Orthodox Church at corner of Wall and Thorne Streets. *Lower left center:* electric trolley cars. Beneath the two poles are watering troughs from which stagecoach drivers refreshed their horses. *Upper right foreground:* Graton & Knight building and smokestack. The first railroad station was built in 1835 on Foster Street near Main Street. A third Union Station opened in 1911 on the southeast side of Washington Square.

3.2. *Background:* residential eight-family double house with basement at 65 Wall Street built about 1896. Photo taken from across the street on rooftop of storefront at 80 Wall Street, 1921. *Foreground, left to right:* John K. Boosahda (now Busada) and Robert A. Boosahda (now Busada).

The Syrian Antiochean St. George Orthodox Church of Worcester, August 10, 1928, A.D.

كنيسة القدّيس جاورجيوس السوريّ الأرثوذكيّة الإنطاكيّة في ورسترماس
في عشرة آب سنة ١٩٢٨ ميلاديّة

3.3. Rectory and church, built 1891–1892. Photo taken 1928, the date of its purchase by the Syrian Antiochian St. George Orthodox Church of Worcester. Its consecration was in 1929. *Left to right:* Friendly House, a community recreation center at its third location (formerly Sisters of St. Anne Convent); the rectory; not visible but located behind rectory and church was a four-story shingled hall used for various cultural and social activities. See photo Timeline.1, where the hall is visible in the upper left background. Now this entire area is the present location of Friendly House. *Standing in foreground:* Rev. Michael M. Husson and Archbishop Victor Aboassaly.

3.4. Flashback to a used-to-be neighborhood, the west side of *el-saha*, about 1880–1905. Facing northwest at junction of Norfolk and Wall Streets was 41-43-45 Norfolk Street. Some subsequent owners after Syiek were Maykel, Kaneb, Peters, and Altif. *Lower left:* steep decline at Bloomingdale Court.

3.5. Flashback to a used-to-be-neighborhood, the east side of *el-saha*, about 1880–1905. Facing northeast at junction of Norfolk where it curves downhill and Wall Streets. *Left to right:* two-horse team and buggy in the distance (building with pointed roof was a stable); flat-roofed building was first location of Thamal Salloum's (David G. Salloum) first restaurant where he served Arabic food; 32-34-36 Norfolk Street double-decker, pathway of horizontally laid railroad ties directly opposite Bloomingdale Court, Wall Street sign on post.

3.6. Grafton Street view of "1901 S. George" commercial-residential double house (5½ stories with mezzanine floor and basement). Granite date-and-name stone is visible above the second-story corner window. Note the curved bay windows on the front façade.

3.7. Wall Street view of "1901 S. George" double house. The building was gutted by fire and demolished in the early 1970s.

Chapter Four
WORK

The immigrant's first phase of earning a living was usually as a merchant of dry goods and notions, commonly called a pack peddler. The peddlers were married couples working together or singly, unmarried men or women, widowers or widows, and teenage boys. They traveled door-to-door to the outskirts of the city and surrounding towns by foot or by horse and buggy and out of state as far as the Midwest by foot or train. They worked for weeks or months at a time before returning home. Peddling was a carryover from *el-belaad,* where it was a normal form of commerce.

From the merchandising earnings the immigrants established retail, wholesale, or export-import businesses. They purchased real estate to rent, and they built residences and commercial-residential buildings. Later many invested successfully in the stock market and participated in community activities.

Peddler: The Door-to-Door Traveling Merchant

In days of limited transportation, pack peddlers played an important function because the wares they sold provided the basic needs of their customers. A peddler filled a *kushee* (box, trunk, or suitcase) and/or a gunny cloth a yard square or larger with corners tied together with dry goods and notions. Often they carried rolled-up Oriental rugs over their back and shoulders. Generally the Arab-American immigrant was a composite portrait of an adventure seeker whose cheerful perseverance, commitment, fortitude, honesty, reliability, and resourcefulness helped in facing the many daily challenges, developing door-to-door sales routes in unfamiliar areas, and overcoming language barriers. The peddler's driving force was to sell, earn money, raise a family, and preserve the family honor. The supportive structure of the biological and extended families influenced the immigrant's progress. In the extended family certain members chose to help care for the family and others assisted in family businesses, while still others were free to venture to distant areas for work. The strong ties of family helped them achieve confidence, unity, and purpose in search of the good life.

Peddling enabled them to maintain their independence and earn beyond a set wage. It provided the freedom to expand and experiment without restrictions or supervisors. Eli S. reflected on his choice of livelihood:

> I can't work for anybody. I could never work for anybody. Nobody could ever tell me what to do. I've got to feel what I'm doing. I liked what I was doing. I loved the challenge of selling from door-to-door. I love my work.

After settling in Worcester, some immigrants continued their trek across the country as itinerant peddlers and then resettled in a place more to their liking. Frequently, however, they continued to consider Worcester as the place of their American roots and kept in touch with Worcester friends by mail and visits.

Accommodations on the Road

Once the merchants established their sales routes, many customers anticipated and welcomed them as friends of the family and extended them sleeping quarters. Sleeping along the way in homes of strangers was a pattern the immigrants brought with them from *el-belaad*. Eli A. B. translated from his father's Arabic-written history of family matters:

> Many people from Mahiethett [today in Lebanon] traveled to Huran [in Syria] to secure work because that land was level and produced good crops, whereas Mahiethett is mountainous. . . . They walked or sometimes traveled by donkey or horse. The journey took a day and a half to two days. They left early in the morning and prevailed upon people along the way to put them up for the night, and their host fed them in the morning.

> Sam G. A. recalled some peddler experiences in this country: Many peddlers slept in different homes. After awhile they got friendly with the families and they would let the people know when they want to sleep somewhere. Fred A. when sitting in a customer's home was tired he would tilt his head and rest it on his arm and that was his hint that he was tired—so the host family would invite the person to sleep over. There was no problem sleeping on the floor or whatever space was available.

Sam G. A. also reminisced about the often-repeated humorous stories the peddlers told when laughing at their own foibles. One story was about the hazards of peddling:

A particular peddler was very, very clean, finicky and fastidious. While in a customer's home one day he wanted a drink of water, anything, so the lady of the house said O.K. I don't know how he asked her for it, but she understood and got him a cup with a handle. Although he was right-handed he grabbed the cup in his left hand to drink on this side, figuring family members drank from the opposite side, but he did not know that she was left-handed. She noticed and said, "oh, you are like me. I'm left-handed." Although he was right-handed he ended up drinking from her side of the cup.

In order to establish goodwill with their customers, as well as from necessity, many peddlers became multilingual, learning the basic conversational languages of English, French, and Italian.

Alice A. talked about her father:

My father was a peddler. They were all peddlers. The peddlers didn't know the language. They had to learn it. They had to learn English. When they went to the store . . . [they] couldn't even tell you what they wanted, so they had to pretend they were a chicken by imitating the sound of a chicken clucking. How else were they going to make their request known? How else could they let the store vendor know when they wanted eggs? They had to imitate the chicken! They had a hard life! Not only that, in those days the roads weren't cleared like they are today. They used the horse and sleigh. They didn't have a car. So the peddlers would go a little way off from where they lived and would get stranded in the snow. They would knock on a door and the people would let them sleep in their home. The residents would take in strangers, as they would feel sorry for them because it was snowing outside.

Some peddlers experienced the blizzard of 1888, one of the fiercest snowstorms in the Northeast. In Worcester the heavy snows and howling winds lasted three days and nights. Twenty-one inches fell and there were drifts ten, fifteen, and twenty feet high. For snow removal equipment there were only horse-drawn plows and shovels. When the horse couldn't move the men would shovel.

Louise Seymour Houghton, author of "Syrians in the United States," 1911, wrote about Arab-American peddlers:

From the charity visitor these peddlers refuse alms and resent any well-meant but uncomprehending attempt to induce them to change their mode of life, to give up peddling and go into a factory, for example. The two points of view are almost ludicrously, if not tragically, apart. They lie in different plains and are incapable of meeting.

The peddler is a free man—more often, no doubt, a free woman. Why should she give up the open air, the broad sky, the song of the birds, and the smile of the flowers, the right to work or to rest at her own pleasure, to immure herself within four noisy walls and be subject to the strict regime of the clock? Why should she who has been a whole person, become a mere "hand," and that the hand of another? To one unfamiliar with the American industrial standard, the American social viewpoint, the proposal is simply incomprehensible![1]

Women's Choice—Merchant or Housekeeper

Adventuresome women often played a leading role in the economic advancement of the men in the family, particularly when the women were first in their families to emigrate and peddle. They introduced men to the merchandising business by having the men accompany them on their individual routes. Other women chose to stay at home and do household work and child rearing with assistance from the extended family. One woman peddler was Mary Gaze (Ghize), "a pedler of dry goods" (*Worcester House Directory, 1894*, 48). She resided at 96 Bloomingdale Road, next to the "Arabian boardinghouse" at 98 Bloomingdale Road at the foot of Bloomingdale Court on Franklin Street. Among her neighbors were other "pedlers," for example, Michael Maykel, Salim Ghiz, Dahar Haddad, and Akil Haddad. A woman's honor, reputation, and the preservation of the family honor was of the highest order and was protected by the community whose members looked out for each other and cheered each other on.

George A. H. remembered his grandmother's peddling:

> My paternal grandmother, Nimry S. H., peddled and spoke fluent French, English, and Arabic and learned these languages in Lebanon. Her husband was Makhool Husson, a first cousin of Reverend Michael Husson. Makhool had a peg leg—like some pirates had, but he was kicked by a horse and lost his leg—and was described as a bull because of his strength and energy. His name was Makhool! Makhool is Makhool and it is not Michael! Because he was more in a leadership role in his village of Aita, he chose to return there in 1890 and his wife, Nimry, remained here. After that he visited Worcester twice. Nimry taught my father the trade of peddling. She used to take my father out to the country pack peddling—selling dry goods. My dad was twelve or fourteen years of age. They would go to Northbridge, Whitinsville, and different towns in the valley.

MaryAnne L. A. told the story of her grandmother, Latifa (Qatifa), and her grandfather peddling notions from their horse and buggy while in the Hopkinton and Milford areas of Massachusetts:

> They noticed scraps of elastics being thrown out from a factory door. Latifa said to her husband, "Let's see if we can ask to have the elastic and we can make something from it." Her wish was granted. They started their business, Adam & George Company, in 1906 by making plain round elastics to hold up hosiery and armbands to shorten long sleeves on men's shirts. From that beginning they made hose supporters and garter grips. They located off Shrewsbury Street in an Italian and Lebanese neighborhood. Immigrant women with their kids picked up the boxes with the elastics and metal loops and took them home to insert the elastic into the loops.[2]

MaryAnne continued talking about her grandmother:

> My grandmother's first name, Latifa [Qatifa], means very light and delicate in Arabic—but she was a heavyset lady, not *qatifa* [velvet]. I loved her.

Alice A. recalled:

> *Mart amma* [wife of my uncle] Elias was a peddler. Others called her Um Dahar-Abdow and we, the young children, called her "Aunt Mary." Aunt Mary used to carry a bundle—a cloth no bigger than a yard square with the corners tied together; in it was rickrack ribbon, buttons, thread, safety pins, elastics, and different things that she sold. The customers used to feel sorry for her. She was old, about eighty years, and no matter whose door she knocked on they always bought from her and besides, they needed the items.

Julia A. P.'s paternal grandmother, Kalaick (Kaneb) Abdow Abdelmaseh, a widow, was first in her family to emigrate from Mahiethett. Kalaick showed the menfolk of the family who followed her how to make a living by peddling wares from house to house. With a similar spirit of adventure as her great-grandmother, Julia left Worcester to seek better economic opportunities in Washington, D.C., where she set up a florist shop. Rose A. G. reflected:

> The flower shop was so successful that Julia sent for her sister, Alice A., and later her brothers and male cousins joined them. Alice branched out and opened a photography studio. Their [spirit of] adventure and resourcefulness led to thriving businesses mostly in the florist industry.

According to Houghton, cited in her 1911 study, "Syrians in the United States," it was not unusual for Syrian women to emigrate first in a family and take up peddling:

> It is not infrequently the case that the eldest daughter will precede her parents, or a sister, or her brother to this country, . . . but a wife never precedes her husband in this way. . . . As for women's work, notwithstanding the constant evidence of the woman peddler, a very small proportion of Syrian women are breadwinners, except as associates of their husbands. . . . Syrian married women are not expected to contribute to the support of the family, except in this capacity: the care of the household is considered their share in the partnership.[3]

Grandmother Peddled, but Not Mother

Amelia G. A. recalled:

> My maternal grandmother went peddling. She was here alone. I don't know any of my grandfathers. She used to live with my aunt and her husband, Angelina R. Mitchell and Nassif Mitchell and family. She was an active lady and small like me, and she did everything. She peddled dry goods, stockings, pins, needles, and other things, and they went out into the towns to peddle. My parents emigrated after my grandmother. My father went peddling, but not my mother. They had good luck in selling. Like if you wanted something and you didn't have the money, he'd give it to you and say, "I'll come next week and you pay me next week." That's how they did it. Most sales were on credit and they trusted people. People were trusted then. My father, when he died, he had quite a few customers that he trusted. We never knew who they were. He never had the names written. I also remember when my uncle died suddenly from an accident, and his family never knew how much money was owed him. He always told his family a lot of people owed him money and we never knew who they were and we couldn't collect the money. Our people were very honest people. They trusted everybody. That's how they were and most people would pay the next week.

Merchants — Men

Bashara K. Forzley's autobiography describes his introduction to merchandising upon his arrival in Worcester:

> Cousins and friends were at the [train] station to greet us. Once the celebrations were over, my relatives initiated me into the "make a

living" group so common among them. . . . Cousin Farrar [Mansour], proprietor of a dry goods store, put five dollars worth of goods into a basket, looped it over my arm, and gently prodded me out into the strange world to sell from door-to-door. Every article was priced in Arabic.[4]

Nora A. H. talked about her father, Ameen A.:

He started peddling at age twelve and no one coached him. He got himself a suitcase and filled it with things like thread and whatever notions women needed to do their sewing, and went knocking on doors. Because the country and the language was so new to him by the time someone opened the door and by the time he thought of what to say in English the door would be closed in his face. After a few days of that, he returned home and decided to rearrange his wares so that his *kushee* would be open when he knocked at the door. The woman would come to the door and immediately her eyes would go to this display. Well, this gave my father a chance to think of the few words that he knew in English. Meantime she had found something in this display that she wanted. So, they understood one another right away and by then he conjured up enough words to get by with and he made the transaction. Anyhow after the first day of this he went home and his sister said, "How did you do today?" He simply emptied out his pockets of the change and put the change on the table. From then on he was this successful salesman.

Alice A. E. reminisced:

My man [husband] didn't know how or where to start as he didn't know how to speak English. What is he going to do? So the old-timers told him, "Go and sell." He started by using something like a box *[kushee]* to carry shoelaces and small notions.

Tanoos (Thomas F. G.)

An elderly non-Arab man who grew up in Whitinsville shared his impression of Tanoos:

I remember a Syrian peddler carrying a big heavy trunk *[kushee]* on his back and having a big bushy red mustache. His name was Tanoos and that is all I remember.

In an unpublished autobiography, Tanoos (Thomas F. G.) talked about the difficulties of peddling, the challenge of traveling, the rigor of winter, and the warm welcome by customers who helped ease these hardships. His experiences were similar to those of other peddlers, and his story was typical of how the support system and group solidarity helped one to continue, grow, and succeed in their business. Tanoos wrote:

On January 2, 1908, I was very happy to receive my state license for selling . . . I purchased notions and dry goods and took two suitcases. One was carried on my back and the other in my hand and off I went to work. Also [other times] I carried cloth by the yard on my back and notions in my other hand. I traveled to Webster, East Douglas, Northbridge, Farnum, and Fisherville. Each day, I traveled to a different town. I went from house to house and asked the people if they wished to purchase anything. I then made my offer in the form of a song, and they all enjoyed this. I continued this schedule for three weeks, but I did not entirely enjoy traveling this route. I then changed my route to Leominster and Fitchburg. Uncle Farrah directed me there. I continued this schedule for three weeks. This did not suit me, either. This was the winter season and I had not experienced such cold and snow. I suffered many hardships with the elements. . . . I then explained my problems to John K. [Hannah K.], whose father was my godfather. He sympathized with me and asked me to come with him to Southbridge. Monsour A. also showed me the various houses that he knew, and I began to work there. I began to like Southbridge, and after one year, I purchased a hand wagon to carry my goods. After two years I bought a horse and a large wagon with eight doors. At that time, I also sold men's suits, clothing, and took orders for women's clothing. A year after that the horse became ill, and I had to take him to the veterinarian. This cost me $5.00 a week, and I had to hire a horse for $2.00 a day. The stable master informed me that my horse would not recover, and I left the horse there. I hired horses thereafter. I used to leave Worcester on Tuesday and stay in Southbridge until Saturday. . . . I hired a horse from the livery stable in Southbridge, and the horse turned out to be a wild horse. While I was in a house selling my goods, the horse, while waiting outside, took the weight and began running with the wagon, which was full of goods. He [the horse] ran across the railroad tracks and the steam car [train] came by and smashed into the wagon, throwing my goods all over the area. When I came out and found this trouble, the only thing I could do was to pick up the goods remaining and begin over again. I encountered many hardships in my daily routine, but I still wanted to progress. . . . I planned to stay in America for about three or four years to work and prosper. I had begun to be homesick for Mahiethett, my friends, and relatives there. But I stayed in the United States and worked very hard. After four years were over, I then decided I would like to remain in the United States and find a "suitable wife" [helpmate and partner].

My hours [of work] at that time were 6:00 A.M. to 9:00 P.M. I enjoyed my work and I began to forget about my other memories of Mahiethett. . . . My cousin Asaffe [G.] and I were partners in the purchase of 72-74 Wall Street . . . a three-family home and a store.[5]

Anthony Moossa

When Anthony "Tony" Moossa, aged 106, was interviewed in the presence of his grandson, Michael, the conversation was exciting and intense. The gleam in the grandfather's eyes made it clear he was pleased with his grandson's interest in his immigrant experience and his grandson's respect for his acumen. A sampling of the interview:

> MICHAEL: They [Arab immigrants] started peddling. Is that right? They started selling merchandise. How did they do that?
>
> TONY: They had a wagon, one-horse wagon, and they lived in it during the day and they go around from street to street and go back and sleep in their own home.
>
> MICHAEL: Did they work together, or did they go separate?
>
> TONY: They worked together. My father and mother worked together and earned the family income.
>
> MICHAEL: Who did you stay with when your parents went peddling?
>
> TONY: I was with my mother's sister. She was an aunt and I used to stay with her.
>
> MICHAEL: Who went over to Clinton Dam, when they were building the Clinton Dam? Who was selling goods there?
>
> TONY: My mother and father and then other people, too. They go there to sell to the men, only men worked to build the dam. They go there from different places. We are Lebanese.

Transition from Survival to Security

While the initial occupation of many Arab Americans was as door-to-door dry goods merchants, a way of surviving in a new and unfamiliar land, they were able to follow that with the more secure (and middle-class) business of setting up a store and owning real estate properties. Relatives and friends in the Americas shared their similar experiences during reciprocal visits.

When Elizabeth A. F. of Spring Valley, Illinois, was asked how immigrants peddled in snowstorms, she responded:

The weather didn't deter them. Snow and cold weather didn't deter them at all. You know, they had one view in mind and one thing only. They had to get out and make a living for themselves and the family and the weather didn't hold them back. My mother [Khazma M.A.H.] used to carry the *kushee* and take the streetcar, get off and walk nine or ten blocks up a hill with the heavy suitcase. They worked hard and were interested in their children achieving academically, although business was a chief attraction. She would tell me how much they bought and what they paid, but she could not write English. She spoke English much better than my father did, although he could read English.

We had our store since 1903 [today called the Emporium]. My father started the store when he could hardly speak English. There was one Italian girl that lived in our neighborhood that he could understand and she could understand him through gestures and motions, and that's how he started the store.

Another example of the continuity and expansion of business from the early peddling days to the third generation was that of Salem Salloom, who spent a few years peddling dry goods before opening his store in the downtown Worcester area. During this period he made several location changes within the same vicinity. The line of merchandise he carried expanded to include yard goods and clothing.[6] His store provided some peddlers with dry goods to fill their *kushees*. Many other merchants before him who owned similar dry goods stores were also jobbers in dry goods and clothing, for example, Issa Kalil at 32½ Norfolk Street in 1900. Dry goods and other items were obtained locally and by trips to New York.

Leather Workers at Graton & Knight

Immigrants from Masghara, now in Lebanon, were skilled leather makers. For most, their attraction to Worcester was the tannery, Graton & Knight Manufacturing Co., manufacturers of leather belting used in all parts of the country. Charles H. recalled:

> Jabour "Joe" Jabour was the "top dog" at Graton & Knight in the tanning department. Over the years he was the highest paid Lebanese-Syrian there at the time. Of course, Fred H. came after that and many others. But Jabour was the original superintendent of our people and a kind man. When he left G&K [Graton & Knight] he opened a coffeehouse, later known as Joe's Spa, opposite 80 Wall Street and next to the "old El." [That was the original location of the celebrated El Morocco Restaurant, a shining example of what Arabs

eat and how they entertain. It was a mecca for stars of the entertainment world. Owned and operated by Paul and Helen (Kalil) Aboody and their children, it grew from humble origins in 1944 and closed after over fifty years.]

Nelson T. Rahaim, an employee at Graton & Knight, left high school in 1926 at age sixteen and earned his diploma at night while working at G & K. He served as a steward in the workers union, was president of the Fur and Leather Workers' Union in 1936, and then for twenty-three years was personnel manager for the company. He described the tanning process in a department:

> The Curry Department [tanning pits] was where the hides were tanned. Tanning pits were about 15 by 15 square and 10 feet deep. They were filled with different acids to cure the hides. Skins were bought raw from slaughterhouses out West, were shipped here and were cured, put in the pits raw, and seasoned to make the leather pliable and strong. In the belting section there was no training, but you were shown how to do it. Skills were learned from practice and working there. The hill [Grafton Hill] was loaded with people who worked at Graton & Knight. It was in business over one hundred years when it was sold in 1961, when it was put out of business.

Six-inch-thick cement walls enclosed each tanning pit; and the flat top of the wall was used as a walking surface. When a hide was removed from the pit two workers each on top of opposite walls used a long hook to remove the same hide and carry it at shoulder height across the pit to the next vat. Each balanced the heavy hide while walking one foot in front of the other. When an accident occurred and a worker slipped and fell into the pit full of hides, skins, hazardous chemicals, and toxic substances and vapors, the worker immediately was pulled out, undressed, hosed down, and flushed with water to remove any residue of toxic chemicals on his skin.

Fred H. reminisced:

> There were jobs at Graton & Knight that were not as hazardous as the tanning pits. The leather belts made were used to make heavy machinery run. Today those machines are run by electricity and that was one of the reasons for G&K closing. Leather was dried by hanging the leather. The ones who worked in the tanning pits could not ride the bus without changing their clothes because of the strong odors from the leather. I was employed at Graton & Knight for forty years, since 1922 until it closed.

The Labor Movement

An early beginning of the labor movement in America was the strike of 1899 in Marlboro, Massachusetts.

Strike of 1899

The strikers included men, women, boys, and girls. A description of a meeting held by the strikers appeared in the *Worcester Telegram,* and some of the headlines read:

> Ring of Victory! Thousands of Men and Women Cheer. . . . Marlboro Skilled Workers in Battle to Stay. Speakers Instill Courage Eloquently. Wages Go Up Elsewhere and Down There.

Excerpted from the article:

> City Hall was crowded this afternoon by shoe workers on strike and their sympathizers to the number of 2000, and their enthusiasm ran high. . . . The meeting was called to order by Mr. Murray [union agent John H. Murray]. He told the audience that he had been requested by City Marshall . . . to ask the audience not to stamp in applauding because the strain of so many people in action at once might prove disastrous to the hall. . . . We have started in on the 17th week of this uncalled for trouble. . . . Before the hearing is over the manufacturers will have to give more fully the cause for posting the notices. Their reason is to enable them to cut the wages from $3.15 to $1.80 a day.[7]

Syrian Connections in 1912 Strike

Some union leaders were Syrians, and many Syrian textile workers were involved.

The Bread and Roses strike was fought in Lawrence, Massachusetts, in 1912. Numerous members of the Worcester Arab-American community kept in touch with relatives and friends employed at these textile mills. Furthermore, a few marriage certificates of Worcester Arab Americans show that either spouse or both worked as mill workers in Lawrence before moving to Worcester. For example, Nazer H. Elais (Nazira Mishalanie B.) resided in Lawrence, and her occupation was "mill operative" prior to her marriage to a Worcester resident.

A *Boston Globe* article on the "Bread and Roses, Too" strike reported:

> Within one mile of the largest mills in Lawrence, people of 51 nationalities, speaking 45 languages, could be found. . . . The Irish

came first, then the Germans, English and French-Canadians, then the real flood—Italians, Greeks, Syrians, Poles, Lithuanians, Eastern Europeans . . .—after almost seventy-five years of submissions—23,000 of those workers struck against unfair wage cuts and oppressive conditions. . . . They faced malnutrition, threats of reprisals and blacklisting, and state militia violence that didn't stop at clubbing children who were being put on trains to the safety of strike-sympathizers' homes in other cities. But the workers held fast . . . threatened capitalism with direct action up to and including general strikes, the immigrants wrote a new chapter in the labor history of the nation.[8]

Excerpted from the *William G. Abdalah Memorial Library Newsletter*, Evelyn A. Menconi, ed., regarding the Bread and Roses Strike:

On Monday, January fifteenth, during a bitter cold spell and a swirling snowstorm, between seven and eight thousand strikers had formed a picket line around the mills to keep others from entering. There were militiamen with bayonets and policemen with firehoses. The strikers never forgot the icy blasts from the firehoses. There was an accidental stabbing of a Syrian boy—John Rami—a sixteen-year-old innocent bystander. He was killed when the militia pushed the strikers with bayonets to get them to move on. He was buried from St. Anthony's Church on Elm Street. There were thirty carriages in the cortege. . . . The strike showed the importance of ethnic organizations in the life of that city during the strike. The Syrian band, meetings beneath the Syrian church, the Syrian relief work, and the Syrian soup kitchens are examples . . . men, women, and children from widely different backgrounds who spoke different languages were able to accomplish their goals despite almost insurmountable opposition, a minimum of resources. . . . The strike lasted ten weeks before management capitulated, and received nationwide publicity and a congressional investigation. The result was a set of new laws, governing working conditions.[9]

Business Networking Centers

The bakeries, restaurants, coffeehouses, and other establishments in the three Arab-American neighborhoods, *el-tellee*, *harrate tahta*, and lower Belmont Street, provided employment for the owners. These establishments also served as networking centers for the exchange of business information and provided recreational and social activities for both local residents and out-of-towners.

Syrian Bread Bakeries

Charles A. George talked about the first Syrian bakery, which also served as a locale for newcomers seeking advice and direction:

> The first bakery I remember was owned by Shaker Saayeke [Syiek] at 41 Norfolk Street with entrance off Bloomingdale Court.

When Kamel Nejaimey, another baker, moved his bakery from the "flat-iron" building to 80 Wall Street, he advertised his product as the "Best Syrian Bread in New England" (pre-1920). Located at the opposite store-front of the building was George Nasif's store, and he advertised as a "Wholesale and Retail Dealer in Dry and Fancy Goods."

Mary K. of Cornwall, Canada, a former resident of Worcester, reminisced:

> Nicholas Kalil started his bakery at 41 Norfolk Street and was the fourth baker to occupy that location with the Bloomingdale Court entrance. After 1924 he moved and set up his bakery at 80 Wall Street, a three-story building that he bought. It had two storefronts at basement level. . . . Earlier El-Hajj AbiSada [Abraham Boosahda] owned the building [80 Wall Street] and operated the first Syrian bakery at that address. His three oldest sons worked there.

El-Hajj's sons in addition to working in the bakery shared responsibilities related to their parents' real estate properties. After school they collected rent and did carpentry work and plumbing as needed.

Restaurants

Many Arab immigrants had learned their trade as chefs in Syria, Egypt, Paris, and Milan.

Eli S. recalled:

> Before he came over to this country, my father, Salem Salloum [also called Thamel Salloum and David G. Salloum] was a chef at the Grand Hotel in Beirut, Syria, where all the dignitaries dined. There's a history about my father that I thought I could mention. He was the first one to have a Syrian restaurant up there on Wall Street and he took care of all the Syrians. They would come there and would have their meals at his restaurant and also meet others. Many of his customers were bachelors. The ones who came here to this country, you see, are those who had the courage to come, to start up anew. It's the courage they had in themselves and believing in themselves.

Well, it's people like them that made the United States a great country, a more-or-less melting pot. America is made up of the best of all countries. . . . Neither my brother nor I favored the restaurant business and my father was there all alone. Then he decided to close his restaurant business and go out selling dry goods.

As Charles A. George reminisced about Syrian food, he smiled and inhaled through his nose as though he smelled the aromas coming from Thamel Salloum's restaurant:

Thamel had nothing but Syrian food in his restaurant. You can smell the food when you go by the place. You say to yourself, "Oh, that smells so good, what's he cooking today?" [laughter]. Someone bought the building and turned the restaurant into a dry goods store and maybe that's why Salloum moved to Kaneb's building across the street in one of the storefronts at 51½ Norfolk Street. He opened a big restaurant there. A lot of people used to go eat there.

Sally H. remarked:

My father, Elias Haddad, was a chef. He was in Worcester and he had his own lunchroom down on Main Street. It was called the Woodbine Lunch. Prior to 1899 he ["Ellis" Haddad] was the cook at City Hotel.[10]

Coffeehouses/Coffee Parlors

Coffeehouses were social institutions where men relaxed over Arabic coffee, mint tea, or lemonade, read Arabic newspapers, discussed current issues, enjoyed poetry or other types of Arabic literature, and played card games or *tawlah* (backgammon played on an elaborate, inlaid, specially marked board). The coffeehouses were often storefronts with only a few tables and chairs.

Michael S. recalled:

My father had a coffee parlor on East Worcester Street, and there was another one across the street. The coffee parlors opened in the morning and closed about six o'clock at night. Sometimes some people would go to the coffee parlor across the street, and another time they would come to my father's. It made no difference. It was all for companionship. We all knew each other. The coffee parlors served as meeting places for folks to sit down and enjoy themselves and talk, talk, and talk. They would finish one cup of coffee and get another cupful.

Occupational Progression and Education of the Immigrants

From the early beginnings of peddling most Arab-American immigrants moved on to other occupations. From their humble origins they rose to personal achievements and activities in many fields of endeavor. A minimal sampling of some of their occupations and education follows.

The *Worcester House Directory, 1900,* included a section titled "A Business Directory of selected names of prominent business houses of Worcester," and under "Dry Goods" a total of thirty-five names were listed, eight of which were names and addresses of Arab Americans.[11]

Prior to 1907 a number of Arab Americans in Worcester expanded their businesses and moved to the outskirts of *el-tellee* or to Main Street downtown. For example, under "Dry Goods" in the "Business Directory" section of the *Worcester Directory, 1907,* a total of forty-seven names are listed, ten of which were names and addresses of Arab Americans,[12] and other business headings listed names of Arab Americans as well.[13]

Certain national directories listed the occupations of some Worcester Arab Americans: *The Syrian Business Directory, 1908–09*[14] listed the various occupations of some Worcester Syrian merchants by full name, address, business, and cities or villages of origin, printed in both Arabic and English; *The Lebanese in America* summarized some of the thriving businesses in 1908;[15] and *Syrians in the United States,* 1911, stated, "In Worcester, Mass., three large factories of white wear and one of overalls are carried on by Syrians."[16]

Some peddlers extended their sales routes from one state to another and stayed away from home weeks or months at a time. For example, Faris George extended his stay in Illinois and died there; his body was returned to Worcester where his wife and son resided.

Tufeek (Taft) A. recalled his father's sales trips:

> After peddling in this area my father, Ameen A., kept going out farther west and peddled as far as Ohio and West Virginia. He got a room in one of the hotels and traveled long distances selling. He had the dry goods—shirtwaists, embroidered items, and other things— shipped to him. He would fill up his two suitcases and go out selling. If he happened to sell all that he had taken with him, he would come back to his room and once again refill his suitcases from the supply of dry goods stored in his room.
>
> After World War I my father ceased selling—you could call it peddling, or more accurately "clothes merchandising," or whatever it

is called today. Anyhow, he was getting more interested in doing more things in another line; at this time he became interested in real estate. He had already bought some property and he extended his interest in real estate and bought other properties in Worcester. Finally he bought some land and a building in Shrewsbury, Massachusetts. We moved there from Worcester around 1919. He built four three-deckers on the land he bought in Shrewsbury, and from there his interests were mostly in buying and selling property. He also invested in the stock market and was successful.

Kenneth K. stated:

My father, Hannah K., was a peddler when he first got here, and then he started buying real estate and building [developing] commercial-residential structures. He continued peddling up to 1924, then continued in real estate and had started an oil business when he died in 1933.

Adele H. A. talked about merchandising Oriental rugs:

Oriental rugs and linens were big items and were purchased from New York importers. Local orders were taken for oriental rugs, as the items were not stocked here. The local peddler goes to New York, places the orders, selects the rugs, and returns with them for delivery.

She continued and talked about some ways by which the immigrants accumulated wealth:

Most of the Arab-American immigrants came with little money from *el-belaad*. They worked hard, very hard, and they made every dollar count. They hardly ever spent money on clothes and luxuries. They sewed most of their clothes. Some of the men were tailors and made their own suits. They were resourceful, raised vegetables, ate food from their gardens and bartered just as they did in *el-belaad*. They swapped services through the barter system. This allowed them to save money and invest it in businesses. Whatever they saved was towards a return trip to *el-belaad* and what was left over was invested in real estate.

According to Charles Nutt, in *History of Worcester and Its People*, 1919, the Syrians were frugal and prosperous:

Syrians.—From time immemorial the Syrians have been traders and makers of rugs. Those who have come to this city are mainly engaged in trade. Their number is not large, but may amount to several hundred. . . . The Syrians of the city are frugal and prosperous, as the officers of all the savings banks and bankers who transmit money to foreign lands, have ample evidence.[17]

Lillian George Shoucair reminisced about her father, one of the early Arab-American developers of real estate property:

> Some people just can't quit. Once my father was successful in one venture, he would take on another. He had a passion to develop property and hired contractors to build commercial-residential buildings. He was several times bankrupt and several times a millionaire. Even in his retirement years in Florida, he still had the ambition to build, but I managed to dissuade him because of his age and finances. Many of his one-to-five-story buildings are still standing in *el-tellee* and other areas. He died a widower in 1959, aged 98, while living with my sister in California.

In 1925 Simon George purchased four parcels of land on Main Street in the center of Shrewsbury, Massachusetts. As the developer of this land he had workmen build a red-brick commercial-residential three-story structure with a balustrade that decorated the rooftop and is still standing today. Since he was limited on the height of the building by Shrewsbury code restrictions, he built it larger lengthwise. The building has a walkout basement on one side and full basements for each of the six retailers on the ground floor. There are four apartments on the second floor with one or two bedrooms. He simultaneously sold dry goods and continued as a developer of real estate. The property was foreclosed, and Ameen A. bought it from the bank. Later in 1983, the son, Taft A., sold the property to an investment company. Simon George was a Worcester millionaire who, according to his daughter, went bankrupt many times in his career but recovered and continued to develop property, maintain his dry goods stores, and peddle. He left a long paper trail in public records of his real estate transactions.

"Dr." Malaky M. (Coury) Shannon (1875–1953) was "the" midwife on *el-tellee*. She delivered babies under challenging conditions, day or night, sunshine or snowstorm. She married an Armenian, Shannanogian, and as a widow put her daughter, Mary C. Shannon, through medical school.

After Charles A. Gammal graduated from Worcester Polytechnic Institute with a bachelor's degree in chemistry in 1920, he was employed as a research chemist and awarded patents on several inventions.[18] He died at age 102 (1897–March 2000). His brother Albert A. Gammal graduated from Massachusetts Institute of Technology, Boston, as a chemical engineer in 1923.

Taft Antoun (emigrated in 1913), after receiving his doctor of medicine degree in 1934, opened his office in Worcester. After moving to Shrewsbury, he served on the School Committee from 1938 to 1947.

Albert G. Swide wrote poetry as an avocation. At the age of eighty-six in 1988 he published his collection titled *Thoughts and Meditations*.

Ice for the Ice Box

James E. talked about how his family got into the ice business:

> The first in my family to emigrate was my grandmother Rogina with her son George. They went out peddling and worked and worked and worked, and finally accumulated some money. Then my grandmother did the buying of real estate, and sent for the rest of her children. After my father, Solomon, settled here, he sent for my siblings and me. By then my four uncles and father were in the ice business and I joined the business. They cut blocks of ice from the pond, delivered it to customers, owned six teams and eight horses. Their first stable was at 13 Norfolk. . . . Our registered trademark was a long diamond-shaped logo with the word "ICE" inside it and was used on our wagons and ice card. When a family needed ice, the card was placed in the front window of their home. The card told the "ice man" the size of the block of ice (100, 75, 50, or 25 pounds) to deliver into the family icebox. . . . Later we owned an icehouse in North Grafton where we stored ice for the summer. The insulation in the icehouse was sawdust between the partitions. There was no ice machinery then . . . it was just the sawdust about fifteen inches thick, and that's what kept the refrigeration there right through the summer. Our business expanded to Esper Bros. Coal, Wood and Ice Company, owned and operated by the five brothers and me.

Moving to Find Work

Nicholas A. stated:

> Immigrants moved to different areas for better job opportunities and to join relatives or people they knew. In 1882 my mother's immigrant family went to Norwich, Connecticut, where there were relatives and work, but some returned to Worcester. This was not unusual, as families moved freely back and forth to different areas mainly because of work.

Alexandra B. remembered:

> Nazira M. B., my mother, who emigrated singly at age seventeen, the first and only one in her family to do so, lived and worked in Utica, New York, for a couple of years with friends from her village. Then, when work was slow, she moved to Lawrence, Massachusetts, worked in a textile mill, and lived with an Eastern Orthodox family. The head of the household was a widower who had been married to a distant relative, and Nazira called him *Amma* Enkhoola (Uncle Nick). She acquired a new family including his children who were Eastern Orthodox and she a Maronite.

Mary (Debs) R. related:

> My grandfather's sister was living in Worcester, and I lived with her when I emigrated at age sixteen. My cousin and her husband came to visit me. They took me to live in their home in Lawrence and introduced me to my future husband. After a month we got married in Worcester and lived in Lowell as that was where my husband worked at one of those textile factories. Our two oldest children were born in Lowell. We came to Worcester for a vacation and when he went back he lost his job as they gave it to someone else. My husband could find no more work in Lowell, so he came to Worcester and lived with my mother's aunt until he found work. Then he sent for our children and me and we joined him in Worcester.

Sadie B. N. reminisced:

> My father, Assad Boosahda [Asa A. Busada] commuted daily between Worcester and Boston to attend Massachusetts College of Optometry. He graduated in 1926 as an optometrist. His business in Worcester didn't do well so he moved to Brooklyn, New York, and then settled in North Bergen, New Jersey, where his practice was successful.

Publishers

Journalist-publishers Aziz G. Francis and Peter A. Shaia published a semimonthly Arabic magazine, *Al-Raudat* (The Meadow), for seven years or more (about 1916–24) in Lawrence, Massachusetts. Francis emigrated from Lebanon by way of Egypt, where he learned his trade of publishing, went to Greece, where he taught Arabic journalism, moved to Manchester, New Hampshire, Lawrence, and then to Worcester, where he operated his printing shop.

Shokri K. Swydan was a writer in Arabic and Russian, a man of many enterprises, and a classical scholar. He studied at Russian-operated schools in Palestine and earned his master of arts degree; his diploma from the Teachers Seminary in Nazareth, Palestine, was printed in Arabic and Russian. The Russian Imperial Orthodox Society of Syria funded and maintained the schools in Syria and Palestine. After graduation he worked at the Russian Imperial schools. During this time Swydan wrote a treatise against the Ottoman rule; his safety was in danger and hastened his emigration from Palestine in 1910. He was born in Judaidet, Marjayoun, Syria (now Lebanon). In Worcester, along with other accomplishments[19] he published two newsletters, one in English and the other in Russian, with his printing press and two manual typewriters, one for English print and the other for Russian. He authored a few books, numerous publications, and many articles in serial form as a regular correspondent for the *Syrian Daily Eagle,* Brooklyn, New York. He also wrote for other Arabic and English newspapers that were published in the United States. In 1937 he donated to the National Geographic Society, Washington, D.C., copies of his books, *Debate against Leo Tolstoi about Faith, Reason, and Prayer, History of the Russian Imperial Palestine Orthodox Association,* and *The History of the Antiochean Orthodox Church, 1672–1850,* which were acknowledged by Esther Ann Manion, librarian at the society.

N. Nasseem and N. Arida were editors of *AL=FUNOON: THE ARTS: An Arabic Review of Literature and Art,* published monthly by Al-Atlantic Publishing Co. in New York in Arabic and English. Among its advertisers was Montauk Theatre, Brooklyn. "Annual Subscription $5 Everywhere." The second issue of the journal was dated May 1913.

Philip J. Ferris was the editor and business manager of the *Syrian-American Review,* published monthly in English and Arabic at Waterville, Maine, by the Syrian-American Literary Association. Its Arabic editors were Massoud Joseph and Rajie Nawfel. The magazine was "Dedicated to good citizenship" and its purpose was "to bring the Syrian Americans in America, and especially in New England closer together, ever mindful and proud of their ancestral ties that should bind them together and ever laboring untiringly for their betterment and advancement as God-fearing and law abiding citizens of these glorious United States." Its first publication was March 1937.

Some historians claim that the founders of *Kawkab America* (the first Arabic newspaper in America) were A. J. Arbeely and his brother Najeeb Arbeely, and that the first Arab editor in America was Najeeb M. Diab, who was an editor of *Kawkab America*. However, Lillian George Shoucair talked about her father-in-law Said (pronounced Sa-eed) Shoucair as founder and editor of *Kawkab America:*[20]

> Said Shoucair was the owner and editor of the newspaper *Kawkab Il-Shareh* (The Star of the East) in Beirut, and because of his outspoken criticisms through his writings of the Ottoman Empire, he was forced to flee to escape persecution. He went to Alexandria, Egypt, and later to New York. He was a pioneer in Arabic journalism in America and the founder of *Kawkab America* (The Star of America) in 1892. The Arbeelys financed the newspaper, later taking more interest in its growth by writing articles and seeking others to write for it.

Lillian George Shoucair substantiated her claim with new research.

South American Connection

Some men maintained two businesses, one locally and one out of the country. Assad K. Abufaris and Michael K. Abufaris established a business in Rio Janeiro (now Rio de Janeiro), Brazil, before 1908, which was registered at Probate Court, County of Worcester.[21] The registration of the out-of-the-country businesses legally protected their Worcester properties. They resided in both places at different periods. The men were comfortable in either setting because of the extended families and similarities in the Arab immigrant communities regarding integration and cultural heritage. However, Michael's wife, Habooba (Rose) S. A., stayed in Worcester with relatives and friends and operated the family grocery store.

Salem Rizkalla also maintained two businesses—a local business and one in Brazil where his four brothers lived. He and his wife, Takala H. R. (daughter of Nimry Saba Husson and Makhool Husson), settled in Worcester and then lived in Brazil for five years. She was homesick for her relatives and friends, so they returned to Worcester. Thereafter, Salem made frequent trips to Brazil to conduct his business while his wife operated their Worcester grocery store.

Budget and Joint Ownership

Whether the woman peddled or stayed at home, she was responsible for budgeting the family finances. Women generally were of strong character, in control of their lives and family affairs, and usually bore as many as three to twelve children. Frequently the husband gave the wife his earnings and she in turn gave him his spending money. In the majority of situations property was in joint ownership with the spouse, widowed mother, and/or son and daughter, for example: "Akil E. Haddad and his wife Najla Haddad"; or "Badaway Abudela, a widow, otherwise known as Badaway Abodeely, and Nassar Abodeely, my son"; or "Simon George and his wife Sarah [Sooriye] George"; or "Shaker Saayeke [Syiek] and his wife Zamorde H. Sayeeke." An example of a promissory note in the name of husband and wife was "Abraham Boosahda and Alexandra Boosahda"[22] for money needed for an addition to a commercial-residential building purchased in 1915.

Children Shared the Work

While attending school older children helped their parents in successful enterprises and rent-producing stores, houses, and commercial establishments. Children did work on the property and worked in family stores, or worked outside the home to bring in additional income. Others stayed at home and helped mothers care for the siblings and do household chores. Some dropped out of college while pursuing medical or scientific disciplines as they felt their parents were too busy in their businesses and needed help. The opportunity to succeed was present, and some children chose to change careers and join the family businesses. Kenneth K. recalled:

> I was in my last year of college studying to be a dentist. My father died and we had started an oil business, which was active and a good opportunity, so I dropped out of college and went into a successful petroleum business. My brothers George completed his studies and graduated as a M.D., Albert went into law, and Mike went into electrical engineering.

Economic Ladder

Multifarious and resourceful, these American entrepreneurs of Arab ancestry used energy, wit, their intelligence, and money not only to survive but flourish. Their successes—in trade as peddlers/merchants, suppliers, storekeepers, realtors, and stock market investors—made demands on their spiritual and intellectual resources; they relied on gut feelings, intuition, and prayer. Their advancement was the result of commitment, discipline, and the support of family and community.

4.1. Peddling with *kushee* and burlap shoulder satchel, 1898. Bashara K. Forzley, aged 14, with *kushee* and rolled gunny cloth bag with shoulder strap, joined the "make a living group." A customer who gave the photo to Forzley a year later took the snapshot. Some of his customers called him "Little Jerusalem" because he was from the Near East (Lebanon). Now the *kushee* is at the Arab American Collection at the Smithsonian Institution Museum of American History.

4.2. Peddling by horse and buggy, 1913. Joseph Namee en route to Whitinsville, Mass.

4.3. On the road showing merchandise, Joseph Namee, 1913.

4.4. Two-horse team and driver, George Esper, of Esper Bros. Coal, Wood and Ice Company, about 1915.

4.5. Journalists and publishers, about 1918. *From left:* Peter A. Shaia and Aziz G. Francis.

Chapter Five
TRADITION, EDUCATION, AND CULTURE

While striving to earn a living, peddling and otherwise, most young Arab Americans had the goal of marriage to spur them on. The marriage customs described in this book followed a traditional pattern in the Christian Arab-American community. (Since many early Muslim and Druze Arab Americans had returned to their homelands or died by the late 1980s, my primary source data on their marriage ceremonies is inadequate.)

Weddings take different forms among Muslims and Christians, but all are occasions for festivity and socializing. A Muslim wedding does not have what Westerners think of as a marriage ceremony. Instead, Muslims have a home ceremony in which the formalities of the religious union are settled prior to the ceremony, when the wedding contract is signed in the presence of a religious functionary and the family members. This is followed by a large reception with dancing, music, feasting, and gift giving. Christian weddings are performed in churches and also are followed by large receptions.

Arranged Marriage

Among both Muslims and Christians arranged marriages and gifts of gold to the bride-to-be were customary. Marriage was arranged through a network of relatives, friends, clergy, brokers, and acquaintances of the prospective bride or groom. There was no dating before marriage. Lori H. commented about arranged marriages in her grandmother's day:

> Oh, that's criminal. How can anyone pick a mate for somebody else? How can your parents tell you whom to marry and all that, but I guess at one time this was not that impractical because they were in a tight community and the unity was important. I guess marriage had a kind of dual purpose as the children were married, and the main purpose was to procreate.

The clergy were among those who helped to arrange and assisted in the marriages by making known the availability of persons from different areas who otherwise would not meet. Very Rev. Michael M. Husson (1860–1939) was well-informed as to who was available for marriage. He was a familiar sight in *el-tellee* with his curly black hair falling below his shoulders, his curly black beard, his long, flowing, wide-sleeved black cassock, and black valise. As stated by Metropolitan-Archbishop Samuel David of the Syrian Orthodox archdiocese of Toledo, Ohio and Dependencies, "Very Rev. Michael Husson, the first pastor of this Church and Parish was the first Syrian Priest to be ordained in the United States." Bishop David also stated that "St. George's Orthodox Church and Parish of Worcester is one of the oldest Antiochian Orthodox Churches and Parishes in the United States." These statements appeared in the *Golden Jubilee 1956* program book of St. George Syrian Antiochian Orthodox Church (now St. George Orthodox Cathedral). Also, Father Husson's name appeared with the designation of Protopriest (first priest) before his name as pastor of St. George Orthodox Church on a few of the early baptismal records of parishioners at Church of St. Mary's Assumption (now St. Mary's Assumption Albanian Orthodox Church) when he was called upon to officiate. Additionally, the consensus of people interviewed was that Rev. Husson was the first resident priest of the Syrian Orthodox Church (forerunner of St. George Orthodox Cathedral).

Some narrators talked about Father Husson's brisk pace when performing his ecclesiastical orders, for example, the blessing of homes with holy water and reciting prayers, and his travels to different localities across the United States to administer the Holy Sacraments of baptism, matrimony, and communion to Arab Americans who were sick or dying.

Michael N. A. recalled the travels of Father Husson:

> It was Rev. Michael who told my family about their relatives living in Cedar Rapids, Iowa. . . . Father Husson came from Worcester and he would travel all over the West because there was no Syrian Orthodox priest. He went from one town to another to do the duties of a priest. There were very, very few Orthodox priests in this country. Besides, Father Husson once a year would travel—he would wire ahead—and he would go to these different towns. Father Husson baptized my sister Mabel, and she was born in Cedar Rapids. He would go out to these places by train. People would give him a few dollars for all he did and then he would be on his way more informed as to the eligibility of those for marriage.

George B. recalled:

The Bishop mentioned to my grandfather [Abraham B.] that there was a well-educated lady and teacher from Beshmezzine [Lebanon] who was living in Pennsylvania, and she would be a good match for his son, Hilal [Harold]. So father and son—my grandfather and my father—went to Pennsylvania to meet the woman. Three days later with mutual consent Hilal and Miryam [Mary], my mother, were married in Pennsylvania and then set up house in Worcester.

According to Tanoos (Thomas) F. George, as related in his autobiography,[1] when he set out to find a "suitable wife," he saw a family photograph on a wall in the parlor at his Uncle El-Hajj B. and Aunt Alexandra A. B.'s home. There and then he decided he wanted to meet the oldest lady in the photo (see photo 5.3).

After corresponding with the family for one year, Tanoos traveled by train with his aunt and Uncle El-Hajj to Spring Valley, Illinois, to ask for the lady's hand in marriage. Tanoos was twenty-two and the chosen bride, Sophia [Sophie] A., was nineteen. The marriage occurred at the bride's church in 1914,[2] and after the ceremonies the newlyweds settled in Worcester.

Tufeek A. recalled:

> My mother came to Worcester at age sixteen and many single men who came from across, naturally, they were looking for a nice girl to marry. Some of them had seen my mother, a newcomer from across, and my aunt says that they had an eye for her, you know. Yes, the eyes of the people were open on her. My aunt persisted that my mother marry and the marriage happened. Now my mother, a girl of sixteen in those days, was not like a girl of sixteen today. She was shy; she couldn't make any objections. She had no free will to say "no, it's too early" or something. She was ashamed to marry. She had no desire to marry at that age but this was the way it happened.

Alexandra B. recalled:

> My mother, Nazira, became a bride in an arranged marriage three years after she emigrated. When her future husband and father-in-law arrived in Lawrence, Massachusetts, to ask for her hand in marriage, they were accompanied by Rev. Michael M. Husson, pastor at Worcester.[3] After spending a few days with her and the family with whom she was living, the groom presented to her the usual gold jewelry as bridal gifts and the marriage took place in Lawrence (see photo on p. v).

Freeda H. W. added:

> After the festivities in Lawrence, Nazira's future in-laws and new
> cousins were gathered in *jiddo* and *sitto*'s [grandfather and grand-
> mother's, respectively] home in Worcester waiting to welcome the
> new member into our family.

Alexandra B. continued:

> Nazira's extended families in Utica, New York, and Lawrence kept
> in touch by reciprocal visits. During her marriage and after bearing
> seven children, she still saved a postal-card photograph of a suitor
> living in Lebanon. Whenever the photo was taken out from amidst
> other photos, her husband smilingly said the photo was of "Uncle
> George," her brother. However, in later years it became known that
> "Uncle George" was one of Nazira's admirers with whom she cor-
> responded in the early days of her emigration (see photo 5.4).

Mae M. M., a neighbor, recalled times from her childhood:

> Every time I catched a glimpse of the new bride, Nazira, and other
> new brides, I would hurry and walk behind them, imitating their
> strut. There were many new brides. It made me feel beautiful and
> grown up and I looked forward to when I, too, would become a
> bride. After all, that was the typical thing to do.

Lillian G. S. spoke of her father, Simon G., who traveled to New York
and hired a marriage broker who introduced him to his future bride,
Sooriya H., of New York (see photo 5.5). The marriage took place at St.
Nicholas Church, Brooklyn, and Archimandrite Raphael Hawaweeny offi-
ciated in 1897. After the ceremony the newlyweds boarded a train to Worcester. Upon their arrival friends and neighbors greeted them, and a musical procession accompanied them as they walked up the hill from Union
Station to *el-saha*. Sooriya's sister Affeza H. married Abraham G. of Worcester. Both women were independent with strong personalities, and active
in the community.

Nuptial Engagement

Alice A. E. recalled:

> Engagements used to be different in those days. We had the priest,
> and he put the diamond ring, the gold jewelry, and the necklace on
> a little tray for blessing and then presentation. I remember the priest
> first took me in the room and asked, "Is anyone forcing you to get

married?" I didn't answer him. I could have said yes as I wasn't interested in getting married. I didn't know whether to answer or not. I didn't answer and later I found out that when you don't answer, that means you approve. It really was a match. That's how they did it in those days. The rings are on the tray and are blessed by the priest. They used to call engagements a half-wedding. The house was full like at a wedding. People are invited to the engagement. It was not like today when they give you the diamond and forget the ceremony. In those days they didn't shower you with gifts at the engagement because at weddings they gave mostly silver and expensive gifts.

Matrimony

Generally the Christian custom was to marry at the bride's church, and it was her choice as to the denomination of the clergy. For example, a bride, Nazer (Nerzeh) Selim—Dadah was her family name—and the groom, Hannah (John) Kanab (Kaneb), were married in 1897[4] at St. Joseph Church (a French-Canadian Roman Catholic parish) by Rev. Jules Graton, its first pastor; the bride was Maronite and the groom Eastern Orthodox. The Maronite church was established here in 1923. After the ceremonies both were members of the Syrian Orthodox Church and later she was an early president of its Ladies Society.

Another wedding occurred at a Baptist church, as the bride was a Protestant and the groom Eastern Orthodox. The *Worcester Daily Telegram* in 1899 carried four consecutive headlines in its reporting of the wedding:

> **All the Hill at Church Ceremony. Dungarvan Turns Out for Syrian Church Ceremony. Peculiar Services Causes Great Interest. Rev. Arthur St. James Ties the Knot.**

Excerpted from the article:

> The Syrian colony of Worcester, about 500 people, celebrated the wedding last night of Faries Abusumra (Abisamra) and Miss Esther [Estelle] Waked [Wakid], Oak Hill. . . . in the presence of the largest crowd that has attended any service in the church, and there also were representatives of many nationalities, including French, German, Syrian, English, Scotch, Irish and American. . . . It was the first Syrian Protestant wedding ever celebrated in Worcester and greater interest was taken in it on that account. It had been reported around Oak Hill that there was to be a wedding, and such an event is so uncommon in a church in that section of the city that everybody,

young and old, attended. Saelem Abusumra, brother of the groom, was best man, and at 8:30 o'clock, he entered the church with the bride leaning on his arm. He was followed soon after by the groom with the bridesmaid, Miss Adella Basila [Bacela], and they took up positions up front.

The article described the conclusion of the ceremony and some attributes of the bride:

Many wedding guests then came forward to shake hands with the young people, and many of them took advantage of the opportunity to kiss the bride, on each of her cheeks. After that, according to an old custom of the nationality, lady friends of the bride sang a number of songs. These were in the French, German and English languages, and "There is a fountain" was sung in Syrian [Arabic]. . . . The company then adjourned to the new home of the bride and groom, 65 Orient Street, where refreshments were served. . . . The bride . . . is brunet, with a fine figure. . . . She was in a magnificent gown of cream colored silk, trimmed with gold lace and satin ribbon to match the gown. She wore a tulle veil, caught up with a spray of orange blossoms, and around her neck was a gold chain attached to which was a gold watch; both were gifts of the groom. . . . The bridesmaid was in black silk, trimmed with silk ribbons, with white bows on her corsage, and one in her jet-black hair. . . . The bride has been in Worcester about three months. She is a talented linguist in the Syrian colony, having been a teacher in a school in Beyroot [Beirut] previous to coming to Worcester. . . . Among those present was the oldest Syrian in Worcester, John Eastley, who is about 73 years of age . . . It is expected the bride and groom will go to Boston tomorrow for three days. According to the custom of the Syrians, the friends made no presents until [they were] about to leave for the night, when they left money and the usual gifts.[5]

The wedding in 1901 of Elias F. Haddad, chef at the City Hotel, and Isabella (Maryam) Ashkar, who originally settled in Rutland, Vermont, occurred at St. Paul Roman Catholic Church (today St. Paul Cathedral) (see photo 5.7). Both the bride and groom were Melkite, and their church was established here in 1923. The headline of the *Worcester Daily Telegram* described their cultural heritage incorrectly as Assyrian instead of "Syrian"— this same type of confusion occasionally occurred in identifying other Near Eastern people, for example, Armenian for Syrian.

Assyrian [Syrian] Wedding. Unusual Ceremony
Performed at St. Paul's Church.

. . . As the bride was unable to speak English, the presence of a priest
of her own nationality was necessary, and Rev. Joseph Yazbeck of
Boston, Chorbishop of the Assyrian [Syrian] missions of the United
States, was called to perform the ceremony. . . . Fr. Yazbek admin-
istering the sacrament of matrimony, and later celebrating a nuptial high mass. The ceremony as performed by the Assyrian [Syrian]
priest attracted many people to the church. The priest, according
to custom, awarded the bridesmaid and the acolytes pairs of white
rosary beads as remembrances of the wedding, and on leaving the
church the wedding party was sprinkled with holy water.

The bride was attended by Miss Amelia Lian and the best man
was Joseph George. The bride's gown was an attractive one of pink
silk, with rich lace and ribbon trimmings. She wore a white veil
symbolic of ancient custom, and wore maidenhair ferns in her hair
and carried a bouquet of roses. The maid was dressed in red cash-
mere trimmed with white satin and white lace. She carried red and
white roses.

After the church ceremony the bridal party went to the new home
of the couple, 121 Shrewsbury Street, where the wedding was celebrated. A dinner was served for the guests and prominent Syrian
citizens responded to toasts.

In the evening there was singing by John F. O'Brien, William J.
Mahoney, Otto Eichoff and Thomas H. Dalling and music by
Michael Kotomy and his sons Zattam and Payes, who played on a
Syrian stringed instrument.

Mr. Haddad and wife received many presents, among them being
gifts of silver and glassware from Robert Kessell, his employer, and a
wedding cake, the gift of Mrs. Kessell. The happy couple will spend
a two weeks' honeymoon in Washington and New York.[6]

Color and style of wedding gowns varied over the centuries, for example,
white or red wedding gowns were worn at the turn of the century, and in the
Worcester area red wedding gowns were worn as late as 1918. Red symbolized joy, life, and happiness, while white represented modesty and purity.
In earlier times white symbolized affluence.

Amelia G. A. talked about her mother's red wedding gown:

Mother wore red velvet for her wedding gown. When my parents
married in 1873 in Syria, Mother's wedding gown was handmade.
Her gown was all done by hand. Every stitch was done by hand.

When we were kids, my sister and I would wear it. We used to try on her gown, wear it around the house, and parade in front of my mother. She used to laugh and enjoy watching each of us prancing around in this beautiful thing. In those days they used to wear flashy colors for wedding gowns. Later the gowns were all in white.

Bashara K. Forzley recalled in his autobiography his betrothal in Lebanon in 1908:

Everything was brought to her [the bride-to-be] ready to wear. Mother, a few friends and I made a trip to Zahlee [Zahle] to buy the jewelry and trousseau. We bought gold bracelets, necklaces, a ring, and the wedding gown, which was a white brocaded satin Paris creation. After all, I was a merchant of cloth in America![7]

The *Zharraghat (tzaghreet)*

Among the early descendants, the traditional way to display happiness in addition to song, dance, and instrumentals, particularly at engagements and weddings, was the *zharraghat*. This is a form of poetic recreation common among Arabs and is carried on from generations in families musically and poetically inclined. The *zharraghat* is made by rolling the tongue against the teeth ridge, thus producing a loud, lateral-type trill that is sustained as long as the breath lasts. Often at the end of each *zharraghat* the women playfully competed with one another to see who could excel in creativity by their recitation of an original verse or poetry in a certain rhyme and meter. In between recitations women danced gracefully while others trilled. The improvisations expressed joy and imparted wisdom and advice in jest for the bride as to how to cope under trying circumstances with in-laws and spouse. Usually the audience knew who the winner would be because of that person's reputation of outlasting most competitors. At the end of each verse the audience joined in rhythmic interplay with cheers of *loola loola laysh*—expressions of approval and pleasure—and/or *ya layli, ya layli* (oh beautiful night). These two activities, the sport of competing and the recitations, created much joviality for all ages to enjoy. An Arab wedding reception or celebration was considered complete with the joyous ululation.

Another Arab tradition performed at the wedding reception was when both mothers of the newlyweds danced solo in front of the couple and conveyed their best wishes for a long life of good health and happiness. Dressed in lovely matronly dresses with their long hair pulled back in a circular pug, the mothers' faces and stances said it all as they danced lithely, swaying bodily with the most emphasis on gracefulness by the use of fingers, arms, and nobility of face.

The men, too, sportingly competed by showing their prowess in solo, double, or folk dancing. They also displayed other talents, for example, singing *ataba* (a song in the best classical music tradition with improvisations of verse and poetry) and playing classical musical instruments. Additionally, at appropriate times throughout the celebration, a man might gently throw a kiss to the bride in appreciation of her beauty. The gesture expressed to the bride, "How beautiful you look and best wishes for your happiness." The bride usually blushed and demurely responded by fluttering her eyelids, smiling, and nodding her head.

Some wedding celebrations were leisurely affairs with weeklong festivities before the wedding. The night before the wedding the bride and the groom's relatives carried on the celebration at their respective homes. During the evening it was customary for the groom's family and friends to visit at the bride's home. Also, when the bride's home was too crowded, the overflow went to the groom's home, and at times the celebration overflowed onto the street and resulted in a parade with song and dance. When this occurred non-Arab neighbors often joined in the dance or just enjoyed the sight of people having a good time.

Position of Arab-American Women within Arab Culture

Arab women were hard-working, devoted wives, mothers, cooks, housekeepers, and businesswomen. Although in public the woman appeared as a quiet and obedient companion to her husband, at home she was in charge. It was often mentioned that women had a strong influence on their husbands, children, and brothers. In many cases, they helped to decide who the son or daughter would marry and whether or not a child continued in school, got a job, or stayed home to help the family in household work or family business. Often the woman was hardy and independent and her main goal was to enrich the lives of the family and extended family with devotion, love, and patience.

There is a popular belief in the United States that within the Arab culture women are treated as inferiors. To address this misconception, Abraham Mitrie Rihbany, an immigrant and author, wrote:

> I never had the slightest reason, nor the faintest suggestion, either by example or precept, to believe that my mother was in any way my father's inferior. . . . I can think of no circumstances in Eastern life which compel a Syrian to think of his mother, sister, and wife

in other than terms of equality in all essentials with the male members of the family. . . .[8] Nor does his attitude toward woman differ essentially from his attitude toward the male portion of mankind. He has one vocabulary for both sexes, with the inclination to be more respectful toward the gentler sex. . . . and there is a multitude of wife-ruled husbands. The family system, however, is patriarchal.[9]

My Mother Was a Saint

A frequently repeated comment by a first-generation American born was "my mother was a saint." A less frequently heard comment was "my father was a devoted and loving man, but I would not call him a saint."

Peggy D. stated:

> My mentor and role model was my mother. My first school, my first church, my first everything, was my mother—and then I went to school and church. She left her mark on me. When I think of her I'm filled with the Holy Spirit. *Ya Rubi* [My God—an expression used as "Thank you, my God."].

Many narrators referred to the hard work of women.

> Adele S.: My mother mixed flour in the evening before going to bed so that the bread dough rose by dawn. At 3 o'clock in the morning she got up and went down to the cellar, and I could hear the swing of the ax as she swung it to break boxes for firewood. Back in the kitchen, she started the fire in the stove and while she baked bread the house got heated before our large family got out of bed.

> Mary D. R.: I didn't wake up by the clock. When the children were still asleep at early dawn, my busy mind awakened me and I baked *khubz marquq* [flat bread with a delicate tang] using a twenty-five pound bag of flour. To get the dough as thin as possible I rolled the dough with a rolling pin. Then I picked up the dough and rolled it over on one arm and flipped it over onto my other arm and repeated this until the dough was paper-thin and about fifteen inches in diameter. Then I placed it on a wooden board with a long handle [peel] and baked it in the oven. We baked many types of Arabic breads at home, but we bought the Syrian bread [*khubz Arabi,* Arabic bread, commonly called Syrian bread and recently called pita bread] from the bakery. Most of the times there were two Syrian bread bakeries.

> Mae M. M.: The women scrubbed everything, boiled it in boiling hot water and on top of that they blued it so the white remained

white, and they starched pillowcases and they starched everything, children's blouses and things. They were meticulous. When they went, the world lost something beautiful.

Breastfeeding

Since breastfeeding was looked upon as a natural act, it was common to see the Arab-American mother breastfeed her baby in public within the Arab-American sections of the city. Some mothers lacked milk and their children were breastfed by other mothers who had an excess of breast milk. At various occasions when the children of both the biological parents and the wet nurse were together, the parents in jest reminded the grown-up children of their special "sibling" relationship.

In Vogue, Woman's Encasement—the Wasp Waist

Clothing played an important part in a person's identity. The Arab-American woman's and man's wardrobes generally blended in with the traditional American style-of-the-day clothing, and in particular for the woman with the proper silhouette such as the hourglass figure shaped by a corset with rigid bones and laces.

> Alexandra B. recalled: To wear a stiff, boned, tight-laced corset was no easy task for Mother. While she pulled the two sides of the corset together and used her elbows to hold the corset tight around her midriff, she used her hands to lace the corset while she inhaled, pulling in her body. To speed up the process I helped her by facing her and pulling on the bones of the corset to get it to pull in her figure while she was lacing. Right before my eyes my mother's matronly figure was formed into the fashion-of-the-day hourglass figure.

> Marion A. B. reminisced: And I remember my mother's corset! In the early days she was able to lace it herself and tie it in front, too. Then towards her later life I had to help her tie it in the back. But she always had about two or three corsets in the closet, and really, she sewed little bags on each corset and when she traveled, she tucked her money in there. When she was hiding money at home, she would have the corsets hanging in the closet and hide the money in the little bags.

Additional Family Tasks

Household tasks were often shared with older members of the extended family. Among the priorities of both parents was usually a constant round

of chores that included crocheting and sewing such household items as curtains, quilts, and family clothing including trousers for the men.

Another common scene in a household was the dressing and cutting
of lamb, the most common meat used in preparation of Arab dishes. The
sheep were either bought at the market or from an Arab American who
raised them on a farm. The task of cutting a leg of lamb was frequently a
chore for the husband, who first skinned it and then, at the kitchen table,
cut the meat into different-sized pieces according to the requirements of
the next few days' menus as planned by his wife. Once cut the meat was
stored in an insulated wooden icebox.

Community Life and Communal Cooking

Many of the women interviewed smilingly spoke of the fun they had when
six to eight neighbors would gather at one of their homes to do communal cooking and bake holiday sweets. They prepared such foods as *tabbuli,* a salad with *burghul* (kernels of dried cracked wheat) and mixed
with chopped tomatoes, finely chopped parsley, and zesty-tasting mint,
minced scallions, lemon juice, and olive oil dressing; *hummus bi tahini,* a
dip of mashed chickpeas/garbanzo beans, *tahini* (sesame paste), olive oil,
and lemon juice and garlic; *warag inab mihshee,* stuffed grape leaves with
diced lamb, rice, mint, and lemon juice; *kishk,* a fine dry-powder blend of
laban (commonly called yogurt) and *burghul. Kishk* was a basic ingredient
in making delicious thick soup that was a mainstay in the winter diet and
used in other dishes as well. Many women recalled making *kishk* as a time
for fun, song, storytelling, and sociability. It was a long process done during the bright dry days of summer at a home that had a flat roof or in a
field that had a piece of flat ground. Alice A. recalled:

> I helped the women make *kishk* on the rooftop. In those days every
> summer, everybody made it. You know *amma* Girgis' house, at 32-
> 34-36 Norfolk Street, well, it was eight apartments, and the women
> of each household took turns to make the *kishk* for each other's
> use. There were about eight women working together sitting around
> white sheets laid out on the roof. The women took the *burghul* and
> *laban,* spread them on the sheets, and rubbed them together. They
> mixed it with their fist. Then it ripened [fermented] and they would
> take a handful—like this and like that—like this and like that. Then
> they let the sun dry it a little and rubbed it again and again. They
> sang and rubbed it like this and then they put it into a sifter so
> that it would become like a powder. They started doing the *kishk*

in the morning when the sun was out. Later about 3:00 P.M. or 4:00 P.M., they folded everything in the sheet, and returned again the next morning to start all over again.

Occasionally a few children came by and would eat the *kishk* raw—before it was dried. It was one of the best times of our lives when we were kids. We used to look forward to it because all the old ladies were sitting down with their legs crossed and the sheet on them and they rubbed the *kishk* and sang. Milhem Jahleelee when he came, he sang for them the *ataba*. It was nice. They had sandwiches, *jibneh* [cheese], grapes, or *loobyee ahtya* [string beans with tomato sauce]; all *ahtya* [Lenten food—no meat] because it was summer. We had good times—we played. It was nothing to come onto Norfolk hill at 11 o'clock at night and we were still playing hide-and-seek.

Mae M. M. reminisced about making *kishk:* My mother took me with her when she was going to make *kishk* and I would be right up there on your grandfather's flat-roofed building [El-Hajj Abi-Saada's, at 80 Wall Street] next to the bakery because the roof was so sunny and wide. I helped the ladies because it was a two- to three-hour chore at a time in that hot sun. I did errands for them such as getting them drinking water when asked. The women's heads were covered with pretty *mandeel*s [head scarves of fine cotton with colorful embroidery, and tatting around the edges]. The women sat in a circle with their legs underneath the sheet that was drawn to their laps. They took the *kishk* and just rubbed and rubbed and rubbed until it was nice and smooth and powdery. Then they used their strainers and they sifted it and all the powder fell through and all the chaff stayed on top and that was used for a certain soup, and the smooth powder was used for thick soup. They didn't waste anything. As they rubbed the *kishk* they talked about family affairs, sewing, what their plans were, and the troubles they had.

Education

Many immigrants were bilingual. Among the languages they learned in their homeland schools or missionary schools were Arabic, Russian, German, English, and French. Margaret J. T. recalled:

As Mother spoke mostly in Arabic I used to think when she referred to anyone as "a smart man" or "a smart woman" Mother meant that those people were literate in English. However, later I learned when she called someone a "smart" person she meant that person was multilingual.

Literacy and Language

There were literate Arab Americans who read and collected books in Arabic and other languages. While many spoke only Arabic on arriving in America, most eventually learned English as well as other languages at school, through neighborhood contacts or at their workplace. For example, those who traveled to neighboring towns and sold dry goods door-to-door in French-Canadian neighborhoods learned French, those who sold in Italian neighborhoods learned Italian, and in mixed ethnic neighborhoods they learned English.

The Worcester Public Library, particularly the Billings Square branch library on Hamilton Street (now George Russell Realty), and coffeehouses were places with ongoing collections of Arabic newspapers and journals from across the United States and abroad. Men gathered in coffeehouses to socialize and get the news of the day. A few immigrants had their own subscriptions.

Tufeek A. recalled:

> I think my relatives must have written letters to me in Arabic. My parents also subscribed to Arabic newspapers in Brazil. My guess is that the newspaper was sent from Brazil just as the newspaper *Al-Hoda* arrived in the mail from New York. Later I know my mother received magazines like the *Readers Digest* translated in Arabic. There was always a kind of literacy in our home.

Literacy and Marriage

Literacy was important to the Arab psyche. Evelyn A. M. reminisced:

> The man who became my mother's husband and my father was originally attracted by her beauty but insisted on putting her through the literacy test before asking for her hand in marriage. To qualify, his future wife had to be able to read and write Arabic. They roomed in the same boardinghouse. One morning when she came down the stairs to go out, his door was purposely left ajar. He had his Arabic Bible in hand and asked if she would kindly read a passage for him. Nazira H. passed the test satisfactorily, and she and Girgis (George) A. married.

Early Arabic Schools and Teachers

While wanting their children to learn English, Arab-American immigrants were anxious to pass on to them their love of Arabic. At first, Arabic schools were conducted privately in the homes of several of the early immigrants with small groups of children attending. However, parents were eager to have their children learn Arabic in a school setting, and this resulted in large classes held on the ground floor at St. George Orthodox Church, 100 Wall Street. Attendance was open to all children. Among the earliest teachers at the Arabic school were Akil E. Haddad, literate in Arabic, Hebrew, Greek, and English, and Estelle (Esther) Wakid Abisamra, literate in Arabic, German, English, and French.

Akil E. Haddad was born in Mahiethett, Syria (now Lebanon). According to several local people interviewed, Haddad was a scholar who had taught at Harvard University at the invitation of a department or a faculty member. He held the teaching position for a few semesters. Several reminisces of Akil Haddad were by his son, daughter, and a former student. His son, Eli A. H.:

> My father came to America under the auspices of the Syrian Protestant College [now American University of Beirut] as a guest teacher to educate students in the Arabic language at Harvard University, Cambridge, Massachusetts. Most of his writings and books were donated to the Widener Library [Harvard College Library]. His granddaughter [Virginia H. C.] saw one of her grandfather's books on display in a showcase at the Widener Library.

> His daughter, Florence H. C.: My grandmother, Badaway Haddad [Abudela, Abodeely], was a widow. Her son, my father, Akil Haddad, was sent to a monastery and from there he went to Harvard as a guest teacher of Arabic. He also was a noted Arabic calligrapher. I remember watching him when he spread out bamboo sticks on the table and shaped them with his knife by chipping at the bottom of each stick until he shaped it the way he needed for the thick and thin lines. He knew just how to turn the stick when he was printing. He printed and designed the primers used at his Arabic classes.

> And his former Arabic school student, Charles A. George: When we were in Arabic school we had parades downtown and our schoolteacher, Akil Haddad, bought everyone in class a cane to use in the parades. He had the whole school march in the parades. Every nationality had a separate place and our schoolteacher used to stand up like a major. He used to be straight as a board, and we all had to walk just like him. He led our group and we were marching straight as boards and we thought we were great. We held the canes in our hands and sometimes we would spin them around. I was about ten years old then and it was about 1910.

Estelle Esther (Wakid) Abisamra was born in Kfarchima, Syria (now Lebanon) (see photo 5.15). Following are several reminisces of her by various individuals.

> A son of her peer, Albert A.: Estelle taught English to my uncle, Milhelm Abdelnour, at the Protestant school in Kfarchima prior to his emigration, and she also taught Arabic and German. She married Faries Abisamra in Worcester in 1900. Many educated women who emigrated taught at schools in *el-belaad*.

> Her daughter-in-law, Lilian (Maloof) A.: My mother-in-law, Esther Abisamra, was the first woman in Worcester amongst our people who could speak, read, and write English, French, German, and Arabic. She was a very learned woman. She helped the Lebanese community in Worcester as many could not read. They were dear but were not as educated. All her family was Presbyterian way back and so was she. Esther had a personality that was very much like that of the feminist movement of today. She was a mother, friend to everyone who knew her, and at the same time a housewife who went out to various functions and women's clubs.

> A granddaughter, Helen K.: My grandmother's collection of books included five volumes of German classics, published in 1847. Estelle Wakid's name is handwritten in Arabic—her first language—on the book covers. One volume is of Phadra [Phaedra, the Greek classic].

Some of the later teachers at the Arabic school were husband-and-wife teams who conducted separate classes, for example, Shokri I. Swydan and his wife, Hafeeza (Khoury) Swydan, and Mitchell G. Chakour and his wife, Adele M.(Kefruny) Chakour. The Chakours taught for twenty-seven years. One of the later teachers, Archpriest Constantine Abou-Adal, was literate in Russian, Greek, Latin, Hebrew, English, and Arabic. Another teacher was Rev. Joseph Ghiz. Mitchell G. Chakour was known for giving books from his collection to some of his students attending the Arabic school. George N. K. reminisced:

> There are eight children in my family, five boys and three girls, and we all went to Syrian school. Mr. Chakour was my Syrian school [Arabic school] teacher. My older sisters and brothers had different teachers. Their classes were held before my time. When Mr. Chakour died I used to talk with his wife and I always called her *Maarmee* [teacher—a title of respect]. I never knew her first name. She was always *Maarmee* to me. She told her children that many of her

husband's books were to be given to me. I received many of his books—God, was I ever glad. I ended up shouting with glee. I built a bookcase with shelving eight feet long and about six feet high with five shelves full of Arabic books. Mr. Chakour collected these books and bought them in this country. He also brought books with him from abroad, from his school and from his town. He had all these books full of scholarly material. Although he was Christian, he also had books about Muslims. You know I feel very very lucky that I could take these books, read and understand them 100 percent. When I read I feel happy and I thank God that my father and mother sent me to Arabic school and glad I had Mr. Chakour to take me under his wing and he gave me all this extra studying to do. I stayed with him until I was seventeen years old and I started with him when I was five. I love Arabic literature, as the heroes are always kind and caring. My father also had Arabic books, and he used to tell me about Abla and Antar of the Antar fables. Antar was a folk hero and a kind of a superman.

Charles C. H. remembered: Mr. and Mrs. Chakour taught at the same time but conducted separate classes. She was very learned and he was very strict. The demand to learn Arabic was great and especially motivated by the parents.

S. Paul H. recalled: I went to Arabic school for nine years and Mrs. Chakour was my teacher. She and her husband taught their children the better things in life such as reading and writing, and gave them a lot of inspiration as they were very knowledgeable and talented in their own right, both in Arabic and English.

Other Arabic school recollections by John K. B., born 1917: I went to Arabic school before the age of five, spoke Arabic at home, and then went to public school where I had to speak English. I learned English without any trouble from the streets as well as at school. I don't remember any conflict whatsoever.

Kenneth K., born 1912: The children went to the regular American school, and then we were at Arabic school from between four and six o'clock at night for two hours every school day. We read a lot from the Arabic books, and we practiced penmanship from a master sheet. So we didn't have much time to play.

Keeping Village Ties

Among the immigrants kinship bonds existed between those who came from the same village or town, as shown by Alice A. E., who reminisced:

Bashara K. F. did good, too. He did much charity work and never told anybody—like on holidays he would come early in the morning, I'm still in my pajamas, and he would leave a holiday gift because he and my husband came from the same village. Just like you. You were born in Worcester and someone else is born in Worcester, the person will give you holiday goods just because you were born in the same place, Worcester. That is the connection. There is no relationship. Just coming from the same little small village. The name of the town is Karhoun. I wonder if it is on the map. It is a small village, spelled K-a-r-h-o-u-n [now Qaraaoun]. My husband, Elias E., did good by himself. He had no one. The only person he knew was B. K. Forzley, who came from the same town, but they are not related.

Gracious Living and Hospitality

Probably what most defined the Arab-American home was gracious living and hospitality. The Arab Americans enjoyed having guests and entertaining people, and it was important to be generous or willing to share whatever one had with others. The gracious living involved a certain amount of ritual. Time was taken to express proverbial Arabic expressions of cordiality, and formal politeness was used during conversation, dance, or music. Dialect and colloquial expressions depended on place of origin; for example, there are varied phrases used to ask or thank Allah for His blessing. Each situation had its appropriate language, and courtesy involved the use of many different consecutive phrases. This type of etiquette would still be experienced if someone walked into an Arab-American home as late as the early 1980s.

Visits

When guest and host initially met they would embrace openly and touch cheeks three times—first the right side, then the left, and then the right. The traditional Arabic greeting usually consisted of at least two salutations and responses, for example:

Greeting: *Ahlan wa sahlan, tafoddal* [male], *tafoddali* [female] (Welcome, do me the honor by entering my home). *Bytee kaennak fee bytak* (My home is your home). *Allah yaatik elafee* (God give you health and strength).

Response: *Ahlan bekum* (Welcome to you). *Tayabe el-hamdulillah* (Praise be to God)[indicates that the respondent is well]. *Neharkum saed wa mubarak* (May your day be prosperous and blessed).

Greeting: *Sabahh el-khire* (May your day be full of happiness). *Allah younam aalyke* (God bestow upon you His bounty).

Response: *Allah kareem* (God is bountiful). *Sabahh el-noor* (May your day be full of light).

If either the host or guest did not feel well, that matter was discussed later and only after solicitously inquiring about family, friends, and affairs.

Table Etiquette for the Uninitiated

An important phase of the welcome was the serving of food that was done in the spirit of thanksgiving. As well as being sustenance, food symbolized life and had important traditional roles in home ceremonies. Generally homes had back and front entryways, and large rooms including the kitchen. When adult guests entered by the front door, they were entertained in the parlor; otherwise, they were entertained in the large kitchen. When the guests were comfortably seated, most likely near the kitchen table or on the kitchen couch, they were served *mezza* (a variety of light nutritious snacks and appetizers), including, for example: Jordan almonds (sugar-coated almond nuts); white raisins mixed with *adami* (roasted chick/ceci peas); pistachio nuts; roasted pumpkin seeds; sesame seed candy; and apricot delight, also called Turkish paste. *Mezza* was usually available in glass jars or tin cans on the closet shelf. When food was served, common expressions were used:

Host: *Min fadlik sharaftena* (Please partake, you have honored us).

The host would invite the guest three times as etiquette, and tradition called for the guest to refuse twice before accepting food. To accept the first time would appear overeager, and a second refusal showed restraint. For example:

Guest: *La, istakther bekhirak* (No, thank you, I am grateful to you). *Ana mabsooton zhiddan* (I am well pleased). *Tafoddal, tafoddali* (After you, I ask you to eat).

After the third invitation the guest would accept the food, and more courtesies were then exchanged between guest and host:

Guest: *Salam dayakoom* (May your hands always be blessed with doing good works). *Kattar Allah kherik* (May God increase your goods).

Host: *Wa ukherik* (And your goods also). *Bitsharriftena mah shoftkoon, el-hamdulillah* (You have honored this household. Seeing you is food for my soul for which I thank God).

When the guest preferred something else to eat or drink, it was requested and the host responded:

Host: *Halatha barikoom* (You have my blessings and indeed your request is granted). *Sahtain* (To your health).

Since the host continued to refill empty plates, guests frequently left some uneaten food on the plate. Toward the end of the visit some drank Turkish (or Arabic) coffee in a demitasse, and some often played a game of *tawlah* or chess. Others smoked a *narghile* (an elaborate water pipe from which smoke is drawn through a decorative flexible tube with a mouthpiece extended from a glass container of water atop of which sits a thumbnail-sized ember of tobacco). It was also common at the end of the meal to see a man remove from his pocket a *misbaha/tasbah* (prayer beads used by many Christians, Druze, and Muslims). Each bead represents a reference to Allah, and in Arabic there are ninety-nine such expressions. A thirty-three-bead *misbaha* requires the cycle to be repeated three times. Aside from any religious overtones, the *misbaha* has a relaxing effect when one rhythmically moves the beads between thumb and index finger.

Expressions used at the end of the visit:

Guest: *Khatirkum salama* (I ask permission to leave). *Bitsharrifna* (We have been honored by your hospitality).

Host: *Anta lateefon zhiddan* (You are extremely kind). *Ana tahhet amrak* (I am entirely at your service). *Wa alaykum salam wa rah matullaha wa baraka tehi* (May the peace and mercy of God and His blessings be upon you).

Guest: *Kattar kherkum* (I am grateful). *Wa salam alaykum* (And upon you be peace).

Visits by Children

Hospitality and endearments were also bestowed upon children, be they relative, friend, or stranger. They were greeted with outstretched arms and were called *ya walidi* (my children). The elders had the shared responsibility for caring for and protecting children. Frequently, the women, and some men, would greet the children with hugs and one or more kisses on each cheek, on the chin, forehead, and on top of the head, and address them with words of endearment: *ya youni* (my eyes), *ya urbi* (my heart), *ya hayathi* (my life). Generally children enjoyed this attention and outpouring of love, however, others shied away from it. They were aware that adults cared about their well-being, and they in turn respected and honored their elders.

Children were served freshly baked cookies or snacks, and then the games and storytelling would begin. A favorite story was about a baby bird that fell from its nest and sought refuge. The storyteller would start by opening the palm of his or her hand and saying that the birdie fell safely into it. Then, with the index finger of the other hand, the storyteller would lovingly stroke the imaginary birdie. As the story unfolded the storyteller's fingers would move up and down the child's arm, and then the cupped fingers of the storyteller would come to rest in the child's armpit, and the storyteller would exclaim: "Oh, the birdie was hiding here in the shelter of your armpit." Then with a swift movement the adult would swing his arm in the direction of up-and-away and open the closed palm of the hand, thereby indicating the baby bird was free and had flown away. As we see, stories were more than told; they were acted out, sung, and even danced.

Community Gatherings

Dance, music, poetry, reading, and storytelling were frequently common components of Arab life at home or at public functions.

Arabic Music

Janet H. S. happily recalled how her household played music and danced together:

> For entertainment we sang our hearts out in the kitchen, and occasionally in the parlor. The music is rhythmic, the lyrics expressive. It makes the feet dance, and lifts the spirits despite hardships.

The *el-ud* and the *darabukkah* are played for their own beauty of sound and as accompaniment to and the inspiration for poetry recitations and storytelling. At certain types of public performances the folk music summons up emotion, similar to other Eastern and Western cultures, and is played for response by the audience. The natural expression is to clap in rhythm with the music, join in with the chorus, dance solo, or do the *dabkah* in front of the auditorium stage. Especially when an artist sings an *ataba* and the audience is overwhelmed with emotion, the audience calls out terms of affection and approval at the appropriate time during certain pauses by the artist.

Arab Folk Line Dance

The *dabkah* is the most popular line dance. It is easy to do and a great way to socialize and meet people. The dancers hold hands or are arm-in-arm throughout the dance. Every two or three steps the dancers forcefully stomp the floor and sway their bodies to accentuate the rhythms of the music. Once the dance starts anyone may join the line and often the whole family, young and old, dance the *dabkah* together. It is especially popular at weddings, *haflah*s (parties), *sahra*s (social gatherings), and *mahrajhan*s (outings). The honor of improvisation is given to the leader, who holds a handkerchief and waves it rhythmically. Usually the second in line leads the rest of the group in varied steps, thereby permitting the leader freedom to perform while the group dances the standard steps of the *dabkah*. Subsequently, the leader joins the end of the line or drops out to allow the next in line to take the lead position. Those who remain seated or standing on the sideline participate by clapping in rhythm with the *darabukkah*. Solo or duo dancing has an air of dignity and physical grace. Solo dance sometimes occurs within a circle formed by the line dancers who stand in place and clap to the rhythm of the music or continue dancing the *dabkah* around the solo or duo dancers.

Historical Dramas Performed in Arabic

For additional recreation, many chose historical dramas with a variety of themes that were great for teaching and learning about one's heritage. A group among them would decide which play to perform, and when the word got around, some people volunteered for particular parts and others were drafted. One of the numerous heroes was Salah El-Deen Yusif ibn Ayyub (Saladin). Different plays based on his life were popular and performed at various times with varied casts and stories. A performance of *Salah El-Deen* raised money to aid the Melkites in the purchase of their first church building,[10] named St. Mary's (now Our Lady of Perpetual Help Church). The cast for this performance was made up of Eastern Orthodox and Melkites. Regardless of religion, people were chosen for certain parts based on their ability to perform, and frequently there was interaction between the groups of various religions.

Albert A. recalled the performance of *Salah El-Deen:*

> In the great Arabic drama *Salah El-Deen,* Salem Kassab played the king of France. Kassab was perhaps the most educated man of all the group that played in that drama. He was a graduate of Antouna,

the French school in Lebanon. He spoke Arabic, French, and English fluently. Kassab never married.

Before emigrating, Aneese Abdelnour lived in Kfarchima [Lebanon], where he played Omad El-Deen, the servant of Salah El-Deen. He still remembered the lines and did not want to study a new part as that was the only role he wanted. A number of people tried out for the part of Salah El-Deen, but they did not have the voice or the stance. The director did not accept them, and so he said to Aneese Abdelnour, "You've got to try out for Salah El-Deen." He did and he got the part—and that's why he played Salah El-Deen. Charlie Husson, who later became a priest known as Rev. Raphael Husson, played the part of Omad El-Deen, the servant of Salah El-Deen.

Elias (Eli) Ghiz was director of the play and also supported it with an advertisement:

> Elias J. Ghiz, Refreshments, Where Leisure Hours Are Interestingly Spent, 69 Wall St., Worcester.

The program book's back page was titled "Our Appreciation from the Committee," and it thanked the patronizers of the program, the cast, the audience, and "the committee who had shown the real spirit of our organization."

When Albert A. was questioned as to why Elias Ghiz's name was not recognized as director in the program book, he said:

> The credit goes to the whole group. The important thing to Elias was the play was a success and the credit went to the whole group who valued each other's involvement. People worked together for the community and the leadership cared more about the promotion of Arab culture than seeking personal recognition.

Another popular historical play, *Haroun El-Rashad* (Harun ar-Rashid), a story of the caliph of Baghdad, was performed by children from the Arabic school. Mary S. reminisced:

> I was in *Haroun El-Rashad,* and that play was put on by Mr. Mitchell Chakour, our Arabic school teacher, who also put on another play at the Strand Theatre in downtown Worcester. He put on and directed plays now and then which were performed by the school children to benefit the school. He took us on field trips with the money.
>
> I have no idea what the name of the other play was at the Strand Theatre, but I took the part of a prince. I remember I unsheathed

the sword and it hit my hat and the hat fell off, and I was wearing long hair at the time. I had pushed the hair up under the hat and it came flowing over my shoulders. Everybody howled with laughter and they had a great time. And I was wearing a mustache to boot. So can you see me with this long hair over my shoulders and a mustache? I guess the sword was too big for a little girl so when I unsheathed it, it hit the hat and the hat went flying across the stage. The mustache did not fall off—believe it or not—only the hat did.

In another play I recited a poem in Arabic about a pigeon, that went something like this: "The pigeon is born free and we hope the people will be free just as you are free to fly wherever you want to go the year round and hope that the people who are enslaved will be free." It was a long and beautiful poem. You know Arabic is a flowery language. The old folks loved the plays. There was no television in those days and many people didn't even have a radio, so this was wonderful entertainment for them.

Adele K. G. stated: My Arabic school teacher was Reverend Joseph Ghiz, and one of the plays our class performed was *Charlotta*, with John Ayoub as the director. He lives in California now. All our plays were performed in Arabic by first-generation American-born children. Most of the kids were bilingual in English and Arabic.

Rev. Polycarpe Warde, the first pastor of Our Lady of Perpetual Help Church, produced and directed dramatizations of Greek tragedies translated into Arabic.[11] Additionally, Shakespearean drama was performed by other Arab-American immigrant groups. Of the thirty-seven Shakespearean dramas, twenty-one were translated into Arabic during the first half of the twentieth century.[12] One of the plays performed in Arabic and directed by Rev. Polycarpe Warde was *The Princess Venus of England*.

Albert A. described the attendance at the performance:

They sold a tremendous number of tickets, and Girgis [George] Abdow, who was one of many leaders in the community, got up on the stage and told the people from Worcester that they sold too many tickets and asked the Worcester people if they would leave and give their seats to the people who came from out of town. The people from Worcester got up and left, and the play was performed again two weeks later for the Worcester folks.

Oratory in Arabic and English

Classical Arabic lends itself to public oratory and rhymed verse. The richness and melodiousness of the Arabic language cause many Arabophiles to get carried away with its style, substance, and passion. Encouraged by an audience that often reacts audibly, orators captivate the listeners by using the voice with equal consistency and sustained animation, making the presentation both aurally rich and revealing of character. Orators speak with drama and emotion in their voices and at times it carries over into their everyday conversation. Their style and delivery with its many nuances and gestures mesmerizes an audience with its drama. In addition to entertaining, orators customarily assist in eulogizing the deceased at wakes and often serve as chanters and liturgists.

People remembered Aneese Abdelnour as an eloquent orator. Usually when Aneese's name was mentioned, someone in the group was compelled to recite poetry or recall a part in a play and recite it with gusto as Aneese did. He was a forceful public speaker who was much in demand at religious and philanthropic functions throughout the area. A quote in the Saint George Consecration book described:

> Aneese Abdelnour—A Glorious Memory—Who served the Arabic-speaking people with his golden tongue and silver pen.[13]

Many other orators were remembered who performed the same services. Included among them were Aziz G. Francis, Mrs. Harold F. Boosahda Sr., née Mary Najjar, Mrs. Abraham I. Haddad, née Nabeha Merhige, and Mrs. Joseph T. Peters, née Annie Bourisk.

Albert Abdelnour used an oratorical style in public speaking similar to that of his father, Aneese, and Albert was in demand to speak, predominantly at sports functions and schools. On occasions when several speakers were scheduled for the same program, other speakers made it known to the host organization that they would speak only if they were scheduled before Albert. For example, Michael F. (an Italian American) stated:

> Who can follow Al's performance and come out ahead? He spoke with such enthusiasm that brought the audience to their feet to applaud his dynamic delivery and spellbinding style. You know, when Al spoke at functions he always recognized his sister Adele in the audience as supportive of most everything he undertook and how important she was to him.

Debates after 1917

Albert A. recalled:

> Debates were a big thing in those early days. Titles of some of the debates were "Was the U.S. Justified to Enter World War I?";

"Should the U.S. Recognize Communist Russia?"; and another debate was "Should the U.S. Give the Philippines Their Independence?" Philip G. Haddad asked many of the girls to debate against the men, and although the women qualified they refused. However, five women and three men debated in *Haroun El-Rashad*, "The Poets," Act II.

Family Conflict: Impartial Party — The Resource Person

Each family group was accustomed to have several resource persons who were acknowledged by their peers to be wise, understanding, and knowledgeable and as such could serve as informal judges, advisers, and peacemakers who could be called upon to settle family problems and local disputes. Usually those chosen as mentors shared the same religion and village of origin as those in conflict. The parties with conflicting ideas were comfortable airing their problems in the presence of an impartial third party who was highly respected, sincere, and committed to strong spiritual values. Conflict resolution was important to the immigrant community that expected proper conduct from its members in honor and respect of family names and reputations.

5.1. Rev. Michael M. Husson (Hussan) (1860–1939), about 1900.

5.2. Certificate of Baptism, 1916. The certificate for Hind-Helene Swydan with imprinted ikon of St. John the Baptist baptizing Jesus Christ. The certificate was printed in English and Arabic, signed, and sealed by Rev. Michael M. Husson.

5.3. "Suitable wife," Sophia, 1913. The Abraham family. *Clockwise top left:* Sophia (Sophie), Louis (brother), Musalam Farrah Abraham (Sam) (father), Milhem Azar (with waxed handlebar mustache, Khazma's father), Henry (brother), Sadie, Elizabeth, Mary (sisters), and Khazma (Emma) Milhem Haddad Azar Abraham (mother, and peddler of dry goods).

5.4. Photograph postal card from suitor in Lebanon, 1919. A poetic message in Arabic was written on reverse side of card by Assad C. of El-Mreijat (now Lebanon) and sent to his friend, Nazira M. B.

5.5. Marriage, Simon George and Sooriya (Sarah) Haggar in her lace wedding gown, 1897.

5.6. Wedding gift and recording, about 1916. Pitcher of green glass with gold design and trim and matching drinking glasses received as wedding gift. Cylinder ten-inch Saidaphon Records recording of Easter hymn *Il-Maseeh Qaam* (Christ has risen) by "golden-voiced" Archbishop Germanos (Shehadi) of Baalbek and Seleucia. Recording was played on hand-cranked Victrola phonograph player.

5.7. Marriage, Elias F. Haddad
(aged 25 years) and Isabella
Ashkar (aged 21), 1901.

5.8 Contemplative bride, Nazira Lian.
Marriage to Charles Syiek, 1917.

5.9. Marriage by bishop, 1926. *Clockwise top left:* Rev. Naum Vangel Cere of St. Mary Assumption Albanian Orthodox Church (location of the ceremony to accommodate about 300 attendees); Bishop Basil M. Kherbawi; Lamise Chakour (flower girl); maid-of-honor n.n., Victoria Shakour (bride); James Kalil (groom); best man n.n. *Background:* the Ikonostasis. James Kalil, fluent in five languages, was born in Palestine and died aged 97. Victoria Shakour Kalil was born in Syria and died aged 93.

5.10. In vogue, woman's dress,
about 1916. Afifi C. Shweire (later
Mrs. Chikri D. Salih).

5.11. In vogue, man's
clothing, about 1916. Eli A.
Boosahda (later Busada).

5.12. In vogue, four women and child, about 1918. *Clockwise top left:* n.n., Shafeeka (Sophie) Trebulsi Bollus, Saada (Sadie) Trebulsi, n.n., Effie Trebulsi Hajjar.

5.13. In vogue, Assafe George and Elias Dahrooge families, 1908. *Back row, left to right:* Malocke George (name at marriage was Mary Arsaaf/Assafe) Dahrooge [daughter of Assafe George and Um Embass, and wife of Elias (Ellis) K. Dahrooge], wearing feathered hat, gold jewelry pin with gold watch, and necklaces, with her husband (married 1906). *Center:* Um Embass Mary (Tekla) Aboassaly-Skaff George (wife of Assafe George). *Front row, left to right,* the George children: John A. G., Thomas A. G., Michael A. G. "Steve," and Charles Bashara A. G. The shepherd's cane was property of the photographer. *Missing from photo:* Assafe George (husband of Um Embass), and son George A. G. The three sons who served in the U.S armed services during World War I were John A. G., Michael A. G., and George A. G.

5.14. In vogue, woman's encasement—the "wasp" waist, 1909. Farrah Abraham (husband), Sophie Khoury Abraham (wife) posed in her fashion-of-the-day hourglass-figure shaped by a corset, and Henry Abraham (son).

5.15. Abisamra family, 1904. *Clockwise:* Esther (Estelle) Wakid Abisamra (mother), Faries (father), Alexandra (later Mrs. Ward Abbott (Aboud), and Victoria (later Mrs. Assad M. Kouri), (daughters).

5.16. Realia montage, 1883–1922. *Clockwise bottom left:* a shaver razor blade, shaving chalk to stop bleeding when the facial skin was nicked by the razor blade, two sharpening stones for razor blades. A piggy bank for bills and coins. Rolled bills were inserted into a hole on the side of the bank, and coins were deposited into a slot on the opposite side, a key to the piggy bank. United States Liberty one-dollar silver coins, 1883, 1890, 1922 (coin collection of Kalil A. B.). Bridal headpiece, gold watch with gold chain worn around the neck, a wedding gift from the groom to the bride, long, narrow, white cloth bridal gloves with rows of tiny pearl buttons, 1916. Mother-of-pearl *misbaha*. A covered maroon leather scapular, and another with gold-threaded border on maroon silk velvet with bound relic of Theotokos (mother of God). The larger silver pocket watch belongs to father and smaller gold pocket watch belongs to son.

5.17–5.23. Children, 1915–1927.

5.17. Raymond J. MacKoul, 1915.

5.18 John K. Boosahda (now Busada), 1921.

5.19 Samuel G. Abdelmaseh, 1914.

5.20 Frances Boosahda (now
Frances Miles LeBesque), 1925.

5.21 *clockwise top left:* Malvina Mitchell, n.n., *middle row right:*
Evelyn Mitchell, others n.n., 1918.

5.22 n.n.

5.23 Grandfather with grandchildren, 1927. *Clockwise:*
Abraham Boosahda, Elizabeth
B., Freda B. (now Dadah) wearing a wristwatch, Rose B. (now
Nicola) wearing a bracelet.
Dresses are eyelet and embroi-
dered. *Upper right corner:* A
typical horizontal grapevine
arbor found in many yards provided grape leaves for cooking,
grapes for eating, and a shady
area where family, neighbors,
and friends congregated for
pleasantries.

5.24. Cast of *Salah El-Deen*, 1924. *Clockwise top left:* Abraham "Doc" Debs, Milhelm Abdelnour, Salim "Sam/Cutie" Abraham, George MacKoul, S. Michael Haddad, James Aboumrad, Albert Abdelnour, Alex Jalboot, William Abdelnour, Robert Boosahda (Busada), Fred Haddad, Nicholas Haddad, Akil Haddad, Aneese Abdelnour, Fida K. Forzley, Rose Jalboot, Mary Saber, Sam M. Kouri, Mary Dowd. The women in the cast were presented with bouquets of flowers in appreciation for their fine performance. Costumes were rented from Fuller Regalia Company.

LIST OF CHARACTERS

1—Aneese Abdelnour
2—Charles Husson
3—Joseph Lian
4—Karam Saad
5—David Thomas
6—Litfy Esper
7—Najeeb Koury
8—Mrs. W. Younis
9—Miss Naphie David
10—Sam Karey
11—Elias Hillal
12—Charles Saliba
13—Moses Eid
14—George Husson
15—Aneese Abdelnour
16—Charles Husson
17—Salem Kassab
18—Joseph Lian
19—Toffie Saad
20—Mrs. E. Abougousl
21—Eva Nasif
22—Jack Njamey
23—Elias Karam
24—James Esper
25—Mansour Moore

HISTORICAL DRAMA

SALAH EL-DEEN

GIVEN FOR THE BENEFIT OF

St. Mary's Chur

Houghton Street

Worcester, Massachuset

POLI'S THEATER
SUNDAY EVENING, JULY 20, 1924

HAROUN - EL - RASHAD
ARABIC PLAY

BENEFIT OF THE SYRIAN
SCHOOL

SUNDAY MAY 23 1925

Rose Jalbot
Mary Saber
Lena Ghiz
Adele Kouri
Madlin Hajj
Delia Mitchell
Alice Moore
Evelyn Mitchell
Raymond Mackoul
Assad Abufaris
Michell Kouri
Miss Louice Sears
Rodney Peters
George Dowd
Philip Nackley
Miss Eva Nackley
Mike Saad

ABU - AL - NAWS ASSAD ABUFARIS

5.25. Pages from program booklets of *Salah El-Deen* and *Haroun El-Rashad*, 1924 and 1925 respectively. Shown are covers and pages with lists of characters.

5.26. Cast of *Princess Venus of England*, 1932. *Top row, left to right:* Edmund Haddad (now Monsignor Haddad), George Lian, Nick Baroud. *Middle row:* Rev. Polycarpe Warde, Herbert Wakeen, John Lian, Charlie Wakeen, James Esper, Mitch Nejemy, Peter Wakeen. *Bottom row:* n.n. Thomas, Effie Nejemy Nakosey, Sophie Hajjar Abraham, Charlie Halal, Edward Salem, Sally Haddad, James Arraj, Mary Hajjar Nejemy.

Chapter Six
AMERICANIZATION

While most Arab-American immigrants retained their Arab culture and ties to their homelands, they nevertheless chose to become U.S. citizens. To do this, they had to file two papers: a Declaration of Intention to become a citizen and, after a five-year residency, a petition for naturalization. The only exception to the residency requirement was made for men who had served in the armed forces. Before 1922, when a husband or father became a naturalized citizen, the wife and children automatically became citizens. The benefits of citizenship were the opportunity to homestead in the West and to vote. For an Arab alien the reference to renouncing allegiance to "Victoria, Queen of the United Kingdom of Great Britain and Ireland" was lined out on the declaration form, and in its place was a handwritten reference to the Ottoman sultan Abdul Hamed (Abd al-Hamid II), who ruled from approximately 1876 to 1909. The declaration of Hanna Abdallah, for example, read as follows:

> United States of America, Massachusetts District, ss. Be it Remembered, That at a District Court . . . at Boston, . . . Hanna Abdallah . . . Pedler [Peddler], an Alien, and a free white person, by his Declaration in writing, on oath, sets forth, that he was born in Syria . . . in the year of our Lord eighteen hundred and sixty and is now about thirty-two years of age; that he arrived in Philadelphia in the District of Pennsylvania . . . in the year of our Lord eighteen hundred and ninety, that it then was, and still is, his bona fide intention to become a citizen of the United States of America, and to renounce forever all allegiance and fidelity to every foreign Prince, State, Potentate and Sovereignty whatsoever,—more especially to Abdul Hamed, Sultan of Turkey whose subject he has heretofore been. He therefore prays, that his said Declaration and Intention may become a record of said Court, agreeably to the laws in such case made and provided.
>
> Whereupon the Declaration of the said Petitioner is admitted to become a record of said Court accordingly.

In Testimony Whereof, I have hereunto set my hand and affixed the seal of said Court, . . . this 24th day of September, A.D. 1892, in the one hundred and seventeenth year of the Independence of the United States of America. [Signed and sealed by the] Deputy Clerk of the United States District Court for the District of Massachusetts.

Citizenship and the Caucasian/Asian Controversy

The reference in the declaration to the alien as a "free white person" was the result of restrictive and amended naturalization laws passed by Congress and the courts. For example, the amended naturalization law of 1870 defined the terms "white person" and "Caucasian" as well as the part nativity played in those definitions. Alixa Naff wrote that although the naturalization law of 1870 stated that free whites and aliens of "African descent or African nativity" could apply for naturalization, it failed to define "white," leaving the interpretation of that term to the subjective opinion of individuals in the courts.[1] Naff continued:

> When in 1899 the Bureau of Immigration initiated the "racial" classifications of "Syrian" and "Palestinian" for immigrants from the eastern Mediterranean provinces of the Ottoman Empire, they were regarded [correctly] as Caucasian. Race did not become an issue until after 1906 when immigrants from western Asia became entangled in new naturalization laws designed to determine suitability for citizenship. . . . Then when Congress and the courts, in order to control illegal naturalization of immigrants for voting purposes, added ethnic origins to requirements for suitability, based on a law that declared Chinese ineligible for citizenship, the problem of race for many non-European immigrant groups surfaced.

In 1910, the U.S. Census Bureau classified peoples from the eastern Mediterranean—Syrians, Palestinians, Turks, Armenians, and others—as "Asiatic." To further provoke the issue, a directive emanated from the Bureau of Immigration and Naturalization in 1911, ordering court clerks to reject applications for first papers from "aliens who were neither white persons nor persons of African birth and descent." The directive was acted on nationwide by a bureaucracy that included bureau chiefs, naturalization examiners, and district directors.[2] The Bureau of Immigration and Naturalization frequently denied citizenship to an alien on the ground that as an Asian-born subject of the Ottoman sultan, he/she was not a "white person." The question of Asian nativity was unresolved, and Asian-born immigrants were vulnerable to nativist interpretations. Ultimately, the question of which "non-yellow" immigrants of Asian birth were "free white persons" or "Caucasians" was addressed in the Act of 1917. It appeared that Syrians and Palestinians were once again proclaimed white persons and their place of nativity, the Ottoman Empire, had no bearing on race.

A later Declaration of Intention form, in this case of Nasif Mitchell, was more detailed regarding the immigrant:

> United States of America, . . . Commonwealth of Massachusetts, County of Worcester ss: In the Superior Court of Massachusetts. I, Nasif Mitchell, aged 56 years, occupation merchant, do declare on oath that my personal description is: Color white, complexion medium, height 5 feet 6 inches, weight 200 pounds, color of hair grey, color of eyes brown . . . I was born in Muhaidtha [Mahiethett], Syria, Turkey [an example of incorrectly not separating province of Syria from Turkey] on the 10th day of April, anno Domini 1867; I now reside at 47 Wall Street, Worcester, Massachusetts. I emigrated to the United States of America from Havre, France, on the vessel unknown; my last foreign residence was said Muhaidtha [Mahiethett]; I am married; the name of my wife is Angelina Rizkallah, she was born at Muhaidtha [Mahiethett], Syria and now resides at above residence with declarant. It is my bona fide intention to renounce forever all allegiance and fidelity to any foreign prince, potentate, state, or sovereignty, and particularly to The Present Government of Turkey, of whom I am now a subject; I arrived at the port of New York, in the State of New York, on or about the 20th day of March, anno Domini 1891; I am not an anarchist; I am not a polygamist nor a believer in the practice of polygamy; and it is my intention in good faith to become a citizen of the United States of America and to permanently reside therein: SO HELP ME GOD. "Nassif Mitchell" Original signature of declarant.
>
> Subscribed and sworn to before me in the office of the Clerk of said Court this 8th day of September, anno Domini 1923. (Signed and sealed by the Clerk of the Superior Court).

The clerk handwrote the reference to the intention to renounce allegiance to "The Present Government of Turkey." Reference to the issue of race and suitability for citizenship was stamped in the upper left corner of the declaration, stating: "NOTICE—Persons who arrived in the United States after June 29, 1906, should consult the clerk before appearing with witnesses to petition for naturalization. No. 27903."

Encounters with Prejudice

The modern nativist movement began in the 1870s when Congress was taking its first steps toward weeding out "undesirable foreigners." Some

Americans complained that there were too many foreigners in the United States and feared that immigrants constituted a danger to the economic welfare, moral fiber, and cultural purity of the United States. While Know-Nothingism waned soon after the Civil War, the nativist organization appeared periodically in Yankee Worcester. In the early 1920s the Ku Klux Klan spread in Worcester County and surroundings. Nativism did not impact greatly upon Americans of Arab ancestry. However, during the process of integration, the learning and practice of one's culture was discouraged by nativism. After World War II oftentimes the descendants were victims of discrimination, myth, and stereotype.

Prospect of Deportation

The prospect of being deported and losing what you had gained was frightening. Such an incident occurred in 1917 and was recalled by Nabeha Merhige Haddad in her autobiography:

> I still remember the day when Cousin Amelia's daughter Alma came home from Grafton Street School for lunch. She was crying as though her heart would break. . . . Between sobs, Alma said that her teacher, Miss Morin, told the whole class that President Wilson [1913–21] was going to deport all the Syrians after the war because they were not doing their share toward the war. . . . First, I thought I would go and speak to the teacher but on second thought, perhaps it's best to write her a little note. . . . I had Alma deliver it to the teacher.

> Excerpted from Haddad's note: In front of a class of children, all of different nationalities, you condemned the Syrian people and told them that President Wilson was going to deport all the Syrians after the war.

> Can you realize the prejudiced feeling you were creating among the children at a time like this?

> With full courage, I shall write and ask President Wilson if this is true. But I doubt our President would say such a thing after I read the beautiful letter [from the President] consoling Mrs. Bayrouty who lost her son George in the war.

> I have two nephews in the service and many of our boys answered our Country's call. All the people I know were proud to buy the Liberty Bonds since they were not eligible to serve in the armed forces.

> Our main concern should be to pray for peace, that this terrible war will be over and our boys come home safely to their loved ones.

Haddad continued: When school was out in the afternoon, Miss Morin came to the house and told me how sorry she was for the mistake. . . . I admired her for apologizing. . . . Mr. Underwood, the principal of Grafton Street School, did his best to encourage and boost the morale of the boys and girls under his care. He told them not to be ashamed of their parents' language but to strive to learn both the English and Arabic. [He further stated:] A person who can speak more than one language represents more than one person.[3]

Asian Controversy

Peter M. A. recalled a frequently told story about Mitchell K. Maykel and Hon. Pehr G. Holmes, a Republican senator (served March 4, 1931– January 3, 1947):

They [the government] were going to classify us, the Arab people, as Asian, but Mr. Maykel visited Congressman Pehr G. Holmes and asked him to fight this thing and make sure we are classified as white and not Asian. I'm as white as anybody who claims to be white is! Our people were going to be considered not of the white race but the senator made sure that we were classified correctly. He was the catalyst behind the movement to classify us once again as Caucasian. I know of this story because I was friendly with Charlie Maykel, the son, and he told me about it, and so did Michael N. A. and my brother Sam. That actually happened.

Czarist Russia Connection

Since the Eastern Orthodox Church was under the jurisdiction of the Russian Orthodox patriarchate in Moscow, cultural exchanges occurred between the Russians and the Lebanese, Syrians, and Palestinians. These exchanges were halted in 1917 following the Bolshevik revolution and the onset of Communist Russia. Because of the fears of the new Bolshevik regime, a "Red scare"—among other things, accusations of disloyalty to the government, subversion, or belonging to the Communist Party—engulfed the United States and branded Eastern Europeans and people who had a czarist Russian connection as un-American and sympathetic to the Russian regime. Consequently, immigrants who had lived in and emigrated from Russia and had in their possession any material pertaining to that country were in danger of being suspected of a Communist connection. For example, in Worcester the "Red scare" threatened some patriotic immigrants like Archpriest Constantine Abou-Adal (born in Damascus, Syria) and Shorkri K. Swydan (born in Judaidet, Marjayoun, now Lebanon). With the probability of the U.S. government bringing charges against them as having leanings toward Russia because of their collections of cherished Russian books and writings, each of them sadly burned their collections, one by one.

In later years when Archpriest Abou-Adal was asked his view of the future, he responded, "It has always been unsure. We who have seen great changes must have great hopes."[4]

The New Citizen and Bigotry

The immigrant was at times looked upon adversely, with hostility and with certain condescension as a foreigner. Even though the immigrant served in the U.S. armed forces and was a U.S. citizen, that person was sometimes still looked upon negatively as a foreigner because of such characteristics as appearance, manner of speaking, and cultural traits. Eli A. B. spoke from personal experience about how some prevailing attitudes toward new citizens had tragic consequences, particularly with the belief that the new citizen could not be a good family provider:

> How can I forget my first-born child [born 1923] from infancy to the age of three when my wife's family influenced her to take the child and move away with no forwarding address? Her family traced their ancestry to a great-great—whatever great he was—grandfather who had gone through the [Revolutionary] war with George Washington. The grandfather died about 1811, I believe. I advertised in newspapers throughout many areas; had detectives on her trail; made many contacts with the wife's family and all to no avail. Frances B. M., my daughter, was given a different surname and was moved to California with her mother. I desperately wanted more so to find my daughter as I was happily remarried to my dear Nellie by whom we have three children. We wanted my daughter to know her family and her relatives and to benefit from my financial success as a builder and contractor. All who knew me shared my pain and sorrow of not knowing what became of my daughter, Frances. This weighed heavily on my heart and mind for fifty-two years and finally father and daughter were reunited. With much gratitude and joy I reintroduced my three-year-old Frances fifty-two years later to my family, relatives, and friends.

World War I Servicemen

In 1917 when the United States joined the Allies in World War 1, many Arab-American men proudly served their adopted country—some enlisted and others were drafted. All men between the ages of eighteen and forty-five were eventually included in three draft registrations, whether they were native born or alien. The first registration was on June 5, 1917, for all men between the ages of twenty-one and thirty-one. The second registration occurred on June 5, 1918, for those who attained age twenty-one after June 5, 1917, and a supplemental registration on August 24, 1918, for those reaching age twenty-one after June 5, 1918. The third registration was on September 12, 1918, for men aged eighteen through forty-five.

M. M. Maloof wrote in the *Boston Evening Transcript* about the intense patriotism and staunch loyalty of the Syrians:

> A splendid example of Syrian patriotism is the proportionately large numbers . . . who have enlisted as volunteers in answer to Wilson's call. The exact figures are not available but it is known that over 300 have gone from the State of Massachusetts alone, which is remarkable in view of their small numbers.[5]

Eli A. Busada stated in his autobiography how his work influenced his choice to serve in the U.S. Naval Air Service.

> In 1917, I decided to build a garage on Norfolk Street, where the Abdows lived and opposite the macaroni shop, on land that was owned by my father. I excavated a good part of it myself. I used the old Ford, taking the body off and replacing it with a flat body that would not be easily tipped over. . . .[6] At that time this country was drafting men. I began to think that I could be drafted and wondered what would become of my garage. I changed my mind and decided to enlist in the branch of the service of my choice before being drafted into the army . . . I decided to enlist in the Naval Air Service, as my experience as a mechanic on gasoline motors would be helpful.[7]

While he (at that time Eli A. Boosahda, now Busada) was at Hampton Road Naval Air Station, Virginia, his group was assigned to a class studying gasoline engines, and his knowledge of Arabic and his drum corps experiences proved to be helpful:

> The instructor spoke so fast that I could not keep up with him. I started writing the words in Arabic by the sound and later when I got back to the barracks, I changed them into English. It worked very well, and the men in class thought I was taking shorthand. Many of the men in class were having the same trouble so they copied from me later. . . . [I] took some men in my company out

to drill because of my experience in the Syrian Fife and Drum Corps.[8]

He continued: . . . [I was] given the second-class machinist's mate rating. I was assigned two planes, one to be ready at all times. Our duty was to escort convoys of ships coming in, or to scout around for German submarines. We carried bombs under the wings of the planes to be released by the observer in the front cockpit, if and when he saw a submarine. That went on until November 11, 1918, when the Armistice was signed.[9]

Albert Gammal was honored in the graduation yearbook, *The Aftermath of the Class of Nineteen-Eighteen of the Worcester Classical High School:*

Albert came from that beautiful and ancient city, Damascus, Syria, to the city of Worcester when he was sixteen years old. He went to the Night School in order to master our language and with his own studying managed to reach the mark for Classical High School. He strove to graduate in one year and a half and had almost succeeded in fulfilling this ambition when he was called for service. Although desirous of becoming an electrical engineer, he has obeyed the call of his country. As a soldier, he will help make the world safe for Democracy, earning the undying gratitude of his fellow-countrymen and of generations to come. May he know that the best wishes of his classmates go with him, and may he return to carry out those plans he has cherished and that now yield to a higher call. "Lost to sight, but to memory dear."

Honored War Dead

On a wall at the Worcester Memorial Auditorium (now Worcester AUD) is a dedication to servicemen from Worcester who made the supreme sacrifice in World War I:

"1917—They Ventured Far in the Cause of Liberty—1918" and made the supreme sacrifice with their last full measure of devotion, and have taken their places among the heroes of war and peace whose lives and deeds reflect everlasting glory on the name of Worcester.

Below the inscription the names of the servicemen are engraved in gold letters, and among the names are those of three servicemen of Arab heritage: George Beyrouty (Bayrouty), Nicholas Malooly, and Toby Nejaimey. Some men of Arab heritage who made the supreme sacrifice but whose names did not appear on that dedication were Michael Katrina[10] and Michael Sednawi.[11]

Nicholas Malooly was honored by a World War 1 plaque in front of the Holden Public Library and was listed in the Holden "Roll of Honor" book as one of five whose bodies were brought back to Holden.

> Alice S. H., niece of Nicholas Malooly, recalled: Before he enlisted in the U.S. Army, there was a house on Bloomingdale Road that was burning and an American flag was hanging on a flagpole from the porch. He climbed up the burning building to take down the flag so it wouldn't burn. On his way down everybody started clapping and cheered him. A crowd had already gathered to watch the fire.

Military Funeral

John L. Bayrouty, brother of George Bayrouty, recalled:

> My father emigrated in 1909. He owned a casino in Antioch, Syria, and he was a Donald Trump [millionaire] of those days. He left Antioch so his son George wouldn't be drafted into the Ottoman army. However, because of George's love for this country and his sense of patriotism, he enlisted in the U.S. Army.

When the body of George Bayrouty was returned to Worcester around 1919, a military funeral took place. Victoria H. stated:

> I remember seeing the color guards and caisson coming up the hill [Norfolk Street] and I shouted to whoever was indoors to "Come see! Come see!" It was a four-horse drawn wagon, that's what they used to put the body on, you know, instead of a hearse. It was a military funeral with soldiers marching. Wakes in those days were held in the home of the deceased for a week usually and, at the very least, three days and nights. That's why the caisson came up to 69 Norfolk Street, the home of George Bayrouty. They put the body on the wagon and took him to church and then to the cemetery. A memorial square in *el-saha* is named Beyrouty [Bayrouty] Square in his honor.

The Beyrouty Square plaque at the junction of Wall and Norfolk Streets reads: "In Memory of Pvt. George Beyrouty, Born July 15, 1895, Killed In Battle, Chatel Chehery, France, October 3, 1918."

The major participants present at the Bayrouty military funeral and the Eastern Orthodox services are illustrated in photo 6.6. In the foreground, on both sides of the semicircle, were members of the U.S. armed services:

Lower left and right: Drummers and other members of the Syrian Fife and Drum Corps; *center of semicircle:* Archbishop Germanos (Shehadi) wore a miter (bishop's crownlike headpiece) and held a crosier (bishop's staff); *right of archbishop:* Rev. Michael M. Husson, resting his hands on the shoulders of an altar boy so the boy can be seen. Throughout the crowd several men—stylishly dressed with shirts, ties, and derbies, or caps with visors tilted to the side or worn straight—carried their babies. Women, too, stylishly dressed, mingled throughout the crowd. For example, *right, third row of semicircle:* a woman wore a hat topped with a cloth flower; next to her was a younger woman without a hat; *center left:* a woman with a wide-brimmed hat and a concentration of women with headscarves. *Mid-center left:* the stone wall (partly still stands) that extends down to *el-saha*.

In the center background was Saint George Orthodox Church and belfry at 100 Wall Street; visible from the second-floor windows were people looking out to get a bird's-eye view of this historic event. To the left of the church in the background was a four-story duplex residential building owned by husband and wife, Abraham and Alexandra Boosahda; to the right of the church was a three-story residential building with porches, wooden railings, and an attached barn. Above the crowd were strings of lightbulbs that illuminated the grounds, and on the outside wall of the church at the second-floor level the lights ended in a design of a cross. The omnipresent American flag was displayed in various places; two were at the base of the cross formed by lightbulbs and directly below were two more flags; and more abounded near the entrance to the church.

Post–World War I Patriotism

Many descendants of the Arab-American immigrants served in World War II and subsequent wars. As in World War I many families had as many as three or four children serving simultaneously in the U.S. military. Among the women who enlisted were two sisters, Celia Debs, master sergeant, U.S. Air Force (died aged 96 in 2001), and Eva Debs, WAVES, U.S. Navy; Ann Haddad, WAVES; Selma A. Chakour, first lieutenant, U.S. Air Force; and Rita J. Abdella, U.S. Marines. Abdella had three brothers in the service, and she was the ninth member of the Abdella family to enter the armed services.

To honor and commemorate the heroism and perpetuate the memories of some of the veterans who made the supreme sacrifice in the service of our country, living outdoor memorials owned by the city were placed at many squares and street corners throughout the city. The granite marker, plaque, and black sign with gold letters were usually placed near an area that held a meaning to the veteran being honored. Some living memorials are "Abdelnour Square," for Captain Underwood J. Abdelnour, USAF, France; "Abraham Square," for Private Abdow Abraham, Marshall Islands; "Arraj Square," for William J. Arraj, Okinawa; "Attella Square," for Private Edwin M. Attella, France; "Esper Square," for Lieutenant Joseph Esper, Germany; and "Kouri Square," for Private William G. Kouri, France. "Wood Square" honored two brothers, Lieutenant Michael Albert Wood, who died in Alabama, and Private Charles Albert Wood, who was killed in Belgium. A third brother, Colonel James Albert Wood, killed in service, was buried in Kansas where he, his wife, and children lived.

Arabic Language Usage in the U.S. Military

Knowledge of Arabic provided special opportunities for some in the U.S. armed services. For example, Tanoos F. George's autobiography referred to his son Michael F. G., who studied Arabic at Princeton University under Professor Philip K. Hitti.[12] Michael F. G. joined the U.S. Air Force during World War II and was sent as an Arabic language interpreter to North Africa.

Community Support Programs

Arab Americans integrated into mainstream America in many ways—by interaction with their neighbors at public and private schools (Grafton Street, Dartmouth Street, and St. Ann schools), through work (peddling, factories, real estate, and the stock market), and at community institutions. Mentors, as well as persons to help with the process of integration, were available within the Arab-American groups and also from community institutions, in particular, the Worcester Employment Society and Friendly House—both were women's organizations founded by the Worcester Civic Club. The object of the Worcester Civic Club was "to do practical work for the public good." Its membership was made up of delegates from the various societies represented in the club and its board "shall never exceed twenty-five members." The Junior League of Worcester, another women's organization, was founded in 1924. At that time it joined the Worcester Civic Club and then in 1928 took on the sponsorship of Friendly House as its project. The Junior League "is exclusively charitable and educational and promotes voluntarism and provides trained volunteers to the community at large." There are Junior Leagues throughout the United States, Canada, and Mexico. Interaction between the women volunteers of these organizations who resided in the prosperous West Side of Worcester and the Arab Americans benefited both the new citizens and the West Siders who also sampled delectable Arab food, enjoyed Arab hospitality, and discovered new cultural traditions.

Worcester Employment Society

The Worcester Employment Society was founded in 1856. Its Woman's Exchange Department provided a sales outlet for articles (fine sewing and intricate lacework, embroidery, and fancy and decorative items) made by immigrant women who were employed to do the work at home. The society's 1886 annual report stated: "This Society does not exist as one more avenue for almsgiving, but seeks by the payment for services rendered to relieve temporary necessity with temporary assistance." According to the society's 1887 annual report, the visiting committee of its Woman's Exchange Department stated that "[e]leven ladies take the responsibility of recommending and visiting the fifty-five women employed and visiting them during the winter." Janet H. S. recalled:

> There were not many clothing stores, so my mother bought material and sewed our clothes. She used to tat handkerchiefs, and other women crocheted fine lace and other items, and they got paid for their work. I know exactly the price she was paid—twenty-five cents for the handkerchief. That was a good price in those days, and it took her two days to tat edgings around the handkerchief. The women used different designs for tatting. They worked quite a few hours at night to do this. The tatting was real fine work with fine thread.

The president's annual reports of 1922 and 1932 of the Worcester Employment Society refer to the fine lace made by the women in its Folk Stitchery Department. The 1932 report states that work was given to thirty women, all foreign born—Syrians, Armenians, Italians, and Swedes, respectively.

The change of purpose of the society as stated in its 1951 bylaws was the creation of the Craft Center (now Worcester Center for Crafts), which is reputed to be the oldest nonprofit educational institution for craft study in the country.

Friendly House

The Worcester Civic Club (Worcester Civic League) founded the Friendly House in 1920, and as of 1928 the Junior League sponsored it. Through the years, Friendly House has served a variety of ethnic groups, and each group has represented a different set of needs reflective of a changing society. In the April 24, 1969, *Evening Gazette,* Mrs. Eugene (Ruth E.) F. Trainor, director of Friendly House, stated that the object of Friendly House has not changed, which is to serve the immediate recreational and informal educational needs of people in the neighborhood.

Some members of the Junior League who were associated with Friendly House beginning in 1928 were literate in Arabic and familiar with Arab culture. They were Mrs. Jeanette H. Campbell, wife of Donald W. Campbell and daughter of an American diplomat, Franklin E. Hoskins, who was serving in Syria at the time she was born;[13] Mrs. William A. Eddy, wife of Colonel William A. Eddy,[14] both of whom had lived in Lebanon; and Miss Marian G. Lantz, born in Palestine of missionary parents. After four years on the staff at Friendly House, Miss Lantz resigned in 1932 to accept an appointment to the faculty of Friends' Girls' School in Ramallah, Palestine.[15]

Mrs. Campbell was a signatory of the November 9, 1928, certificate of incorporation of Friendly House for the purpose of "the educational, social and family betterment of residents of the City of Worcester."

Nabeha Merhige Haddad, a long-time volunteer at Friendly House, stated in her autobiography:

> Before long Friendly House was bringing joy into the lives of the children and helping to mold their character. Friendly House was soon receiving the same respect as the Church.[16]

Arab Americans owned each piece of real estate at the various locations of Friendly House. It had three addresses. The first was a one-room storefront at 57 Norfolk Street, owned by Jacob Lian, and the baby clinic opened across the street at 46 Norfolk Street, which was owned by Francis and Soriye Abdow. Then Friendly House and the clinic moved to 37 Norfolk Street, which was owned by Kalil J. Haddad, and the next move in 1929 was to 38 Wall Street, the former three-story convent of Saint Ann (Little Franciscans of Mary, p.f.m.), then owned by the Syrian Antiochian St. George Orthodox Church. In 1972 Friendly House moved into its own new quarters at 36 Wall Street. Today Friendly House is a multiservice center and includes family shelters and transitional housing. It is also a history of Worcester as it continues to attract people from all walks of life. Since 1969 Gordon P. Hargrove has been the executive director of Friendly House.

Alice A. recalled the early period of Friendly House when the Junior League was involved:

The Friendly House opened a clinic for parents to bring their babies once a week to have the baby weighed and examined, and all it would cost is twenty-five cents. The Arab-American mothers wouldn't do it—they could not take time out—they couldn't be bothered. They just didn't see the need for this type care. The Junior League women would help the doctors by getting the babies and undressing them. Later the clinic had a nurse there constantly. . . . The Junior League women donated a lot of good clothes to give away—you know, how they do now at the Friendly House on Wall Street. They brought shoes and I used to look through the bags and the shoes were from Paris. So it happened that we were supposed to go there and get the clothes. None of our people would go and get them—we never even applied for welfare. We never accepted any of the clothing. I don't know if we were too independent and had too much pride in feeling that we are able to get along without handouts.

Alice continued:

The Friendly House taught handicraft, piano, and other classes. I liked the weaving and nature class. We weaved straw around a tray. Once that was done we were taken to Beaman's farm to pick milkweed. It's just like silk. We would open it, lay it all down, and it was so beautiful—then it was time to go look for the butterflies, and when they died we would lay them down on the tray and put a glass on the butterflies and it was gorgeous. It was really nice. It was really pretty. All the Syrians had them—the kids made them. Cousin Julia, Ann, all of them used to make them.

George N. K. talked about the planned trips that the Junior League women had at their homes. They picked up a few kids at a time to spend the afternoon at their homes with planned activities. He commented, "We had a wonderful time. I guess they took us for a day from home to show us there is another life to strive for."

One of the many other field trips included a large group of boys and girls under the guidance of Samuel Karakey, recreational instructor at Friendly House, and Enis G. Johnson, instructor. They toured the *Worcester Telegram* and the *Evening Gazette* newspaper plant and WTAG radio station next door. Apparently the instructors had no problem handling the large multicultural group of young people, a total of sixty-three, forty-seven of whom were Arab American and thirteen of Italian, Irish, Russian, and French heritage.[17]

Among the activities of winter 1946 at Friendly House was an art class for junior high school girls conducted by Irma Kalil and boxing and physical fitness classes under the supervision of James Debs.

The Junior League invited mothers of Syrian children who attended classes and clinics at Friendly House to a "Syrian Night" evening, and in the afternoon to an open house when mothers visited regular classes and inspected an exhibition of sewing and crafts by the children. On another day the mothers of Polish and French-Canadian children who attended Friendly House were entertained at an afternoon tea.[18]

Boy Scout Troop 72

Friendly House sponsored Boy Scout Troop 72 of the Worcester Area Council in 1932.[19] Its first scoutmaster was Russell P. Talbot and assistant scoutmaster was John K. Boosahda (Busada). Troop numbers were picked arbitrarily and not in sequence. The first Boy Scouts of America organization was incorporated in Washington, D.C., in 1910[20] to provide effective character, citizenship, and personal fitness training for boys. Shortly thereafter Girl Scouts of the USA was established in New York in 1912 with similar goals. Subsequently in 1911 Worcester was one of the first cities to develop a Boy Scout movement when Troop 1 was formed at Park Church. By 1918 the Boy Scouts of America Worcester Area Council had established fifty-one troops.[21]

John K. B. talked about interest in forming a Boy Scout troop:

> We needed a scoutmaster who had to be twenty-one years of age. I was under twenty-one at the time. Russell Talbot agreed to be scoutmaster, and we had to form a committee. We were able to get the husbands of some of the women who were active in the Junior League and some Arab Americans to serve on the committee.

Troop 72 was officially transferred from the joint sponsorship of the Friendly House Board and the Syrian American Association to the sole sponsorship of the Syrian American Association. In 1941 the troop was under the sponsorship of St. George Syrian Orthodox Church and then the Cathedral.[22] After thirteen years as a devoted scoutmaster, Russell C. Talbot tendered his resignation and continued to serve on the troop committee. John K. Boosahda (Busada) was inducted as the new scoutmaster. The assistant scoutmasters were Frederick C. Assad and Fred V. (Vladimir) Swydan. Junior officers were Herbert Swydan, Abraham Boosahda (Busada), and James Haddad. The troop received much recognition for the troop's rating under the Worcester Area Council (now Boy Scouts of America Mohegan Council, Inc.) rating plan. The third scoutmaster was Vladimir Swydan, and the troop remained under his able and dedicated longtime leadership until it ceased to exist in about the mid-1980s.

Besides the many Arab Americans who aided in the Friendly House programs and volunteered their professional services in medical and dental clinics and other programs, Friendly House also attracted non–Arab Americans from the community at large who shared their experiences and expertise at Friendly House.

Kindergarten Class—Worcester Public School

Miss Helen Kenney, kindergarten teacher who taught at Grafton Street School from 1925 to 1970, described activities such as visits to homes of the children by kindergarten teachers, mothers' visits to the school, interaction between a grandfather and his grandchildren, and excursions away from school:

> We visited the immigrant parents in their homes, and they knew we represented the school and were pleased. They had lovely lace pieces such as curtains, shams, and pillowcases; other pieces enhanced tables and chairs. They gave presents of handkerchiefs trimmed with lovely needlework lace. It was intricate work and very nice and pretty. They also did tatting. . . . Before the days of the parent-teacher associations the kindergarten teachers occasionally invited mothers to programs held at the school. On one occasion our supervisor talked about her travels to Syria and Italy and that pleased the mothers. Then she talked about the values of education for young children. . . . The head of physical education in the city schools heard a teacher talk about the different names of the children, and he said: "It seems to me you've got all the prophets in here. You've got Moses, Abraham, and all the typical biblical names." And we did have! I remember one child was named Abraham, and then there was a Moses Haddad and a lot of the real old-fashioned names. . . . This quite elderly man who used a cane walked down along Wall Street, and at times when we were out at recess his twin grandchildren, Harold and Raymond [birth names Peter and Paul], would see him and he was so glad to see them. He would just beam and he'd come to the gate and I can remember they both went to him and each kissed the back of his hands. I suppose that was an old-world custom that they had for children to show respect to the elderly. It was new to me and I was impressed and enjoyed it. . . . One

time we took the children to C. T. Sherer, a three-story department store, to see Santa Claus. I don't remember how we got there, but it seems to me it was too far to walk and we probably took a trolley. One little boy had never been in an elevator, and it was a big elevator in the store, and we went in it and he said, "Oh, Miss Kenney, it [the elevator] makes my stomach afraid, you know that?" C. T. Sherer's used to invite all the kindergartens in Worcester to come and each child received a toy or something. . . . We tried to widen the children's environment a little bit, too, by taking them on a few excursions.

Church-Related Programs

The spirit of ecumenism existed in the matter of church school training and other youth activities. The Eastern Orthodox children from *el-tellee* attended Sunday school at either Oak Hill Baptist Church on Orient Street or the Methodist Episcopal Church (now the Covenant United Methodist Church) on Hamilton Street. After Sunday school classes the children walked to St. George Orthodox Church at the corner of Wall and Thorne Streets to join their families at liturgy. Nuns from St. Stephen's Church (Roman Catholic) crossed over to Arthur Street to conduct Sunday school classes at Our Lady of Perpetual Help Church (Melkite-Greek Catholic). For the seventy-fifth-anniversary celebration of the founding of Covenant United Methodist Church, Rev. Herbert A. Wheeler composed the history of the church in poetry, which included the following verses about the Syrian children attending Sunday school:

> Since the Orthodox Church on Wall street
> Had no church school where children could meet,
> In our Sunday school they were enrolled
> Until these children were twelve years old.
> And because our church, they did attend
> They're part of our history we contend.
> And a reason why we believe it,
> They often return for a visit.

Rev. Wheeler recalled:

> When I was going to Sunday school I had a lot of Orthodox Syrian boys and girls in class with me, and that was shortly after the Covenant Congregational Church on Houghton Street and the Methodist Church on Coral Street united as one church on Hamilton Street

in 1917. The Syrian children kept coming to our Sunday school until they were twelve years old. We figured they were part of our church, even though they considered themselves Orthodox.

Subsequently the Arab-American churches conducted their own Sunday school classes. However, some children continued to attend other Sunday schools where they were comfortable and later joined the Protestant or Roman Catholic churches where they began at Sunday school. There was community between churches.

Community Interaction at Public Celebrations

Participation in community public observances was considered a patriotic endeavor and an opportunity to become part of the whole community in pleasurable activities. The following are some examples.

President Roosevelt's Welcome

In her autobiography, Nabeha (Merhige) Haddad stated that her husband, Abraham Isa Haddad, and Mitchell K. Maykel were among the people who marched in the parade when President Theodore Roosevelt visited Worcester on September 2, 1902, as guest of Senator George Frisbie Hoar. She described the reception given the president, stating that

> [never] in the history of Worcester was so much enthusiasm shown to an individual as was given the nation's Executive. From the booming of 21-guns [salute] announcing his arrival at Barber's Crossing until his special train pulled out slowly at Union Station nearly one hour late, with the cheers of thousands ringing in his ears.[23]

The local newspaper *(Worcester Telegram)* headline told the story of the president's welcome to the city: "Thousands, Tens of Thousands, Greet Him as He Rides, in Triumphal Car." After the parade President Roosevelt was a guest at Senator George Frisbie Hoar's home along with the two Syrian children, the Nemrs (also spelled Namers), whom the president saved from deportation. The president had earlier expressed a desire to meet the children.

The Syrian American Drum Corps

The Syrian American Drum Corps, formerly called the Drum and Fife and Bugle Corps, reorganized in 1938 and participated in parades, public celebrations, and competitions throughout New England. It won numerous

prizes and trophies for its members' fife, drum, and bugle playing and drill-
ing. Their participation in exhibitions and competitions was generally sanc-
tioned by the Massachusetts Fifers and Drummers Association. In September 1942 the corps performed at the Syrian Day entertainment as part of
the "September Is Salute to Our Heroes Month" staged in front of the city
hall to honor those in the service of the United States during World War II.
Also, a Syrian American Drum Corps Honor Roll was unveiled in the early
days of World War II. Included in the program was the recitation of a poem
composed by one of its members and addressed to "The Members of The
Syrian American Drum Corps in Service":

> We were once so proud and gay [happy],
> Never faltering in spirit or way.
> Ours were the heights of glory
> With a happiness endless in story.
>
> Thence came the fire of war
> Its flames spreading so near and afar,
> Feeding on those so dear and sweet
> Sparing none who nears her heat.
>
> To you, our pals, who have been swept away
> In our memory you linger from day to day,
> It is for us to remember and let fall a tear
> For yours is a friendship to cherish and to hold dear.
>
> Fear not old pals, the time will come
> When these flames will die and your work is done
> Back to us you'll return, to God we pray,
> And once again we'll be proud and gay.

The poetry was signed "from your *PALS*."

Alice A. recalled:

> The Syrian American Drum Corps had the Haddads, the Syieks, the
> Abdows, the Dowds—there were so many more. There were non-
> Arab kids, too. They bought themselves fancy uniforms with red
> and gold jackets and wore tall hats with the gold braids. They also
> had uniforms with which they wore red berets tilted to the side.
> They were all so handsome in their uniforms.

Harold F. B. II reflected:

My dad played the drums in the drum corps and he kept the drum in a closet at home. I was a kid and whenever I opened the closet door I'd be confronted by this humongous drum compared to my size. I'll always remember the sight of the drum close up. Whenever I saw my dad in the parade he would appear a giant to me banging away at the drum while marching. I was so proud of him.

Sylvia H. remembered:

When I was nine years old and I would hear the drum corps in a distance as they were practicing on Orient Street, I would run into the house and come out with a broom and start marching in front of the drum corps. I had grand visions of being a majorette twirling my baton, imitating the ones I saw in the many parades in Worcester. The drum corps did not appreciate my talents and would prod me with their drumsticks to get out of their way. My vision of being a drum majorette was more overpowering than the prodding, and I continued until I was exhausted, much to the relief of the drum corps.

The corps disbanded in about the early 1950s.

Syrian American Club

In the years after World War I, the Syrian American Club held its meetings at various storefront locations on Wall Street, starting from the upper end to a storefront across from Thorne Street near the lower end. In about the mid-1930s it purchased a newly constructed (1930) one-story building on Plantation Street. Membership was open to Syrian, Lebanese, and Palestinian people. However, membership also included non-Arab-American spouses: French, Italian, Lithuanian, Irish, and others. Charles A. Gammal, one of the founders, stated:

The reason for the founding of the Syrian American Club was political . . . [it] represented 124 members. It was not founded as a charitable organization, as our people were active in that regard. We encouraged people to vote, invited politicians to speak at our functions, and distributed campaign literature.

Later the club was called the Syrian American Association and was affiliated with the Syrian American Federation of New England.

In 1930 during the yearlong celebration of the tercentenary anniversary of the founding of the Massachusetts Bay Colony in 1630, the association participated in a local parade. It entered a float that depicted an American historical scene and won second prize for the best-decorated float. By the end of the seventeenth century the Bay Colony was the largest and most powerful English colony in the "New World." The float was a replica of Diggory Sergeant's log cabin with his nameplate attached to the outside of the cabin. He lived on the high ridge of Sagatabscot Hill in the southeast part of Worcester in the northern end that is known as Union Hill.[24] It was on this elevation that a Native American murdered Diggory Sergeant and "his children were taken captive by the Indians at Worcester in 1704 and carried to Canada."[25] Ten members of the association were on the float dressed as Diggory Sergeant, his wife, and their five children or as Native Americans. To commemorate this and similar encounters, Hon. Edward L. Davis built as a memorial in 1889 the Davis Tower[26] — a castle-like structure made entirely of boulders and topped with flat-rock parapets in Lake Park on the site of Samuel Lenorson's home, where his 12-year-old son, Samuel Lenorson Jr., was kidnapped in 1695 "by Indians and taken to Canada." The tower was demolished about 1971.

Mary S. stated:

> Sally A. A. and I were the children on the float. The presentation of the first prize was made at Grafton Street Junior High school. I was asked to say something in Arabic, which I did. Our group also put on a skit.

Syrian-American clubs and associations existed in many cities where a good number of Arabic-speaking people resided. To bring local clubs together under one affiliation, the Syrian and Lebanese American Federation of the Eastern States was founded in 1932.[27] In 1934 the name changed to Syrian-Lebanese American Federation of the Eastern States.

In 1945 the Syrian-American Association of Worcester, later known as Syrian-Lebanese American Association, held a series of dinner meetings at Putnam and Thurston's restaurant to honor recently discharged World War II veterans. The association members were represented by Frank F. George, president, and Martha M. Abdella, vice president.[28] A eulogy in memory of the men who gave their lives in this war was read, and tribute scrolls were presented to the guests, followed by a special program.

At the installation of the 1947 officers of the association, the newly organized Syrian and Lebanese American Association Auxiliary (women members) officers were also installed.[29] In its first year the auxiliary launched a program that included the establishment of a "camp fund through which 20 boys and girls enjoyed a vacation at a summer resort." Within a year from its founding the club's membership was 125.[30]

The Federation of the Eastern States under the auspices of the Syrian-

Lebanese American Association of Worcester, Mass. (now defunct) held its twelfth annual three-day convention in Worcester in 1948.[31] Other regional federations developed, and in about 1950 a National Association of Federations of Syrian and Lebanese American Clubs was formed and included the Southern, Midwestern, and Eastern Federations. The National Association of Federations held its 1950 annual convention of Arab Americans from around the country in Lebanon. In 1955 the Western Federation joined the national organization. The monthly publication *Federation Herald* of the Eastern States was dropped in favor of the *National Herald* of the National Association. Its purpose was to

> pool together the talents of United States citizens of Arabic-speaking background for the good of America and for the objective of a peaceful and prosperous world. It is devoted to the principle of what is in the best interest of all the American people. . . . It seeks to interpret America to the Arab countries of the Middle East and the Arab countries of the Middle East to America. . . . (It) has acted and does act as an effective medium of informational and cultural exchange between the people of the United States and those of the Arab states.[32]

Many of these clubs and associations no longer exist. Instead, individual members—as well as members of active federations—join other Arab-American organizations throughout the country such as the Worcester County chapter of ALSAC (American Lebanese Syrian Associated Charities), which organized locally in January 1958. Regarding the gradual demise of the local Syrian-Lebanese American Association, Kenneth K. stated:

> Everything leads into an intricate pattern. Most of those who left from working within our local association went to become early volunteers for ALSAC, and that's where some placed our energy. We were devoted to ALSAC.

Over the years these and other Arab-American private-sector organizations interacted collectively at public celebrations. In 1942, some participated in a three-hour entertainment program in observance of "Syrian Day" as part of the "Nationalities Days" at city hall to spur sales of war savings bonds and stamps. General chairman was George J. Lian. Arab-American activities and organizations included the Syrian-Lebanese Federation of Eastern States, a drill by the Syrian Boy Scout Troop 72, and a Syrian sword and shield dance team with John Fayard and Walter G.

Thomas on one team and Joseph Sear and brother George Sear on the other.

Rededication of the Worcester Memorial Auditorium

The Friday night program, "Festival of Nationalities," held at the three-day rededication of the Worcester Memorial Auditorium on its twenty-fifth anniversary, included approximately twenty-one nationality groups that performed in an international dance program. In an article on September 27, 1958, the *Worcester Daily Telegram* described the event as follows:

> But in some groups, variety was the rule. No two women in the Syrian-Lebanese, Albanian or Armenian groups were dressed alike. . . . Their costumes were elaborately decorated with sequins, ribbons, or jeweled embroidery. . . . An Armenian-Lebanese-Syrian dance group gave a musical interpretation of a courtship. . . . A solo Syrian Dance was [given] by Vina . . . Master of Ceremonies was Walter J. Moossa.

Headlined on the same page was "Syrian Band Includes Derbekees *[Darabukkah]*, Oud *[Ud]*," and the story showed that love for Arabic music transcends nationality:

> Although the four-piece unit headed by John F. Awad has played at Syrian weddings, and other festivities hereabouts, last night was the group's debut before an Auditorium-size audience. . . . Robert G. Lotuff and J. Anthony Thomas, Worcesterites of Syrian ancestry, played the two *derbekees*. But the remaining two instruments were played by two young men Italian-Americans Jay Pichierri and Joseph Marsello.[33] (See photo 6.15.)

> Excerpt from the *Evening Gazette,* September 27, 1958, related to the variety of dancers: City Manager McGrath termed Worcester "a melting pot for democracy." "Our city is built of 29 nationalities," he said, and described the fusion of peoples which takes place in a city like Worcester "an asset to Americanism."[34]

Another example of how Arabic music transcended nationality was the extraordinary Pyramid Dance Group of non–Arab Americans wearing a variety of gorgeous handmade costumes, who danced to the accompaniment of Arabic music. Introductions to the performances were by Melanie Lajoie—of French-Canadian heritage, director-dancer and founder of the group—who with gracious hand movements, then with folded hands and a bow, said *"Salam"* (May well-being, happiness, and peace be upon you).

Lajoie taught Middle East dance at her studio and at Worcester Public Schools night classes, and her dance group performed at many charitable community functions.

At the 1959 Fourth of July celebration, the Syrian-Lebanese Folk Dance Group performed and was presented a "Recognition of Good Citizenship" plaque on behalf of the City of Worcester. It read ". . . for your contribution of time and talent to a worthy community program."

The Worcester Music Festival

For the past 102 years the Worcester Music Festival has been held annually in the Worcester Memorial Auditorium. It offered one month of musical performances until 1973, and more recently for one week annually. As the finale to a week of Music Festival concerts in 1973, a "Festival Casbah" party by invitation was sponsored by the Music Guild of the Worcester County Music Association. Casbah featured the attractions of traditional Arabic music, food, and dance.[35]

In 1979 Nita B. Dowd (Mrs. Charles Dowd) was elected president of the Music Guild of the Worcester County Music Association, and another top officer elected was Mrs. Henry B. Abusamra (Hind-Helene Abusamra), nominating chairman.

Other Leisure Activities

Fred R. Aramony recalled his young adult days growing up in *el-tellee* and the camaraderie between men and women friends during the 1930s. He put his recollections into a song titled "Song Reminiscences of the Thirties," which was sung to the melody of "Those Were the Days, My Friend."

> Verse 1
> To a Grafton Tavern, We Would Go
> For a Pot of Beer, A Coin We'd Pitch:
> A Toss-up, and a Toss-up, "Odd Man Pays"
> Was It Ralph, Bill, George, Jimmy or Mitch.[36]
>
> REFRAIN
> Those Were the Days, My Friend,
> We Thought They'd Never End.
> We'd Sing and Dance Forever and a Day.
> We'd Live the Life We'd Choose,
> We'd Fight and Never Lose.
> Those Were the Days,
> Oh, Yes, Those Were the Days.

Verse 2
To Johnny Hynes, A-Dancing We Would Go
Or Marshall's, Or Duggan's You Would See
A Lad of Talent, Spinning His Tales,
And Lassies Circling Joking Leo D.[37]

REFRAIN

Verse 3
To Rizkalla's Barbershop, We'd Go
For Chemin De Fer. A Game You'd Like
Whose Turn Is It Now, For Morris Plan.[38]
Was It Jimmy, George, Mitch, Bill or Mike.[39]

REFRAIN

Verse 4
And to Dungarvan Hill We Would Go
For Kalil's *Kaack* [*kaak*, anise bread], *Fatayie* [*fatayer*,
    pie/turnover] or Hot Bread [Syrian],
Or to Coffeeshops or Joe's or Awad's
Or Paul Aboody's Famous Tablespread.

REFRAIN

Verse 5
To the Family Theatre, We Would Go
Or to the Strand, or Poli's Johnny Jones,
For Johnny Jones a Jesting Name Became
To Abo, Ralph or Ara's Kidding Tones.[40]

REFRAIN

Verse 6
Oh *Dabky [dabkah]* Queens, OCTAVIAN Maidens![41]
Your Ways Mystique, We Dare Not Tally,
Oh Sirens—Mary, Marion and Both Adeles
Delia, Ann, Louise and Sally.

REFRAIN

Verse 7
On Easter Morn, A-Marching We Would Go,
To Open Homes, A Friendly Welcome Scene,
Echoing, *"Masseeh Kalm," "Harkan Kalm,"*

[*Il-Masih qaam, Haq qan qaam*. Christ has risen. Response: He
   has risen indeed.]
Or *"Kull Sinny Wa Antum Sallimeen!"*
[*Kul assenat wa antum assalam*
May God's blessings be with you yearlong].

Musical Shows

The musical show was a transition from the Arabic classical drama to English drama and musicals. John K. B. recollected:

> Some shows were set up so that the proceeds were given to the
> church for its charitable work. I do know that Mike Dowd [Michael
> Dowd] was behind it all. He took approximately a year in prepa-
> ration, and no sooner one was finished, he started the next one. I
> believe the performances took place at what was called at that time
> Mechanics Hall in downtown Worcester. Most of the talent was
> local. They did from time to time bring in some personalities. The
> shows were complete sellouts and the whole community was in-
> volved in them, and in this way people were able to show off their
> talents. I don't know how many people recall all the time and effort
> Mike Dowd put into them. He put a lot into them. He had some
> help, but I believe that without his driving force these shows would
> never have been successful. Perhaps this was good training for Mike
> Dowd's success as vice president of the Worcester Music Festival
> working along with other community leaders.[42]

Testimonials and Banquets

Testimonials, banquets, and other activities were often held to honor Arab
Americans who were considered outstanding in the community or served
the community at large. For example, a 1918 newspaper article titled "Worcester Boxer Aviator to Receive Royal Welcome on His Furlough Home"
reported that a musical reception and a banquet was planned in the young
man's honor. "The Syrian American Drum Corps will lead the way in es-
corting Boosahda [Eli A. Busada] from the station to his home and the tri-
umphant aviator-boxer will ride in [an] open automobile decorated with
American flags."[43]

Another example of a testimonial was described in a multiheadlined
newspaper article as:

> CONGRESSMAN THEIR GUEST. Hon. Samuel E. Winslow Ad-
> dresses 200 Members of Syrian Brotherhood Society. GATHER-

ING PLANNED AS A TESTIMONIAL. St. George's Church Crowded in Appreciation of Work He Had Done in Their Cause.

Excerpted from the 1920 article:

> . . . . a testimonial to Col. Winslow for the interest he has taken in the Syrian-speaking [Arabic-speaking] people and the number of instances in which he has been of service to them officially and individually. . . . Col. Winslow was greeted at Norfolk Street by the Syrian-American Drum Corps of 12 pieces, led by Henry Abdelmaseh, and a parade was formed, including the members of the society. . . . The congressman was given a rousing ovation by a crowd of hundreds of men, women and children of the neighborhood, for whom there was no room at the meeting. The program opened with the singing of "America." . . . President Sroor Peters presided, and a number of other prominent members of the society spoke briefly, emphasizing their devotion to America as their adopted country, extolling Col. Winslow and appealing to the audience to support the Republican party. Officers of the club said that while it was essentially non-partisan, with no political tests for membership, all its members were strong for the Republican ticket . . . secretary Shokri Swydan then translated Mr. Winslow's remarks on the League [of Nations] and other points in his address for the benefit of those who had an imperfect understanding of English . . . Henry Abdelmaseh spoke briefly, declaring that the stars and stripes stood in the best sense of the slogan for "All for one, and one for all." . . . James Kalil who came to America from Jerusalem said that friendship was emphasized in the Arabic language. . . . A large bouquet of flowers was presented to Col. Winslow at the conclusion of his talk. He afterward greeted with a handshake hundreds of children who crowded around him, and was entertained at a Syrian tea by Mr. and Mrs. George M. Abdow and family at their home, 32 Norfolk street. . . . Col. Winslow also was present by invitation at the wedding of Charles G. Debs and Miss Jennie Fatool in St. George's Church following the meeting.[44]

A third example of a testimonial was sponsored by the American Lebanon Club honoring Right Rev. Monsignor Joseph Saidi (now Chorbishop Saidi) of Our Lady of Mercy Church at the Sheraton Hotel, Worcester. He had arrived recently on his second trip here. According to an article in the *Sunday Telegram*,[45] invited guests included Bishop Thomas M. O'Leary of Springfield; clergy from six local, out-of-town and out-of-state parishes representing Maronites, Eastern Orthodox, and Melkites; presidents of three local Lebanese and Syrian American organizations; and Rev. William Casey S.J., president of Holy Cross College.

Other invited guests included Governor Robert F. Bradford, Mayor Charles F. Jeff Sullivan, Congressman Harold D. Donohue, Judge Eli Shannon [Elias F. Shamon] of Boston . . . and District Attorney Alfred R. Cenedella. Walter J. Moossa was toastmaster, Patrick J. George, general chairman, and Philip M. Massad, member of the committee in charge of the testimonial. The committee included some of the immigrant-founders of the church established in 1923: Patrick J. George, Assad Hilow, Joseph Abdella, Michael Daboul, Anthony Massad, Joseph Dadah, and Joseph Lotuff. Another founder of the church was Joseph John George.

Another example of a banquet was the celebration of the consecration of St. George Orthodox Church held at the Sheraton Hotel when the guest speaker was Worcester County sheriff William A. Bennett.[46] Ernest J. G. recalled with pride one of the comments the sheriff made:

> I have never seen any of your names on our court records and I don't see a familiar face here, which is a sign that your names do not appear on court records and you don't appear in my court.

Examples of church-related testimonials that honored women for their good deeds were for Miss Mary Dowd and Mrs. Constantine Abou-Adal.

Model of an Outstanding Organization

ALSAC, the American Lebanese Syrian Associated Charities, was founded nationally by Danny Thomas, whose parents were born in the village of Becharre (Besharri), Lebanon. ALSAC was incorporated in October 1957 to support and maintain the soon-to-be-constructed St. Jude Children's Research Hospital in Memphis, Tennessee (opened in 1962), as a nonprofit, nonsectarian, charitable corporation. Danny Thomas enlisted the help of the American Lebanese Syrian community nationwide as the main fundraisers—united on a national basis in a common American cause. St. Jude Children's Research Hospital is an international leader in research on leukemia and other catastrophic diseases of childhood. Children of all faiths and races are admitted and treated free of charge. ALSAC broadened its volunteer base and included all multicultural people to assist in fund-raising, and the acronym now also stands for Aid to Leukemia Stricken American Children.

The Worcester County chapter of ALSAC was organized January 1958 at the Shish-Kabob Restaurant and elected its first president, Dr. George C.

Dowd. For many years, until 1987, Albert E. Maykel served on the national board of governors of St. Jude Children's Research Hospital, and since 1989 Joseph G. Hyder has served on its board. Hyder, the Central Massachusetts coordinator for ALSAC, is a former host of his television and cablevision shows and a weekly hour-long radio program of Arabic music. Genevieve Thomas is president of the Worcester County chapter of ALSAC and a key volunteer since its inception.

To Date or Not to Date a Non–Arab American

Occasionally, a first-American-born-generation male married a woman outside his culture. George S. talked about dating a non-Arab woman:

> I didn't really date a lot. I didn't want to date seriously, and if I went out with a Syrian woman it had to be a serious date. You didn't go on a date with a Syrian woman and redate her and redate her and then say, "I'll see you later, Charlie, goodbye." With somebody outside our culture, you could go out and have a date and think nothing of it. If you want to say goodbye, you said goodbye, and there was no strings attached. So, I went out with a few women—none of them Lebanese or Syrian. I finally met my wife, fell in love, and got married. She was my Uncle George's secretary and not an Arab American. When you start to go out with an Arab-American woman and after going out two or three times, the parents want to know, "Hey, what's your intention?"
>
> There is more freedom dating other than our people. You don't feel obligated to marry the woman if you went out with her. You date one of our women only with the consent of the parents. If you started dating one of our women and don't marry her, there is all kinds of stories that would go around. By going with an Arab-American woman the men put themselves into an obligation and they probably would wind up with someone they didn't want to marry; so you don't want that lasso around your neck. Of course, there are many men who married our women and lived happily. So, like my father dating my mother, after going out together two or three times they got married because my father liked my mother and she liked him.

For a woman who was a first-American-born generation, to marry outside her culture was rare, and it was not until about the late 1930s that marriage to a non-Arab more frequently took place.

Multicultural Reunion

Members of the Nostalgia Night Association hold a reunion every five years generally of former neighbors who lived in the multicultural Norfolk–Wall Streets neighborhood. Hundreds of people attend to share fond memories of growing up on "the Hill" (Oak Hill) and to have an occasion to keep in touch with people whose paths do not cross but who have good memories that linger. Nostalgia Night's inception was in 1980. It was held at the former Bianchi Macaroni factory on Norfolk Street that housed the Knights of Columbus, a charitable organization. The multicultural group includes Americans whose heritage are Arab (Syrian, Lebanese, and Palestinian), Italian, Irish, French, Polish, Lithuanian, and others. Although each group has a strong national culture, together they have a rich ethnic mix. The homogeneity is less ethnic and more cultural.

6.1. Elias Khalil Coury (Eli K. Coury), U.S. Army. *Background left:* fourth story of eight-family residential double building owned by husband and wife Abraham and Alexandra (Abraham) Boosahda. *Background right:* bulbous oriental lantern, bell, and cross topping the two-story brick and wood-shingled Syrian Orthodox Church at 100 Wall Street.

6.2. Joseph S. Peters, U.S. Army. The sword was worn when dressed in full military uniform, about 1917.

6.3. *Left to right:* Charles A. Gammal plays *el-ud*, while picnicking and drinking soda with his brother, Albert A. Gammal, a World War I soldier, and a neighbor, Rofan Haffty, about 1917.

6.4. *Left to right:* Eli A. Boosahda (Busada), U.S. Naval Air Service, and Emil Souda, U.S. Army, about 1917.

6.5. Albert A. Gammal, U.S. Army, dressed in full military uniform, about 1917.

6.6. Participants at World War I military funeral, 1919. A religious service was held on the grounds of the Syrian Orthodox Church in conjunction with the military funeral for George Bayrouty.

6.7. American cuisine cooking class at Friendly House, 37 Norfolk Street at side entrance off Bloomingdale Court, 1923. The class, *clockwise top left:* Clara Haddad, Lydia Orfalea, Lena Ghiz, Rose Bacela, Ann Abisamra, Helen Ghiz, Rose Ezen, n.n. Saad, n.n. Saad, Mary Kourey, Matilda Haddad, Sally Haddad. Entire class not present. *Clockwise top left:* The boys/brothers/a future husband were at play in the street and ran uninvited to get into the picture: Bobby Esper, William "Barney" Orfalea, Philip Corey, n.n. Kalil, n.n., Mitchell Estephan. *Mid center:* The sign on the wall in Arabic read *Menzel El-Sadiq* (House of Friends) and was translated as "Friendly House." *Foreground:* The class posed in front of a low stone wall which still partially stands; however, the building has been demolished. When cooking it was the custom of the day to cover the hair with a white headscarf and wear a large white apron.

6.8. Practicing at Friendly House for the city's snaps tournament, about 1935. *Clockwise left:* teenagers and preteenagers, Albert Dahrooge, Abraham K. Boosahda (Busada), Raymond Boosahda, Philip Dahrooge, Harold F. Boosahda II, Mesale Bonardi, Michael MacKoul, Michael K. Boosahda, and Edward "Pat" N. Salem. Snaps is a competitive game played by the snap of the index finger and thumb at wooden rings (about one-quarter-inch thick by one inch diameter) to get the rings into net pockets located at corners of a table. Photo taken in basement level at Friendly House, 38 Wall Street.

6.9. American Red Cross class at Friendly House, 1928. *Top row, from left:* Claire J. Lavallee, Elizabeth Hyder, Margaret Samara, Lamise Chakour, Edna n.n., Miss Marion G. Lantz (instructor), Helen Haddad, Pauline Popro, Louise Aikely, Alice Massey. *Middle row, from left:* Adele Haddad, Georgianna Aboumrad, Bertha Peters, Margaret Haddad, Lillian Altif, n.n., Margaret Saad, Selma Hajjar, Doris Lavallee, Hind Helene Swydan, Louise Haffty. *Bottom row, from left:* Mary Carota, Adele Dowd, Mary Haddad, Yvonne Reyes, Erma n.n., Janet Aboumrad, Sophie Conte, Janet Haffty.

6.10. Members of Drum and Fife and Bugle Corps, about 1923. *Left to right:* Robert A. Boosahda (Busada)and Naimer Haddad posed in early corps uniform. Above their visors was an emblem of an eagle with outstretched wings. The reverse side of the photo read: "Our hands are on our fifes." *Background, left to right:* This barn with vertical wooden slabs was located on Rondeau Court behind 80 Wall Street. Uphill in the next yard was a three-story wooden residence with vertical porch railings. The horizontal wooden lattice was a typical grapevine arbor.

6.11. Members of Syrian American Drum Corps (formerly Drum and Fife and Bugle Corps, and Syrian Fife and Drum Corps), 1941. *Clockwise:* Joseph G. Nassif, Edward J. Salem, general chairman; Joseph Arraj, William N. Rezuke, Michael S. Abraham. This was the committee that arranged a field day and competition at East Park, Worcester that was attended by groups from Massachusetts, Rhode Island, and Connecticut.

6.12. Prize-winning float by the Syrian American Association for Tercentenary Massachusetts Celebration parade, 1930.

6.13. Seated on parapet of Davis Tower at Lake Park, 1931. *Left to right:* Edmund Shoucair (son of Said Shoucair) and wife, Lillian George Shoucair.

6.14. Festival of Nationalities, Arab folk line dance (the *dabkah*), 1958. *Left to right:* Salim "Sam" Lotuff (leader), MaryAnne (Lotuff) Awad, Jane (Esper) Scheffel, Vina (Mrs. Thomas Haddad, née Florence Abdo), George Abdo (bandleader and composer of Arabic music).

6.15. Arab music played by Arab and non-Arab musicians, 1958.

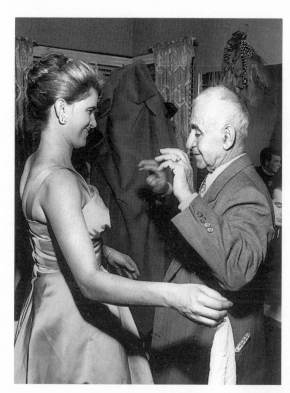

6.16. Duo Arab dance by old and young, Arab American and non–Arab American, late 1950s. At Shish-Kabob Restaurant, Shrewsbury, Mass., there was an open dance floor for all patrons to enjoy dancing to Arabic music. *Left to right:* n.n., Ameen A. The restaurant was owned and operated by John and MaryAnne (Lotuff) Awad. The renowned El Morocco restaurant was famous for this type of participation.

6.17. Arab culture portrayed through music and dance, 1973. Evelyn Abdalah Menconi, reading consultant and media specialist, leads non-Arab students, a mixed group from grades four to eight, in an Arabic folk dance. Studies of other countries and cultures were integrated into the school's reading programs.

6.18. Worcester woman knighted by church at St. Nicholas Cathedral, Brooklyn, N.Y., Dec. 30, 1951. Associated Press. *Clockwise left:* Metropolitan Antony Bashir, Archbishop of New York, North and South America; Archbishop Samuel David (standing behind conferee; his bishop's headpiece is visible); conferee Miss Mary Dowd, president of the Charles Dowd Box Company, founded by her father. Excerpted from the *Telegram & Gazette*, n.d.: "Miss Dowd has been widely known for social, religious, and philanthropic activities in Syrian Orthodox parishes both in the United States and abroad."

6.19. Testimonial honored Mrs. Constantine Abou-Adal, née Nady Daniloff-Domnena, wife of Archpriest Abou-Adal, about 1955. *Clockwise:* Rev. Thomas Ruffin, David C. Dowd, Metropolitan Antony Bashir, Mrs. Harold F. Boosahda, née Mary Najjar, honoree Mrs. Abou-Adal, Archpriest Constantine Abou-Adal, and Monsignor Edmund G. Haddad.

Chapter Seven
LEGACY AND LINKAGE

The descendants of the early Arab-American immigrants who emigrated from 1880 to 1915 are generally proud people. They love their Arab heritage and warmly embrace their American nationality. Their elders influenced them by establishing linkages to their social and cultural heritage through language, food, family record keeping, music, photos, traditions, and holiday celebrations.

Language

When Very Rev. Michael M. H. died, his collection of Arabic books was given to his daughter, Ethel H.M.K. When Ethel died, the family decided Sam S., a nephew, should acquire the collection as Sam had been fluent in Arabic since the age of eight and additionally chanted in Arabic at church. Violet N. S., the widow of Sam S., reflected on the collection:

> Owning the books gave Sam so much joy. He enjoyed them so much and would read from them daily. Some books are so ragged you can tell they have been used so much. You can tell the books have been through a lot of hands. Some look brand new and have beautiful covers. One of the books had the family tree in Arabic, and Najib Saliba translated Sam's family's genealogy for me into English. Najib found a book that my father, Moosa [Moses] N., who resided in West Virginia, gave to Father Michael. Evidently when the priest was in West Virginia, my father had given him this Arabic book and it had my father's name on it. At that time neither my father nor I had any idea that I was going to end up marrying Sam S., a relative of Rev. Father Michael M. H.

Mitchell G. Chakour was known for giving books from his collection to some of his students at the Arabic school. John K. B. wrote on the inside page of one of the books given him: "This book belongs to John K. B. I received it from Mitchell Chakour, my Syrian School teacher on Halloween night, October 31, 1928, at the masquerade party."

George "Bitar" P. was among others who had a fine collection of Arabic books that included books published in 1905 and in later years.

Children used many Arabic words in games and were amused when parent or grandparent used an Arabic word during a conversation in English. Some children who were not aware that many English words are derivatives from Arabic would ask an adult relative what the Arabic name was for candy, potato, sofa, Messiah, myrrh, tariff, algebra, or carafe. The response would be *qandi, batata, suffa, Il-Masih, myrra, tarif, al-jabr,* or *gharraf,* respectively. The children laughed because they thought the adult was making fun by repeating the English word with an Arabic accent, when in fact the English word was derived from Arabic and the adult had responded in Arabic. They were not aware of the commonalties that bind the two great languages and that a considerable number of English words are derived from Arabic, which for centuries was the world's lingua franca.

Food

Both Arab and non-Arab loved to visit an Arab-American home because of the hospitality and abundance of delicious food that guests were served. Appetite aside, food represented much more than the means to stay alive and healthy. As with many other ethnic groups, food was part of their cultural social system. Peoples of the Near East have mingled through centuries of interchange, and some Arab recipes are similar to the Armenian, Assyrian, Greek, Turk, and others.

Arabic food is prepared with much variation based upon the geographic location of birth in the homeland. Some tasty and nutritious Arab dishes frequently appear under their Arabic names in healthy American diets, on school menus, at public functions, in nonethnic restaurants, and stores. Some of the most popular are sold as:

Appetizers—*hummus bi tahini, baba qhannuj* (eggplant finely blended with *tahini* and pungent with lemon juice and crushed garlic); *falafel* (ground fava beans, sesame seeds, spices, and chopped parsley, shaped in small balls or patties).

Salads—*tabbuli; suf* (similar to *tabbuli* but with chickpeas—also called garbanzo beans or ceci—instead of tomatoes). Both salads are served with lettuce, grape leaves, or cabbage leaves to scoop up the salad from one's plate.

Entrees served with Syrian bread—*waraq inab mihshee; mujaddarah* (lentils, burghul, and brown rice, olive oil, chopped onion, and julienned onion browned and sprinkled on top).

Desserts—*baklawa* (crunchy layers of thin, fluffy pastry sheets, sometimes called filo dough or strudel dough, with ground walnuts or pistachio nuts); *mahallabiyeh* (a delicate pudding of rice flour and milk, lightly flavored with fragrant *mazahar*, which is orange blossom water from the petals of the flower, and decorated on top with almonds or pistachios).

Commercial Bread Baking

Most bread was baked at home except *khubz Arabi* (Syrian bread), which is about one-quarter inch thick and seven inches in diameter. The bread is quickly baked at 600 degrees. The rapid baking contributes to the special feature of the bread's separation into two layers yet still joined around the edges. It is often called pita or pocket bread.

A feature article about Syrian bread in a local newspaper in 1967 carried the following headline:

> Call it Syrian, Call it Lebanese, Call it Arabic, but . . . BOY, THAT'S BREAD!

Excerpted from the feature article:

> If you're Syrian, you call it Syrian bread. If you're Lebanese, you call it Lebanese bread. And if you're neither one, you probably call it just plain good . . . and some call it "Jesus Bread" because of New Testament references to Jesus having eaten it . . . George Salloum, proprietor of George's Bakery at 321 Grafton Street, explains how he makes the bread the same way as his parents in Lebanon . . . How he does it is something of a trade secret, he said, because each baker has a few tricks of his own, which he guards carefully and doesn't even divulge to his apprentices . . . Said George, "In my place I am the bread."[1]

Bread Baking at Home

Bread baked in the home was usually of many varieties and came in various sizes and shapes. Bread was served at all meals, and before breaking bread it was a tradition to make the sign of the cross over the bread and to say the blessing, *bism Illah* (in the name of Allah). Some of these breads are *kurban* (one-inch-thick, soft bun-type bread flavored with orange blossom water, also used as Holy Bread in church services); *kaak* (about four inches in diameter and made with anise seed, milk, eggs, rose water, and crushed *mahleb,* which is black cherry kernels); and *fatayer.* Most *fatayer* are about seven inches in diameter: *fatayer joban* (crumbled Syrian cheese pie); *fatayer laham* (a closed, triangular-shaped savory meat pie with diced lamb, pine nuts, diced onions, and allspice); *fatayer sabanegh* (spinach pie); *fatayer simsum* (sesame seed pie); *fatayer zahtar* (thyme; a pie made with a spice mixture usually including powdered robust sumac berries and sesame seeds).

Sfeeha is an open circular or square meat pie with ingredients similar to *fatayer laham* except that diced tomatoes are added. It is often called *laham ageen.*

Khubz marquq, a flat bread with a delicate tang, was generally used to spoon up certain foods when eating a meal or at parties. It is often called *lavash tannour,* mountain bread, or roll bread, particularly when the contents of a sandwich are rolled inside the bread. Non-Arab and Arab bakers commercially make *khubz marquq* and Syrian bread—both breads are popular with diet-conscious people.

Shared Recipes

Members of the Ladies Society of St. George Syrian Church (now St. George Orthodox Cathedral), wanting to share the recipes of their parents as a legacy for future generations, published a cookbook, *Syrian Cooking,* in 1962. The preface stated:

> Many aspects of our culture have become Americanized. Middle East cookery remains unchanged, handed down through the generations. Many of these recipes originally stemmed from religious ceremony, others were of medicinal value. Many are attached to the occasion of a newborn child, the cutting of the first tooth, the *sahra* or the Easter holiday. Preparation of these foods by our ancestors required many, many hours and sometimes days. Today, with the advent of modern cooking implements, it is a relatively simple chore.

The same organization, later known as the Women's Club of St. George Orthodox Cathedral, published a 1978 edition, titled *Syrian Lebanese Cooking.* It included many new recipes, and, because families were smaller, the number of servings in the earlier recipes was reduced. The artwork throughout the cookbook was by Emily (Swide) Boosahda (Mrs. Leo S. Boosahda); and one of the chairpersons of the Cookbook Committee was Margaret (Haddad) George (Mrs. Philip F. George), who stated in the preface, "We did a lot of testing and tasting."

Mrs. Salem Ayik (Mary Ayik), an early immigrant, won a prize for her stuffed squash recipe from the "Food by Arlene" column in the local newspaper. This event was covered in a 1973 newspaper article titled "Generation-Old Syrian Recipes Remain Timely for Ayik Family," with an accompanying photo of Mary Ayik and her great-granddaughter, Jennifer, sampling a Syrian meat pie. Excerpted from the article:

> Serving dinner to about 50 persons constitutes just an ordinary Sunday for Mrs. Salem Ayik. Mrs. Ayik self-admittedly loves people and loves to cook (in that order), so it is always time for company in the Ayik's home at 158 Norfolk Street. . . . Mrs. Ayik said she raised her eight children on exotic ingredients, such as dried rose petals, pine nuts, semolina, saffron, lentils and a spicy condiment, simply labeled Syrian pepper. . . . The Ayik home is equipped with three stoves to make the preparation of large quantities of food less hectic. Large-scale food shopping also is a must for Mrs. Ayik.[2]

Family Record Keeping

Many families kept records of their history and genealogy. These included official documents, family trees, notebooks, diaries, and letters. Families kept a history or genealogy written in Arabic in their Bible or Quran. Some records were translated into English and distributed to family members to encourage the continuation of this tradition. Bashara K. Forzley, Eli A. Busada, and Nabeha (Merhige) Haddad (Mrs. Abraham I. Haddad) were among those who have self-published autobiographies. An autobiography by Thomas F. George and a collection of diaries by Fida K. Forzley are as yet unpublished. Fida Forzley stated:

> I have diaries now since 1917. I put them in Arabic and now I have translated them into English. After my wife and I are gone, our children will throw away all of the diaries, thinking they are of no value. Children today don't care very much about their history.

> Fida's wife, Rose (Forzley) Forzley, interjected: No, they are in English now. So maybe they'll keep them, maybe.

It may take time for children to learn to appreciate the importance of preserving family history. Contrary to what Fida Forzley expected, Fida's grandson now living in Florida is keeper of the diaries, which are treasured by him and Fida's family. Many children wrote papers for their schools regarding their immigrant relatives, for example, "Biography of John Salem," by his son, Edward Salem; "The Uncalled-For Tale," by a grandson, John K. Boosahda (Busada); and "The Life Of Peter Paul Massad, 1795–1890," by a great-grand-nephew, Robert B. Massad.

The paternal side of Edward G. Hyder's family, the AbuHider of Baskinta, Lebanon, traced their roots back to 1650. Families in America with AbuHider lineage celebrated their first reunion in Worcester in 1998.

Resourcefulness

The immigrant family was extremely resourceful at meeting its many needs. Making enough money was difficult; it made them learn to live frugally and develop ingenuity at making do in hard times. They raised chickens and planted vegetable gardens and orchards. They sold crocheted and hand-tatted lace, sewed clothing by hand for the family, made household furnishings, did carpentry and plumbing jobs on their real estate holdings, built foundations and stone walls, trimmed the hair of their children and neighbors, and repaired shoes. Often they performed services in exchange for a reciprocal commodity.

Even after becoming wealthy, a few maintained these habits throughout their lives. Some of the descendants felt their well-to-do ancestors should have lived in a more "Madison Avenue" manner. For example, a great-grandfather's ingenuity at repairing shoes was of no consequence to a fashion-conscious great-grandson, who in viewing a 1917 photo taken of four of his great-uncles and great-grandparents at the onset of entry of the United States into World War I, exclaimed:

> Wow! There's a patch of about one inch square on Great-Grandpa's right shoe. How could he do that? He is so well dressed and has his pocket watch chain visible, his wife has a Victorian lace, high-collared blouse, and bouffant coiffured hairstyle, and his sons are formally dressed. They look so regal, but yet Great-Grandpa is sporting a high-laced shoe with a visible patch. How could he do that?

There was anger and disappointment in the great-grandson's voice. His dad explained:

> Although your great-grandfather was a successful real estate investor after his beginnings as a peddler, he retained his simple lifestyle and still repaired his shoes and those of his family. The only time one would receive a new pair was when you outgrew the shoes you were wearing, and that frugality and practicality was their style of living.

Religious Celebrations—Christian and Muslim

Easter is the most celebrated holiday in the Christian calendar with its Midnight Mass, Easter egg tradition, holiday foods, and visits with relatives and neighbors. In 1947 the *Worcester Telegram* wrote about Syrian Easter customs:

> [Mrs. Abraham I. Haddad, née Nabeha Merhige, talked about visitations at Easter time.] "The first house visited is always a home that has felt sorrow or the loss of a loved one during the year. Visitors have the thought of giving hope and encouragement to the family. . . . Every friend is visited and no one is slighted. When a family has many friends the visits may go on for several days. Any misunderstandings that may have occurred during the year are rectified and friendly relations again established. . . ." Friends of Mrs. Haddad say that she is interested in many things outside her home and care of the family. She is active in church work and civic affairs and has cooperated in many projects relating to America and World Unity. They will also tell you that she does her full share in all things in which she takes part.[3]

Ramadhan, the ninth and holiest month of the Islamic calendar, commemorates God's revelation of the Quran to the Prophet Muhammad. The most celebrated Muslim festivals occur during Ramadhan. Based on the lunar year, Ramadhan and its holidays fall at different times each year. The festivals are Id al-Fitr (Eid al-Fitr), the Feast of the Breaking of the Fast marking the end of Ramadhan, and Id al-Adha (Eid al-Adha), the Festival of Sacrifice and commemoration of the pilgrimage to Makkah. Muslims of North America unite with over a billion people worldwide in the yearly observance of these celebrations. Ramadhan is a time of self-denial, charity, and collective celebration. The dawn-to-dusk daily fast of abstinence from food and drink begins with the sighting of the new moon and ends with the sighting of the next new moon, twenty-nine to thirty days later. *Iftar* is the breaking of the fast at sunset during Ramadhan when the Muslim traditionally begins dinner with milk or tea and a few dates, a bowl of soup, or apricot juice, and then eats a full meal. According to the *Arab World Studies Notebook* (AWAIR),[4] Islam regards fasting as a means of achieving spiritual, moral, and physical discipline of the highest order. Seeking to please God through righteous living is required, so Muslims perform acts of piety and charity as well as depriving themselves of food and drink. Fasting, being an outward manifestation of an inner yearning to be closer to God, is considered especially meritorious in the Muslim faith. The month of Ramadhan also has the social virtue of creating new bonds of understanding between all classes of people. The fast, practiced by rich and poor alike, reminds the more fortunate members of society of the pangs of hunger that the poor suffer. Ramadhan, therefore, is especially a month of charity.

Id al-Adha follows the Hajj. It commemorates Ibrahim's (Abraham's) obedience to God as shown by his willingness to sacrifice Ishmael, his son by Hagar (Sarah's handmaiden), and God's mercy in substituting a lamb for Ishmael. Abraham is patriarch of Christian, Jew, and Arab. For Muslims, particularly those who made the Hajj, the day begins with a sacrifice of an animal in honor of God's mercy. One third of the meat is shared with the poor and the remainder is shared with neighbors and family. This holiday is celebrated in much the same way as Id al-Fitr, with special foods, gifts for children, and general merrymaking.

Id al-Fitr marks the end of Ramadhan and begins a three- to four-day celebration. The time of Ramadhan and its culmination in Id al-Fitr brings thoughts of spiritual fulfillment and its joys. Elaborate dishes are served at large banquets to which relatives and friends are invited. At the beginning of the day each member of the family performs an act of charity for the poor. The early-morning prayers are said and the day is celebrated by visiting family members and friends, making special foods, calling those who are far away, and sending letters and cards to those they will not see.

On September 1, 2001, the United States Postal Service released a first-class postage stamp honoring Eid al-Fitr (Id al-Fitr) and paying tribute to the estimated 6 million American Muslims and 1.2 billion Muslims worldwide. On these festival days, Muslims greet each other with "Eid mubarak," which means "blessed festival." This phrase appears on the stamp in Arabic calligraphy, based on the classical Ottoman style of calligraphy in gold on a blue background. The Postal Service issued this stamp as part of its holiday celebration series.

Advanced Age

We usually know our parents or grandparents only in their mature years and do not readily recall that they, too, were once young and vibrant. Frequently, the descendants—the children of the immigrants—were not interested in learning about the successes and triumphs of the elderly. The children's concern was to be identified as American and not foreign. Consequently, they never knew about the productive years of their elders. It was common to hear descendants say in interviews that they wished they had been older when their parents and grandparents were still living, and then they probably would have been interested in their stories. Alexandra B. recalled her grandfather:

> My only recollection of my grandfather is that of an old man who always wore a black suit. Because of old age he moved in with my family and most of the time his black trousers were soiled.

However, her cousin Sadie B. N. filled in the gaps in her knowledge of family history and recalled this same grandfather:

> My mother always reminded me that Grandpa owned fourteen rent-producing properties, and at one time owned all the houses on Rondeau Court, and he was seriously thinking of changing the name from Rondeau Court [extended from Wall Street to Orient Street] to Boosahda Court.

Marion A. B. recalled a man who was highly respected in the community and had his own business:

> I remember my father as an old man who could hardly walk, and as he got older he spilled things on his clothing. He was just—"old"— that's the way I remember him, not for all the hard work that he did, and all the property he had bought and sold that kept his family comfortable in food and clothing.

An Old Man—Three Views

S. R. simultaneously owned and operated a few successful businesses, and his name appears in numerous public documents such as business directories and real estate records. He was a respected family man. A. A. described him as:

> [a]n old man and not in the class with his peers who were outstanding people and more intellectual than he, such as Yacoub (Jacob) Lian and Aneese Abdelnour.

> Another narrator remembered S. R. in a different way: He was one of the early pioneers who arrived during the latter quarter of the nineteenth century. To my knowledge he wasn't a pack peddler and I believe his first business was operating one of the early "Arabian boardinghouses."

> A granddaughter, Bernice E. P., views the same person: He was a tall, handsome man, and I remember mostly his dark blue eyes that

always twinkled when he spoke. In his old age he was no longer the tall, slender man, but shrunken and short in stature. I loved him.

Centenarian

Anthony "Tony" Moossa, a centenarian, was photographed while seated comfortably with three generations of his family. Although his hands were curled in a relaxed position, Alexandra B. noticed his beautiful smooth hands with long, slender, straight fingers. She motioned to the grandson, Michael, to have his grandfather's fingers outstretched while resting on the armrest of the chair instead of with the fingers curled. Michael positioned himself directly in front of his grandfather, and with a smile he looked into his grandfather's eyes and with the grandfather smiling back, Michael gently held his grandfather's arms, outstretched his fingers, and placed them on the armrest. The gentle touch encouraged the grandfather to oblige. Moments later, however, when the grandfather did not see the need to hold his fingers outstretched, he raised both arms with a quick gesture that indicated he would pose in his own comfortable position. His gesture suggested "How dare we indicate how he should position his hands!" His zest and mindset made those present laugh and he joined in on the laughter. Whenever Moossa was asked about his good health, he responded, "I'm going for 200, God willing." Moossa died the year after the photo was taken.

Some women centenarians who died at age 106 were Julia (Thomas) Aboody, widow of Charles Aboody, and Almaza (Forzley) Forzley, widow of Bashara K. Forzley. Almaza Forzley was honored on her 100th birthday at St. George Orthodox Cathedral Auditorium by over 500 well wishers. When Almaza's family told her of the planned celebration, she was pleased and described what she would like to wear: an ankle-length purple velvet dress with a matching purple velvet hat. Her aura at the celebration was elegant and regal. After dinner people wished her well and identified themselves in English, and to each she smilingly recalled in Arabic, "You are *bint* (daughter of) . . ." or "*ibn* (son of) . . ." and gave the full names of the parents. Surnames of Arabs are almost always expressed even after marriage as daughter of or son of their father or mother.

Badaway Mary (Haddad Abudela) Abodeely, widow, died in 1966 at age 101 at her daughter's home in Cedar Rapids, Iowa, and her body was shipped to Worcester for burial near her other children. Angia Angelina (Haddad) Abodeely, widow of David Abodeely, died at age 100.

Nonagenarian

Michael Sulvane was the topic of discussion during a mid-afternoon in 1988 at Steve's Spa, a small Italian-owned restaurant located on Shrewsbury Street. An Italian American woman seated at a table with friends talked about the "old days." In particular she talked about Michael Sulvane, an Arab-American immigrant whom she had seen that morning doing his grocery shopping at the age of 92. She reminisced:

> In his youth Michael Sulvane enjoyed athletics and won awards and titles in bodybuilding. He was sort of a pied piper when kids were around because they walked behind him imitating his erect stature by holding their chests out with shoulders held back, swinging their arms and giggling. In those fleeting moments it was apparent they imagined they too would be in bodybuilding and have the same muscular physique as he.

> Alexandra B. recalled: Later that evening as Sulvane walked into a restaurant, an Italian father accompanied by his three young sons touched Sulvane from behind to get his attention. He said he wanted his sons to see the man after whom he used to run and strut hoping that he, too, when he got older, would be as strong and muscular as Mr. Sulvane. Mr. Sulvane thanked the father for his kind words and then turned to a friend and said: "Because now I am an old man no one speaks to me or even says hello unless I'm with someone. I thank God for my good health, my family, and church."

Mr. Sulvane died in 1990, aged 97. His brother Leo Sulvane was a World War I veteran, served in France with the Yankee Division, and during World War II received commendations from the navy for specialty work. He died at age 93.

> Nicholas A. talked about his visit to a nonagenarian: After being away in New York for twenty-five years and returning to live in Worcester, I stopped by to visit Um Mikhail [mother of Michael A.]. Her age was 95 and she recognized me. Can you imagine that! She always invited guests to sit in the shade of the garden in her backyard off Acton Street and served them aromatic Turkish coffee. She smoked the *narqhile* and in later years, to give the appearance of modernity, she would occasionally smoke a cigarette. I was saddened to learn she died that same year. Old age didn't hold her back from the sheer pleasure of working with the soil and enjoying her beautiful flowers and fresh vegetables. Her final wish was granted.

She died suddenly doing what was most pleasurable for her, digging in her garden.

Takala M. (Husson) Rizkalla, who owned and operated a market on Wall Street, died at age 97.

Nellie M. (Haddad) Bourisk, born in Worcester, moved to Lewiston, Maine, taught bookkeeping and commercial studies at Bryant Pond High School, Bryant Pond, New Hampshire, and served as secretary of the Lewiston and South Portland, Maine, chapters of ALSAC, St. Jude Children's Research Hospital. She died at age 96 in Lewiston and was buried in Worcester.

Malocke (George) Dahrooge was treasurer of Public Oil Co. (founded by her husband Elias K. Dahrooge) until 1977, ten years prior to her demise at age 96.

Catherine Anna Hilow, who had fifteen great-grandchildren and was a longtime volunteer with children at St. Vincent Hospital, died at age 95.

Amelia (Ghiz) Aboud volunteered for more than twenty years and continued beyond the age of 87 when she received an award from the Worcester Area Retired and Senior Volunteer Program (RSVP). Five days weekly she traveled by bus to visit elderly people in the city who were confined to their homes. She died at age 92.

Public Personalities of First-American-Born Generation in New England

Contributions were made by the first generation of Arab Americans born in this country beyond the scope of employment, through their community service, personal achievements, and activities in various aspects of living. For example, Michael N. Abodeely graduated in 1926 from the Boston University Law School. College days were over and he returned to Worcester and was admitted to the bar of Worcester County in 1927. He was mentioned in the selections for the "All American" football eleven of 1924.

After college James Batal held successive positions in Massachusetts as reporter, editor, and publisher in the newspaper world. In June 1945 he was awarded a Nieman fellowship in journalism at Harvard University. He authored *Assignment: Near East* (Friendship Press, New York, 1950), and he served as executive secretary of the Syrian and Lebanese American Federation of the Eastern States and as editor of its magazine.

Francis "Frank" Maria spoke out for Arab Americans and for peace with justice in the Middle East for nearly half a century. He served on the

General Board of the National Council of Churches and its Middle East Committee and on the U.S. delegation to UNESCO, Paris, in 1960, and in 1985, he attended the United Nations Special General Assembly in Geneva, Switzerland, on the subject of Palestine.

Mary C. Shannon specialized in obstetrics and gynecology starting in 1937 and practiced for fifty years (died 1987). In 1925 she received a medical degree from Middlesex School of Medicine in Boston and in 1961 was named in *Who's Who of American Women*.

George Lutfy Esper, a civil engineer, began his career as a road construction inspector for the Metropolitan District Commission in 1927. In 1930 he joined the Massachusetts Department of Public Works in construction of the Boston–Worcester Turnpike and the Southwest Cutoff, and in 1937 he supervised the construction of roads and bridges. He retired after forty-four years with the Massachusetts Department of Public Works.

Some served the government in elected office, in state-appointed office, and on boards of institutions, for example: George J. Abdella was elected city councilman for Ward 4 in 1939, starting his term in 1940, and he served for six years. In 1954 he was elected as alderman (at that time councilmen and aldermen served in different branches of elected city government) and was the governor's appointee as chairman of Gardner State Hospital Board of Trustees. In 1934 and 1935, Abdella worked as a page at City Hall.

George J. Lian was first state appointee named as trustee of Westboro State Hospital in 1946 and was chairman of the three-member board of appeals. In 1954 George J. Abdella was appointed to its board. Walter J. Moosa was chairman of Lake Quinsigamond Commission, 1954.

Governor-appointed judges in central Massachusetts courts were Walter J. Moosa, Albert E. Maykel (earned a juris doctor degree in 1929 and was admitted to the bar at age 23), Ernest S. Hayeck (appointed 1970), Joseph L. Lian Jr. (appointed 1990), and Charles A. Abdella.

Kuson J. Haddad was mayor of Marlboro, Massachusetts, from 1960 to 1966 and from 1984 to 1986.

Albert A. Gammal Jr. had a long career of public service as an elected Worcester state representative, the top aide to U.S. Senator Edward W. Brooke, regional administrator of the U.S. General Services Administration in Boston and Washington, and a U.S. marshal in Massachusetts, until he joined the Federal Emergency Management Agency in 1979. Additionally, he was chairman of the Worcester Board of Election Commissioners and served as a trustee of Gardner State Hospital for sixteen years.

Some from New England who worked in our nation's capital were John

Sununu, who was governor of New Hampshire from 1983 to 1989, elected chairman of the National Governors Association in 1987, and then appointed as White House chief of staff to President George Bush; and George Mitchell, a Democrat from Maine and U.S. Senate majority leader (retired 1994).

Some Arab Americans from across the country who work in our nation's capital are former U.S. senator Spencer Abraham (Michigan), now secretary of energy in President George W. Bush's cabinet; Mitchell Daniels, director of the Office of Management and Budget under President George W. Bush; Donna Shalala, former secretary of health and human services, who served under President William J. Clinton; and Rep. John Elias Baldacci (Maine), Rep. Pat Danner (Missouri), Rep. Chris John (Louisiana), Rep. Ray LaHood (Illinois), Toby Moffett (Connecticut), Rep. Nick Rahall (West Virginia), Darrel Issa (California), and former Rep. Mary Rose Oakar (Ohio), who served sixteen years in the House of Representatives. Helen Thomas, dean of the White House press corps, has covered eight presidents since 1961.

Among the early local women who graduated from college in the early to middle 1930s—when nationwide it was not popular for women to attend college—were teachers Martha Abdella (now Bates), Mary Saba, Malvina Mitchell, and, as a registered nurse, Bertha Peters (now Najemy). Nora Antoun graduated from the Fine Arts School at Carnegie Tech (now Carnegie Mellon University) in Pittsburgh, Pennsylvania, and transferred to New York University in New York City in the late 1930s and early 1940s. She, Nora Antoun Hakim, served on the Shrewsbury School Committee (1968–74) and on the Finance Committee (1976–88). At about the same time Tony Thomas of Shrewsbury served on the Finance Committee and thus, on the committee of nine members, two were of Lebanese heritage.

On the national and international scene:

Rosalind Elias, mezzo-soprano, born in Lowell, Massachusetts, was a star at the Metropolitan Opera and sang in major opera houses in the United States, Europe, and South America.

Henry Awad moved from Worcester to a milder climate in California. He married, and with his wife Blanche (Barhoum) Awad founded, published, and edited the *Star News and Pictorial*, a bimonthly tabloid English newspaper published in Hollywood, California. For ten years from January 1953 it reported about Arab Americans in the United States and provided news from abroad; its circulation was international. From about 1946 to 1950 Henry Awad was the owner and operator of the Middle East Restaurant at the Hotel Warren, Front Street, Worcester, which featured Arabic food.

William Aramony, a Worcester native, was the first president from New England of the United Way of America, the National Association of United Way Organizations, from 1970 until he resigned in 1992. Under his leadership the association evolved from being primarily a fund-raising organization to one that assumed a larger role in community planning and addressed health and human care services. In addition, he was president of United Way International.

Kahlil Gibran, of Boston, is an internationally known sculptor and author. His technical skill is characterized by his works of ingenious complexity of texture, resulting in many awards for excellence, exhibit prizes, a Guggenheim fellowship, and honorable recognition from the National Institute of Arts and Letters. He is the cousin and namesake of the philosopher and poet Kahlil Gibran.

Ralph Nader is a nationally known consumer advocate, environmental advocate, and leading opponent of "corporate welfare." Nader was a U.S. presidential Green Party candidate in election 2000.

Among the scholars and authors:

Richard P. Mitchell (1925–83) earned his master's and doctoral degrees from Princeton University, where he received a Ph.D. in Oriental languages and history. He was a professor at the University of Michigan, an author, diplomat, professor, and Muslim scholar and worked for the U.S. State Department in Washington, North Yemen, and Kuwait from 1958 to 1963. Among the books he authored was *The Society of Muslim Brothers* (originally published in 1969 and published as a reprint by Oxford University Press in 1993). As oftentimes repeated in the community, his sister, Malvina Mitchell, contributed considerably at the beginning to further his education. In 1952 he studied under a Fulbright fellowship.

Richard T. Antoun received his doctoral degree from Harvard University. He is a professor of anthropology, recipient of many awards, and a prolific writer, having authored many books. Recently he completed the manuscript "Transnational Migration in the Post-modern World."

Among the musicians of renown are Emil Haddad, an octogenarian and acclaimed jazz musician who has performed nationwide and still performs locally. Maxine George (now Hattem) founded Maxine King's 12-piece All Girl Orchestra based in Worcester in the 1940s. The orchestra played gigs in New England, in New York, and at military bases. Her four brothers were in the U.S. military and enjoyed the orchestra's music. Every Sunday morning she was the organist at St. George Orthodox Church. Around 1939 and 1940, when she was just out of high school, she had practice sessions with Emil Haddad on the trumpet, Richard Haddad on the saxophone, and her brother Michael on the trumpet at their homes or at an empty store owned by Emil Haddad's parents. They did gigs together

Anthony J. "Tony" Agbay (1925–88) was a musician for more than forty years in bands throughout New England, had an 18-piece band called Tony Agbay and the Continentals, and played for a wide range of charitable benefits. In a statewide recognition program in 1985, Agbay was selected as "Worcester's Hometown Hero" and honored by the governor of Massachusetts in an official statewide tribute. In 1988 friends of Agbay celebrated a daylong Tony Agbay Memorial Tribute with a city-sponsored thirty-unit parade on Main Street to Mechanics Hall where musical entertainment was held nonstop until 10 P.M.

Among those who have received local distinguished-achievement awards:

Anthony J. Stevens of Springfield and Worcester, Massachusetts, was recipient of the Isaiah Thomas Award in 1983. Stevens was the first ethnic (non-Anglo-Saxon) person to receive this award for outstanding citizenship. The first awardee in 1950 was George Booth, the publisher of Worcester's morning, evening, and Sunday newspapers. Stevens also actively participated in ALSAC.

David G. "Duddie" Massad was very entrepreneurial, very, very enterprising, and a very, very, very quiet philanthropist.

J. Richard "Dick" Nedder was the honoree at an ALSAC Worcester chapter fund-raiser banquet in 1984 for his active support of central Massachusetts charitable organizations and St. Jude Children's Research Hospital. Nedder began his career as a salesman for the Thom McAn Shoe Co. of the Melville Corporation in a downtown Boston store in 1944, and some thirty-seven years later he was named president of this retail shoe chain.

Women recipients of achievement awards included Anne Swydan, manager of Swydan Marketing Communications. Swydan was honored by the United Way as the longest-serving volunteer at Friendly House, where she had served on the board of directors since 1948. Florence Haddad Chrzsiewski was director of volunteer services for twenty-two years at St. Vincent Hospital. She continued volunteer fund-raising activities at the hospital after retirement. While working at the hospital she developed and implemented a volunteer-grandmother program that received national recognition from AARP (American Association of Retired Persons). Lydia

(Haddad) Rankin was honored after her retirement as chief librarian of Boeing-Vertol in Pennsylvania when the library was renamed the Lydia Rankin Technical Library in 1974.

Among the visual artists and art educators is Terri Priest, founder and partner of Fletcher/Priest Art Gallery, whose work has been exhibited throughout the United States and abroad. She is active in community organizations and is the recipient of many awards. Her maiden name, Khoury, translates to "priest" in Arabic, the early occupation of her family. Emily S. Boosahda is founder and owner of Studio 31 Gallery and recipient of many awards. Her work has been shown nationally and in Italy and Russia.

Public Personalities of the Second-American-Born Generation in New England

Arab Americans continue to live lives of accomplishment and service as the second generation born in the United States. Among them are Jeanne Shaheen, governor of New Hampshire; John E. Sununu, U.S. representative from New Hampshire; and Stephen G. Abraham, elected to the Worcester City Council.

Authors include John Najemy, who writes on the Italian Renaissance and classical history; Robert E. Najemy, who writes on understanding our selves and life issues; Clifford Hakim, who writes on working successfully in a changed world and conducts seminars; and David Williams, poet and author. Walter E. Haddad was featured vocalist with the Tony Agbay Continentals band radio show, vocalist with the George Gregory Orchestra, and singer at charitable functions.

Grandsons Converse: Second-American-Born Generation

Donald J. Peters, attorney-at-law and a deacon in the local Orthodox cathedral (now Rev. Father Ephraim, a practicing attorney and recipient of many community and social services awards), recalled:

> I never knew my grandfather, Joseph S. Peters, as he died six years before my birth. I have a large photo of him in his World War 1 uniform on my living room wall. He influenced me without my knowing him personally, and to have my children look at that photo of their great-grandfather, who actually fought in World War 1 for this country, makes me realize that all immigrants of every nationality really sacrificed and were motivated. Because of these sacrifices, we have the opportunity to pursue education and help in the community.

Edward G. Hyder spoke about music and legacy:

> My father had a grocery store, and it was pretty much focused on American products. It was a very busy store, and the only time we had to relax together was on Sundays before attending church services. We listened to music on the Arabic Hour broadcast out of Pawtucket, Rhode Island. We also played classical Arabic music, Armenian and Turkish records. I grew up with the influence of all those different musicians. Although neither of my parents played music instrumentally, they played it on the stereo. I play the *darabukkah* and the American drums. When aunts and uncles visited we always played the Arabic music. My mother also listened to and got me interested in jazz. When my mother's brother, Eli, was going to school on the West Coast, he was involved in recording some top musicians. We always had record albums of American musicians.
>
> When I was growing up there were quite a few picnics and *mahrajhan*s held by various organizations and churches where we had live Arab vocalists and musicians. Arabic music, like a lot of world beat music, has a great rhythmic base so you don't only hear it, you feel it. My father, fluent in Arabic and still is, at the age of ninety years old, always heard the words. I was fascinated with the melody and the beat.
>
> No matter what you were going to do it was important to the family that you get a college degree. I have a bachelor of arts in history and Middle East politics, but I went into groceries. After I graduated in 1972 I visited Lebanon and I returned as a gift wholesaler of imported gold, silver, copper, and brass items. Since I had learned from my father and uncles the grocery trade, I decided to combine the gifts and groceries, but I did it with Arabic groceries, not the American line as they had when I was growing up.

Christian C. Coury talked about linkage:

> As I got older and became more politically aware, I realized that there was a substantial gap in my knowledge of the historical and social development of the Arab world. My main objective in receiving my master's degree in Arab history at Georgetown University was for personal enrichment: to understand my culture, my heritage, and develop an appreciation of how Arab society abroad developed. I consider the Arab-American community to a certain extent as an extension of the Arab communities overseas. I understand where my family came from and appreciate the development of our culture historically. In my own mind there still is an important link with the community overseas which I hope we don't lose.

My parents influenced me as a youngster, especially my father. In his own way he was extremely proud of being an Arab American and it was obvious to me just from the personal discussions that we had. He was proud of his knowledge of Arabic. He had a good working knowledge of the language and he traveled over there when he was in the U.S. Navy during World War II and spent a considerable time in the Persian Gulf and Iraq. I think because my father could communicate in Arabic with the people in the Gulf and in Iraq, that kind of reinforced his own personal pride in his knowledge of Arabic. Although my father was American-born, he felt a very strong link over there. Of course his father, Elias Khalil Coury, was the immigrant and a World War I U.S. veteran. My dad grew up in an immigrant home.

Denial of Ethnicity

The process of Americanization and assimilation was so strong, with some children growing up in two cultures—life at home and life away from home—that it caused conflict and denial. To be considered a "foreigner" was not fashionable. Some people who wanted to be considered "American" even denied their heritage by refusing to eat Arab food in public, because it was "foreign" when in reality only Arab food was served in their home. But others were proud to be recognized as Arab Americans and felt enriched by their Arab heritage.

The Worcester Link

Pride in the Arab heritage was evident in a speech given in 1980 at the St. George Orthodox Christian Cathedral banquet honoring parishioners eighty years of age and older. The guest speaker was Very Rev. Michael Husson, archpriest and dean of St. George Cathedral, Miami, Florida, cousin and namesake of Very Rev. Michael M. Husson (1860–1939). Other Worcester-born priests who were relatives were Rev. Raphael Husson of West Virginia and Rev. Nicholas Husson, who served in Wichita, Kansas, from 1938 to 1945. Excerpted from Archpriest Michael Husson's speech:

> This great hill overlooking the city of Worcester has produced a wealth of talent and professionals. I have been everywhere in America—Detroit, El Paso, Houston, Los Angeles, Oklahoma City, you name it and I've been there. And everywhere I go when I tell people that I'm from Worcester they say: "Oh, you come from *el-tellee*." Most of the cities in our country where we have people of our particular ethnic group have had people who have either lived

here or passed through here. But the glory of Worcester lies in its people who came from across the water, with deep faith, who were religious to the nth degree, and with the foresight to educate their children. And what a history we can put together—lawyers, doctors, dentists, judges, professionals in every field, businessmen of all sorts. And what impresses me most, my dear friends, is that all of us came from meager beginnings. None of our parents came to this great land with more than a gunnysack filled with personal belongings for good grooming.

Another excerpt from Very Rev. Husson's talk: We must remember those of eternal memory, who have long been gone to their rest. All of these wonderful people believed in seeking first the Kingdom of God. It is indeed good for us to be reminded from time to time of the significant work done by so many fine people. The benefits and privileges that you now enjoy are not by achievement alone but also by inheritance. You are today enjoying privileges and benefits that you not only earned but which are yours by the grace of God and the labors and sacrifices of those gone before you. Surely, these great benefactors of St. George Cathedral did not fail in their God-given duty, realizing that they would not be building for themselves but to the glory of God for all ages. And the task is still ahead and it is a big one. Continue in your zeal and endeavor. Love your country, your church, love your leaders, and love one another. You and your children's children can enjoy the great years yet to come.

Heritage Link

There are many examples throughout this book of how the Worcester experience was generally representative of Arab Americans in North and South America who emigrated during 1880 to 1915 and their descendants. Sadie B. N. of Kansas gives one more in her letter of August 1995:

I just came back from a convention at Cedar Rapids, Iowa, of people who emigrated from Ain Arab, the village just above Mahiethett. People came from Brazil, Canada, England, and all parts of the U.S. There were over 500 people. So many of them started as pack peddlers and now many are attorneys-at-law, doctors, and all prosperous business and professional people, either active or retired. There were Abodeelys and Abdelnours who relate with Worcester and so many more.

More than a century has passed since the immigrants settled in New England and integrated into the society of their adopted country. Generally their descendants and recent Arab immigrants enjoy Arab culture and traditions. Often those not literate in Arabic but who understand the subtleties of the language and want to more deeply convey their thoughts pepper their English with Arabic expressions of commendation, endearment, generosity, hospitality, and respect. In closing I, as an American third-generation descendant of Arab immigrants, wish the readers *Salam alaykum* (May well-being, happiness, and peace be upon you).

7.1. Arab foods great for nutritious snacks, 1972. Evelyn Abdalah Menconi serves Arabic appetizers *(mezza)*. *Clockwise from right:* shrimp, Friday omelet *(ihjee)*, cheeses, Syrian pizzas *(zahtar* pie and *sfeeha)*, Syrian bread, tomato and cucumber platter, olives, bride's fingers. The platter in center holds *kibbee* (ground lamb meatballs) and spinach and meat pies. Bowl contained a yogurt dip.

7.2. Resourceful family, 1917. *Clockwise top left:* Harold F. B., Eli A. B., Asaad "Asa" A. B., Kalil A. B. (sons), Alexandra née Abraham B. (mother), Robert A. B. (son), El-Hajj Abraham Boosahda (father) wearing leather-patched shoe, an example of his resourcefulness. Missing were the two older children, Affoumia (later Affoumia Abdelmaseh) and Miryam (later Mary Haddad).

7.3. Celebrated 106th birthday, 1988. *Clockwise top left:* Karam G. Moossa, son, Michael Moossa, grandson, Lauri Moosa, great-granddaughter, Anthony Moossa, honoree.

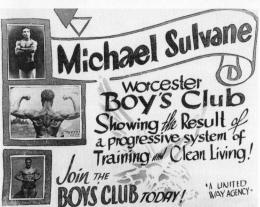

7.4. Bodybuilding at age twenty-two, 1918. In later years this advertising poster—"Michael Sulvane, Worcester Boy's Club, Showing the Result of a progressive system of Training And Clean Living!"—was made to encourage membership in the Boys Club (now Boys and Girls Club of Worcester), a United Way agency. Sulvane was the recipient of many awards for his bodybuilding techniques and meditation, including a 1936 Serviceland award from the Young Men's Christian Association (YMCA).

7.5. All-Girl Orchestra, 1940s. Seated at piano second from left: Maxine King (now Maxine George Hattem) with musicians from the 12-piece Maxine King and Her All-Girl Orchestra.

7.6. "This great hill," a section of *el-tellee* and The Meadows, 1988. *Top:* Orient Street and beyond. *Bottom:* lower end of Shrewsbury Street. *Left vertical center:* snow-covered Bloomingdale Court declivity extending from *el-saha* to Franklin Street. *Horizontal mid-center:* trains in motion on railroad tracks that separate *el-tellee* from *harrate tahta. Clockwise, upper left to right:* rear view of Bianchi (Italian American family) three-story home at 55 Norfolk Street; flat-roofed Bianchi macaroni factory built 1912; across the street is four-story tenement, 46 Norfolk Street, built by Francis Abdow and his wife Sooriya Sarah (née Hajj) Abdow, about 1920. Its first story was the site of the first Friendly House clinic for children. The hillside includes the famed El Morocco Restaurant and its large three-level sloped outdoor parking lot. The parking lot directly behind the restaurant was previously the site of the first Syrian Orthodox Church at 100 Wall Street. *Top right:* steeple of St. Joseph Church (Roman Catholic, French Canadian parish), Hamilton Street.

7.7. "Love Your Church" (a place of worship), ecumenism continues, 1975. *Clockwise left:* Rev. Charles J. Aboody (now Archimandrite), Melkite; Chorbishop Joseph Saidi, Maronite; Rev. Paul Moses, Eastern Orthodox; Deacon Edward Kakaty (now Archimandrite), Melkite.

7.8. "Love One Another," first American-born generation, 1994. *Background:* The large cast-iron cross originally topped the steeple of St. George Orthodox Church (formerly St. Joseph Church, built 1892 at corner of Wall and Thorne Streets, destroyed by fire 1978). Shown are descendants of the early immigrants from Eastern Orthodox, Melkite, and Maronite parishes. *Back row left:* Janet (Haffty) Samara, Marion (Abdow) Busada,** Helen (Boosahda) Hamwey, Albert Abdelnour, Charles A. George (age 96), Rev. Michael Abdelahad of St. George Orthodox Cathedral, Frank F. George, Lena (Dadah) Pike, Edward N. Haddad,* Mabel (Paquette) Abdella, George N. (Bob) Kalil,* Hind-Helene (Swydan) Abusamra. *Seated:* Fred Haddad (age 89),** Lillian (George) Shoucair (age 89).
[* wore shoulder sash of the Orthodox Brotherhood Society (now Syrian Brotherhood Orthodox Society, s.b.o.s.)
** wore lapel badge of the Young Mahiethett Society.]

Addendum I
PRIVATE-SECTOR ORGANIZATIONS

A. Syrian Brotherhood Orthodox Society

The Orthodox Fraternal Association and Orthodox Charitable Association, founded by a group of men in 1905, later became known as Orthodox Brotherhood Society and is now known as the Syrian Brotherhood Orthodox Society (s.b.o.s.). The first edition of the bylaws of the Orthodox Fraternal Association and the Orthodox Charitable Association, in 1905, began with a quotation from the Bible and an introduction:

> "Blessed are the peacemakers, for they shall be called the children of God."
> We glorify the Lord who has enabled us to undertake such a moral Christian and national service, established for a charitable assistance, with fundamental rules of charity and peace: hoping from Him to inspire us to organization and continuance on the identical intention which we have declared.
>
> After compliments: these are the rules of our Association, which we have composed faithfully and sincerely, to become our followed golden rule, hoping they will be satisfactory, and leading to the progress of our enterprise.

The following are excerpts (not in sequence) from the bylaws.

CHAPTER I. The Purpose of the Association and the Motive to Its Establishment

Article 1. To purchase a cemetery to the title of the Orthodox religion for burying the dead of all Christian religions of the Syrians, building a tomb therein.

Art. 2. To build a school for the Syrian children in Worcester, where they will be taught both English and Arabic languages if the aid of the generous party make it possible.

Art. 3. To aid the poor people, visit the sick . . .

Art. 4. To provide reconciliation and peace wherever it concerns the welfare.

Art. 5. This Association should have twelve officers, a Treasurer and a Secretary, to manage its affairs and reserve its rights. Also they shall have a special hall where they hold their special and regular meetings.

Art. 6. No useless name shall be given, as "Active Members" and "Members of Honor," but all the brothers should concentrate into one member and one hand, doing all that leads to the public welfare.

Art. 7. The Treasurer and Secretary will be elected annually by the members, according to the excess in nomination.

Art. 8. People of selfishness and tumult will not be taken in, but all should solemn God and love each other.

Art. 11. All officers should speak wisely within and outside of the meetings.

Art. 13. Every member should observe the regulations and never speak against the Association, because our attempt is to love each other so that its light will shine among others . . .

Art. 14. Disputation, quarreling, scoffing, and smoking are strictly forbidden in the side hall.

Art. 15. No bad talk allowed against anybody for the Association is only polite, breeding and charitable.

Art. 16. It is forbidden for the clergy to meddle in the affairs of the Association, and are not permitted to be present at any of its meetings.

Art. 17. And if any of the latters has any business within, he can dispose [it] with the officers.

Art. 18. Meetings will be held at one P.M. every Sunday, and last an hour and one-half, totally devoted to manage its affairs.

CHAPTER II. The President and Officers

Article 2. It shall also elect a trustworthy and wealthy Treasurer, a man of emulation to his patriots.

Art. 6. The Treasurer cannot draw any money from the bank without the signature and seal of the Association.

Art. 8. The books should be examined every eighth meeting, and a statement of the accounts should be given.

Art. 9. The Clerk shall write down the minutes of every meeting, which will be recorded in the minutes book after being declared and signed.

Art. 11. A statement should be printed and distributed every year to members and others, bearing an account of the income and expenses.

Art. 12. Every officer shall attend the meeting, and none but the important apologies of absence will be accepted.

Art. 13. Absence of three alternative meetings without a cause will lead to fifty cents forfeit; if refusing to do so, isolation will occur.

Art. 18. If an officer wishes to leave his position for some purpose, the assembly will appoint a substitute by nomination.

CHAPTER III. The Duties of the President and Officers

Article 1. The President must conduct the meeting very respectfully and solemnly so that no one shall get disgusted.

Art. 2. He must also demand the minutes of a previous meeting to be read loudly, and other motions will be recorded then.

Art. 4. If nine of these officers are present they can hold a regular meeting.

Art. 5. Every officer in this Association must give an oath for reserving of the rules and accomplishing his moral duties.

Art. 6. All the officers should attend to what the President suggests.

Art. 7. Whoever has any motion to say must stand up and take permission from the President, then his proposition will be heard.

CHAPTER IV. Moral Duties

Article 1. The twelve officers must be good hearted, all honoring each other.

CHAPTER V. Calling the Meeting to Order, Contributions and Boons

Article 1. The meeting should begin and end with prayer.

Art. 2. No meeting will be executive unless the regular prayer is told.

Art. 3. The membership fee in this Association is fifty cents (50 cents) for men, to be paid in advance, and twenty-five cents (25 cents) a month for contributions receipted . . .

Art. 4. Ladies' and Children's contributions are ten cents (10 cents) a month, any other donations will be heavenly rewarded.

CHAPTER VI. Burying the Dead

Article 1. The Association will accept any alms in the memory of any deceased.

Art. 2. If a poor member of the Orthodox religion dies, it is the duty of the Association to render him or her financial assistance after investigating his or her condition.

Art. 3. All the officers [fourteen] should march in the funerals of members of the parish, poor or rich.

Names of the original twelve officers, the Treasurer, and the Secretary of the Orthodox Charitable Association listed in the first edition of the By-Laws:

Sahad Aboumrad [Saad Abo-Murad], Treasurer

Jos. M. Ghiz [Joseph Mitrie Ghiz], Secretary

Farris A. Moore [Ferris Abraham El-Murr]

Abraham Aboosada [Abraham Boosahda]

Solomon Ferzly [Forzley]

Jibran J. Shakoor—Jibran Yakob Shakour [Gabriel J. Shakour]

Jos. M. Thabet [Joseph Michael Tabett]

Nassif N. Khoury [Nasif Nicola El-Khoury]

Khaleel Samara

Abraham Aljamal—Abraham Abdo El-Jamal [Abraham Gammal]

Abdalla J. Ghiz [Abdallah Joseph Ghiz]

Saleem Abosamra

John Hadad [Abouasaly J. Haddad]

Chaleel Samara Batara—Khalil Samara Abotara [George Samara]

Names of newly elected 1906 officers were published in a second edition of the bylaws, and five were reelected from a total of fourteen:

David Saloum [Salloum]

Jacob Khoury

Habib Mackoul

Kalil J. Haddad

Abouasaly J. Haddad

Abraham Bousada, Treasurer [Abraham Boosahda]

Joseph Nesf Jbale

Ameen E. Forzly [Forzley]

Beshara K. Forzly [Forzley]

Thomas Haddad

Joseph M. Thabet

Gantous Haddad

Abraham Gammal, Secretary and Clerk

Abdalla Ghiz [Abdalla Joseph Ghiz]

The third edition of the bylaws included a name change to "Syrian Brotherhood Orthodox Society of Worcester, Mass.," a Commonwealth of Massachusetts charter of incorporation dated 1932, and indicated that the organization was founded in 1905. The bylaws were printed in English and Arabic by the Syrian Press, Boston, Massachusetts. "The Aim of the Society" was similar to those of its predecessors (Orthodox Fraternal Association and its affiliate Orthodox Charitable Association) with a few revisions:

ARTICLE II. Aim of the Society

Sec. 1. The society is a religious, charitable and independent organization, its faith and religion being the Eastern Greek Orthodox Faith [now called Eastern Orthodox; "Greek" referred to the language spoken during the early Syrian Orthodox Liturgy].

Sec. 7. To preserve peace among the members of the Syrian race of Worcester.

Sec. 8. To maintain a library composed of both English and Arabic books for the benefit of the members of the society.

ARTICLE III. Rules of Membership

Sec. 2. That he or she be a resident of Worcester, Massachusetts, or a resident of some other city besides Worcester, providing his name has been recommended by one or more members of the Board of Directors.

ARTICLE IX. Emblem of the Society

Upon the acceptance of the application of a new member and his paying of his first membership fee, the new member shall receive the society's emblem which he shall wear on his coat, said emblem consists of the letters s.b.o.s. [Syrian Brotherhood Orthodox Society] on a round disk with a Hand Clasp signifying Brotherhood and Charity.

B. Young Mahiethett Society

The Young Muhaiti Charitable Society, later known as the Young Mahiethett Society, was founded in 1916 and continues to the present.

The following excerpts, not in sequence, have been selected from the first edition of the 1916 Constitution.

Introduction. In the Name of God the One

With the help of God we have come together and extended to one another the hand of cooperation, for the purpose of establishing a society for mutual love and help, and called this society "The Young Muhaiti Charitable Society." Its object is to help whomsoever comes to it. In the grace of God the officers of the Society were elected in perfect order and decorum, and with the unanimous consent of those present, whom God inspires to found this society in love and righteousness. Him we do ask to prosper it and guide it in the path which will be useful to all. Amen.

The Great Oath

I swear by the honor of humanity, and the honor of my parents that I will enlist in this society with perfect willingness, and be a faithful soldier among its members, zealous for all things that pertain to its affairs.

ARTICLE I. THE PURPOSE OF THE SOCIETY

Its Golden Rule consists in cooperation, love and good doing.

1. To bring together its members, the young men of Muhaithite [Mahiethett], in fraternal love, and for the things that are useful and which tend to preserve the honor of its sons.

5. The treasurer of the society must be one whose integrity is testified to by others. His period of office is for six months.

7. The society will not accept in its membership those who speak against it, or incite trouble. Any one under suspicion in these matters must be investigated by the society, and if found guilty will be fined, and if he revolts against the society he may be suspended. But if he repents of his own accord and apologizes, the society may consider the question.

8. Suspension signifies denial of its legal privileges. The suspended one has no right to demand what he had granted to the society.

9. Every person of Muhaithite [Mahiethett] extraction has a right to belong to this society, and to contribute to it.

11. When one reaches the age limit of forty-two he may neither elect or be elected, excepting those who founded the society, but may be considered as an honorary member.

12. No one is allowed to speak against the society, or against any body, for the purpose of the society is moral, educational and charitable.

14. The regular meetings of the society are held every Sunday at one o'clock in the afternoon. The duration of the meeting is one hour and a half . . .

15. An annual meeting of the society will be held on the day of its founding, to commemorate it . . .

16. Every member has perfect freedom of speech, within propriety. The President has right to stop any member if he violates this condition.

17. NOTICE—If, God not permitting, the society, for some extra reason, dwindles to three members, the same cannot spend the money of the society except

on charitable projects, in behalf of those who helped financially and morally. For sake of removing all misunderstanding, all transactions must be made public.

ARTICLE II. THE PRESIDENT AND HIS DUTIES

1. The President must be an honorable man, alert in his duties as a presiding officer. He must also be an upright example to others, free of pride or prejudice, and in all ways walking in accordance with the Constitution.

3. The President is not allowed to undertake any activity without the knowledge of the society . . . and retain his status as a president by not partaking in the discussions. If a quarrel should take place, he must do his utmost to remove misunderstandings, and fine the guilty one when he ascertains his guilt by a careful investigation.

5. The Secretary must be a well-educated person, strictly keeping the internal and external accounts of the society . . .

7. The Secretary must take down every thing that takes place in the society, whether it be lectures or propositions. When signed these records will be kept in a book of records.

9. Beside three members whom the society elects for that purpose for the period of one year, nobody has any right to use the society's signature or draw of its money from the bank.

10. The society should have a seal of its own, in the Arabic and English languages. The same should be kept with the Secretary.

11. All the members of the society are one in the station of love, lest there be preference of one over the other.

12. The society accepts no one as a member who is below the age of twenty-one.

ARTICLE III. THE DUTIES OF THE MEMBERS

5. If a member is entailed in some outside quarrel, it is the duty of the society to defend him. But if it is proven that the member himself was to blame in starting the quarrel, the society should chide him and fine him the regular fine.

8. If one wishes to resign from the society he must submit his excuse. If his excuse is accepted, he may resign, otherwise the society will not permit his resignation. Under all conditions he should respect the station of the society. If the resigned one desires to be an associate member he may do so.

DISCUSSIONS AND DEBATES

3. To rejoice with those who rejoice, and weep with those who weep is one of the fundamental principles of the society. For this purpose the society designates special persons from among its members.

4. If a member is taken sick, and remains one or two weeks without work, the society should offer him three dollars, beginning with the second week, for a period of four weeks. And if he is laid further without work, the society should look into his affair.

6. Membership fee for men is one dollar, and the monthly fee is fifty cents. Whoever pays more than that, the amount will be recorded in the book of contribution. But no one has any right to demand back what he had voluntarily contributed.

7. Membership fee for women and children is ten cents and above. But they have no right to hold office or become members.

[A 1962 brochure of the Young Mahiethett Society's Annual Installation Banquet stated that St. George Church of Worcester derived its name from St. George Church in Mahiethey [Mahiethett]; the second Sunday after Easter was proclaimed by the society as Mahiethey Day in Worcester; the year 1961 found the society in the hands of the second-generation members; plans were being formulated to establish a sound Scholarship Fund. The brochure included a snapshot of the village of Mahiethett and listed the names of some of the founders who organized the Young Mahiethett Society: Mansour H. Abdelmaseh, Moses Haddad, Thomas F. George, Abraham F. Haddad, Kantous Haddad, Nicholas Haddad, Joseph Mackoul, Naif Abdow, Essa Kalil, Nicholas Kalil, Charles Abouasaly (Haddad), Ferris Abdow, Farah Abraham, and Kalil Boosahda.

Addendum II
THE MIDDLE EAST AND THE ARAB WORLD
AFTER WORLD WAR II

The founding of the State of Israel in 1948 led to numerous wars between Arabs and Jews in the Middle East. In the course of the conflict Israel occupied Arab lands. Today some Arab land in Palestine, Lebanon, and Syria still remains under military occupation by Israel.

The Difficult Present for Arab Americans and American Muslims

The Arab-American community, Christian and Muslim, is outraged and agonizes over the tragedies that have befallen their relatives abroad. Arab Americans are appalled by the defamation, dehumanization, demonization, denigration, hate crimes, and harassment of Arab and Muslim people to justify Israeli occupation of Arab land; and they are appalled at the unconditional and uncritical support for Israel and lack of even-handedness in the Arab-Israeli conflict by the U.S. government. Yet despite this extremely negative defamation and stereotyping, their loyalty and support is to America first as they love and respect this country. This loyalty and love of America have been passed down from earlier appreciative generations who emigrated to America looking for a better life, the majority of whom found it here.

However, after the 1967 Israeli-Arab war, some first- and second-generation American-born members of the Arab-American community became more aware of and sensitive to their Arab heritage. In Worcester a few leaders were critical of the injustices perpetuated on Arab people and the invasion of their homelands. They called for reform of the one-sided U.S. foreign policy in the Middle East. But for other Arab Americans and American Muslims, the false stereotypes and myths about the Arabs and Muslims caused them to be more embarrassed than motivated to question the veracity of the statements. Their leadership was small in number, and they did not form an organization; they began to have an impact beginning in the late 1960s. Local individuals brought speakers to the area to educate the public on the realities of the Arab-Israeli conflict and on the denial of human rights to the Arabs and Muslims. They encouraged concerned people to make personal contact and to correspond with their congressmen, to write letters to editors, and to demonstrate. The leadership also connected with national organizations such as the American Palestine Committee, founded in 1967. Its executive director was Norman F. Dacey, an author who was renowned for his penetrating studies of the American legal and political systems. Other organizations with which they connected were the Association of Arab-American University Graduates, Inc. (AAUG), incorporated in 1967, and Search for Justice and Equality in

Palestine/Israel (Framingham, Mass.), founded in 1972. Its executive director is
Edmund R. Hanauer. His organization "believes that justice for Palestinians and
security for Israeli Jews are not mutually exclusive, but interdependent."

In the early 1970s a local organization was formed, Americans for Peace and
Justice in the Middle East, under the same small local leadership. It was dedicated
to the cause of a just Palestinian-Israeli peace, and its motto was "Justice for the
Palestinians is the best security for Israeli Jews." One of the speakers it sponsored
at a local college on May 8, 1975, was Dr Fayez A. Sayegh, a former member of
the Palestine Liberation Organization Executive Committee and a member of the
Palestine National Council. The local organization disbanded when its few members joined other large national organizations such as the American-Arab Anti-
Discrimination Committee (ADC) founded in 1980.

The ADC New England Chapter was founded in 1982, and its coordinator was
George R. Najemy. Some work of the chapter was with injured, innocent Lebanese children from abroad who lost eyesight and/or limbs during the war. The victims and family members were housed locally and provided with transportation to
a Boston hospital. The chapter donated to the city of Worcester an elm tree that
was planted on the Common behind City Hall. It was a memorial with a plaque to
honor the victims of the invasion of Lebanon and was a symbol of hope, not just sor-
row—a hope that justice through peaceful means and equality will be achieved in
that part of the world. (*Sunday Telegram,* "Elm Tree Planted on Common as Symbol
of Hope for Lebanon," June 12, 1983). In subsequent years, the plaque was removed
for political reasons, and the tree was dedicated anew to another organization.

At a time when Arab bashing, myths, and stereotypes about Arabs and Arab
Americans abounded in the United States, the city of Boston planned a yearlong
"Festival Bostonian" celebration in conjunction with the American Bicentennial.
Judith "Judie" Leon was chairperson of the Arab-American Planning Committee
for celebration of Arab culture during the month of January 1976. The committee
was committed to displaying to the American people the profundity, dignity, and
refinement of its people and the Arab culture. Gala events were held at various sites
including the State House.

On October 6, 2002, hundreds of American Muslims and non-Muslims from
the United States and about fifty other countries gathered in Washington, D.C.
to celebrate American Muslim Heritage Day, which was proclaimed by the city's
mayor in recognition of American Muslims' contributions to the economic growth
and development of this country. This proclamation was proposed by the American Muslim Society under the leadership of Soheil Ghanouchi, president, Saleh
Nusairat, chairman of the project, and Alameddine Kaddoura, project manager.

Annotated Suggested Reading

Ibish, Hussein, ed. *1998-2000 Report on Hate Crimes and Discrimination against
Arab Americans.* Washington, D.C.: ADC Research Institute (ADCRI), 2001.
The report outlines the major challenges facing Arab Americans when dealing with other sectors of American society, including individuals, corpora-
tions, news and entertainment media, educational institutions, law enforce-
ment, and the government. ADC tracks patterns of discrimination and bias

against Americans because of their Arab ethnicity. ADC hopes this report will serve as a contribution to help develop a truly tolerant America, free of hatred, bias, and prejudice. It is also intended as a contribution to the literature on intolerance in general.

"Flash Point! Bomb Injures Officer." *Boston Herald*, August 17, 1985, front page.

"After Friday Blast." *Sunday Boston Herald*, August 18, 1985, front page. "[F]rag-ments of the bomb [9-inch bomb that exploded prematurely] were found at a West Roxbury [Mass.] office building which houses an Arab-American group . . ." Two Boston bomb squad technicians were severely injured when attempting to diffuse the bomb. After the blast, a bomb threat by an "anony-mous caller to police emergency 911 said there was a bomb in a Back Bay doughnut shop. . . . The manager of the shop, a Middle East immigrant, refused to comment on the threat." A half-hour search by police turned up no explosives.

Fact Sheet on Alex Odeh. Washington, D.C.: ADC Research Institute (ADCRI). Infor-mation is drawn from press reports by American-Arab Anti-Discrimination Committee. On October 11, 1985, in Santa Ana, California, "A powerful pipe bomb was trip-wired to the door of his [the Western Regional Director of ADC, Alex Odeh's] office . . . killing him and injuring seven others . . . [and caused massive damage to the building]. This was one of a series of pipe bombings believed by the FBI to be the work of the same person or group. A pipe bomb, similar to the one that killed Odeh, was placed at the door of the ADC office in West Roxbury, Massachusetts, in August 1985."

Washington Report on Middle East Affairs, published nine times yearly. Washington, D.C.: American Educational Trust (AET), a nonprofit foundation incorpo-rated by retired U.S. foreign service officers to provide the American pub-lic with balanced and accurate information concerning U.S. relations with Middle Eastern states. AET's Foreign Policy Committee has included former U.S. ambassadors, government officials, and members of Congress.

Raheb, Mitri. *I Am a Palestinian Christian*. Minneapolis: Fortress Press, 1995. Raheb raises crucial issues of biblical definition and theological interpreta-tion. The work is relevant to Western Christians and particularly to Jewish-Christian relations. He writes out of a situation of existential relations with Muslims and Jews, challenges Christians with fresh insights into the cul-tural diversity of Christian faith, and invites a trilateral dialogue among Christian, Jew, and Muslim.

Antoun, Richard T. *Understanding Fundamentalism: Christian, Islamic, and Jew-ish Movements*. Walnut Creek, Calif.: AltaMira Press, 2001. Compares the three fundamentalist movements and shows how all three share common characteristics. In each tradition, fundamentalists seek purity in an im-pure world, attempt to make the ancient past relevant to their contempo-rary situation, look to move religion into every aspect of life, and actively struggle against the aspects of the modern world they regard as evil.

Genealogy
EXPANDED KINSHIP IN ONE FAMILY

The marriage between Abraham BOOSAHDA and Alexandra (Eskandara) Farrah ABRAHAM resulted in the expanded kinship and family bonding through marriages of their children to spouses in the United States and Canada, except for the oldest child (1a), who married in Mahiethett (now Mhdsie, Lebanon). Parents and children were born in Mahiethett, except for the youngest child (9a), who was born in Worcester, Massachusetts. Family members who emigrated to Worcester were buried there, except for Eli (6a) and Bousaada (9a). Named after deceased family members were Bousaada (3a) after his grandfather; Assad (8a) after his brother (5a); and Bousaada (9a) after his brother (3a).

The dates used are according to the Gregorian calendar although some dates were originally stated according to the Julian calendar. Pope Gregory established the Gregorian calendar in 1582 c.e. when ten days were dropped from the Julian calendar and thus the Gregorian calendar corresponded to the solar year. Britain and the American colonies adopted the Gregorian calendar in 1752.

> Bousaada HANNAH (El-Hajj), paternal father
> Birth: n.d.
> Place: Mahiethett, Rachaya, El Wadi, now Lebanon
> Married: Affoumia ABRAHAM
> Died: January 1889
> Where: Mahiethett, Lebanon

Husband	*Wife*
Abraham BOOSAHDA (El-Hajj)	Alexandra Farrah ABRAHAM
Birth: February 1857	BOOSAHDA
Married: January 24, 1884	Birth: March 1859
Emigrated: 1893	Married: January 24, 1884
Returned to homeland June 16, 1897	Emigrated: 1905
Second emigration to Worcester 1900	Died: March 5, 1940, aged 81
Died: October 26, 1940, aged 83	

Children

1a Affoumia BOOSAHDA
Birth: February 11, 1886
Married: Monsour Hannah ABDEL-
   MASEH
Date: 1899, aged 13
Where: Mahiethett, Lebanon
Emigrated: 1908, aged 22
Died: September 21, 1966, aged 80

2a Mary BOOSAHDA
Birth: July 24, 1888
Emigrated: 1900, aged 12
Married: Moses Hannah (Murkoos)
   HADDAD
Date: December 4, 1904, aged 16
Where: Worcester, Mass.
Died: September 17, 1961, aged 73

3a Bousaada Hannah BOOSAHDA
Birth: n.d.
Died: March 16, 1889, shortly after birth
Where: Mahiethett, Lebanon

Twins

4a Kalil Abraham BOOSAHDA
   (Khalil, Charles)
Birth: February 15, 1890
Emigrated: 1900, aged 10
Married: Nazira MISHALANIE
Date: November 4, 1916, aged 26
Where: Lawrence, Mass.
Armed services: Inducted U.S. Army,
   World War I
Died: March 1, 1987, aged 97

5a Assad Abraham BOOSAHDA
Birth: February 15, 1890
Died: February 16, 1890
Where: Mahiethett, Lebanon

7a Harold Frederic BOOSAHDA
Birth: April 17, 1898
Emigrated: 1905, aged 7
Married: Mary N. NAJJAR
Date: January 20, 1922, aged 24
Where: Johnstown, Pa.
Died: April 27, 1968, aged 70

6a Eli Abraham BOOSAHDA
   (Eli A. BUSADA)
Birth: November 7, 1892
Emigrated: 1905
Armed services: Enlisted U.S. Navy,
   World War I
First Wife: Desire BROWN
Date: December 20, 1920, aged 28
Where: Washington, D.C.
Second Wife: Nellie WILLIAMS
Date: September 2, 1932, aged 40
Where: Washington, D.C.
Died: November 6, 1986, aged 94
Buried: Clinton, Md.

8a Assad Abraham BOOSAHDA
(Asa A. BUSADA)
Birth: October 14, 1900
Emigrated: 1905, aged 5
Married: Nina Helen NASIF
Date: July 22, 1924, aged 24
Where: Montreal, Canada
Died: May 26, 1961, aged 61
Where: North Bergen, N.J.

9a Bousaada BOOSAHDA
(Robert A. BUSADA)
Birth: December 22, 1908
Where: Worcester, Mass.
Armed services: Enlisted U.S. Marine Corps, World War II
Married: Matilda TEHAN
Date: August 31, 1947, aged 39
Where: Washington, D.C.
Died: October 15, 1983, aged 75
Buried: Washington, D.C.

The biological family of Alexandra Farrah ABRAHAM BOOSAHDA (3b) settled in Spring Valley, Illinois. She and her half-brother Farrah ABRAHAM (5b) settled in Worcester, Massachusetts, where her husband and two children resided.

Ibrahim (Abraham) FARRAH, maternal father
Birth: n.d.
Place: Mahiethett, Rachaya, El Wadi, now Lebanon
Died: 1902
Where: Mahiethett, Lebanon
First Wife: Mary ABDELMASEH   Second Wife when widowed: Nimry
Aboassaly FARIS

Children

1b Khalil Farrah ABRAHAM
Birth: n.d.
Married: Nahkle ABDELMASEH
Died: n.d.
Where: Mahiethett, Lebanon

2b Musalam Farrah ABRAHAM (Sam)
Birth: 1843
Married: Khazma Milhem HADDAD
   AZAR
Died: March 5, 1930, aged 87
Where: Spring Valley, Ill.

3b Alexandra Farrah ABRAHAM
   (Eskandara)
Where: Worcester, Mass.
Birth: March 1859
Married: Abraham BOOSAHDA (El-Hajj)
Date: January 24, 1884
Emigrated: 1905
Died: March 5, 1940, aged 81
Where: Worcester, Mass.

4b Ferris (Faris) Thomas GEORGE
Birth: n.d.
Married: Sayoud BOOSAHDA
Emigrated: n.d.
Died: November 1, 1905
Where: Spring Valley, Ill.
Buried: Worcester, Mass.

5b Farrah ABRAHAM
Birth: 1878
Married: Sophie KHOURY
Date: n.d.
Where: n.d.
Emigrated: 1905
Died: February 1960, aged 82
Where: Worcester, Mass.

6b Nimery FARRAH
Birth: n.d.
Died: n.d.

Genealogy sources: Inspired by the encouragement, recollections, and records of Eli A. Busada Sr. and his wife, Nellie (Williams) Busada; family records in Arabic by Abraham Boosahda (El-Hajj); recollections and records of Sophie (Abraham) George, Nina (Nasif) Busada, and other immigrant relatives; and Charles C. Haddad, first-generation American born in Worcester. Compiled by Elizabeth Boosahda, 1970–75 and ongoing.

TIMELINE OF EASTERN ORTHODOX SYRIAN CHURCH
(now under Antiochian Orthodox Christian Archdiocese)

An Overview and Selective Chronology

As in all historical work this book may contain blatant oversimplification, but the overall perspective is valid. The sequence of occurrences and brief timeline of Christianity and Islam and a few key events of the Eastern Orthodox (Syrian, Lebanese, and Palestinian) are part of the heritage and history of the Near East Arab Americans referred to in this text. The immigrants described herein primarily came to the United States to seek a better life and then return to their homeland. Most did not come because of political or religious persecution.

As learned from history, certain significant events acted as a catalyst to create divisions that had an impact on them. This is a universal phenomenon and not unique to any specific group. The timeline is provided to provide the backdrop for their actions.

Old Testament Era

Prophet Ibrahim (Abraham) was patriarch of the Arabs (Semites) through his first son, Ishmael (Ismael), whose half-brother was Isaac.

First Century c.e. to Tenth Century

33 C.E.   The One Holy Catholic and Apostolic Church was established. (Catholic: the universal, ancient, and undivided Christian church).

34   The single ancient body of Christendom was divided into patriarchates (sees) of the three main centers of the Roman Empire: Alexandria, Rome, and Antioch. The apostles Peter and Paul founded the Patriarchate of Antioch. Followers of Jesus were first called Christians (Acts 11:26) at Antioch (Syria). (Now Antioch is in modern-day Turkey and the Antioch patriarchate is in Damascus, Syria.) Later Constantinople (ancient Byzantium, modern Istanbul) and Jerusalem were added as patriarchates.

303   The world's first officially Christian nation was Armenia, stretching at that time from the Black Sea to the Caspian, when King Tradt (Tiridates III) made Christianity the state religion.

325   The Council of Nicea, the first of seven ecumenical councils.

431   Council of Ephesus.

451   The Council of Chalcedon, called to clear up misunderstandings over the nature of Christ. As generally perceived this council marked a major splintering of the unity of Christendom as some churches went their separate ways on doctrinal grounds.

610   Allah (God) revealed His word to the Prophet Muhammad through the angel Gabriel. The monotheistic religion was called Islam.

632   Muhammad died. Islam was established and expanded, not merely as a faith but also as a state and, increasingly, as a civilization. Its spoken and written language is Arabic.

787   The era of ecumenical councils ended at Nicea.

842   The word "orthodoxy" was first used in connection with the First Sunday of Lent. By orthodoxy it was understood the whole body of dogma was upheld by the churches in communion with Constantinople. The name is from the Greek "ortho," meaning correct or true, and "doxa" meaning belief.

Religion in the Near East was complicated by the schisms within the various religious groups. National churches were founded by those who left the Holy Orthodox Church because of decisions made at one of the church councils, for example, the Nestorian or East Syrian Church, the Coptic Church of Egypt, the Armenian Gregorian Church, and the Jacobite or Syriac Church. The Greek Melkite-Catholic Church (Byzantine rite and liturgy in Arabic with some fragments of Greek) is an example of one of those groups that left ancient churches and are in communion with Rome but use their native language instead of Latin. Their country of origin was Greater Syria and Egypt.

Eleventh to Nineteenth Century

1054   The Great Schism. The Roman Catholic Church and the Orthodox Church (known as the Eastern Orthodox Church or the Greek Church because the Orthodox Church was predominantly Greek-speaking) separated after the first 1,000 years of essentially being one Church. The great forces that drew them out of communion with each other sprang from deep-lying causes that had been in operation over several centuries. For example, Rome claimed a universal papal supremacy. The Orthodox Church accepted the decrees of the first seven ecumenical councils and remained faithful to the One Holy Catholic and Apostolic Church. The Orthodox Church contains many Arabs and includes the Greek Church in Turkey as well as the Russian Orthodox Church. Both the Eastern Orthodox and the Roman Catholic churches claim to be the one true church of Christ.

1095–   Crusaders from Western Europe conducted a series of Christian military
1291   expeditions in a campaign to reclaim the Holy Lands from the Muslims. This added to the estrangement between East and West.

1517   Martin Luther nailed his Ninety-five Theses to the door of the Roman Catholic church in Wittenberg, starting the Protestant Reformation.

1529   The Church of England began pulling away from Rome.

Orthodoxy in North America

1794   Orthodoxy was introduced to North America through Alaska, then a colony of the Russian Empire. In 1793, by directive of Empress Catherine to Metropolitan Gabriel of St. Petersburg, the abbot of Valaam Monastery was instructed to recruit missionaries for the colony in Alaska. On December 25, 1793, eight priest-monks from Valaam Monastery left St. Petersburg for America. After a journey of 293 days and having traversed one-third of the world's circumference while never leaving the Russian Empire, they arrived at Kodiak on September 24, 1794. One member of this original mission, priest-monk Herman, was canonized as St. Herman in 1970.

1885   (or earlier) The Syrian Orthodox Church of Worcester (now St. George Orthodox Cathedral) was established under the Orthodox Church in America (OCA) and its multilingual and multinational North American diocese under the jurisdiction of the Holy Synod of the Russian Church, Moscow.

1895   The Russian Holy Synod assigned Archimandrite Raphael Hawaweeny as head of the Syro-Arab Christians (now identified as Eastern Orthodox) in the North American diocese. Archimandrite Raphael arrived in New York on November 2.

Twentieth Century

1904   Bishop Tikhon of the Russian Holy Synod consecrated Archimandrite Raphael Hawaweeny as bishop of the Syro-Arab Mission in North America. Bishop Raphael was the first Orthodox bishop of any nationality to be consecrated in the United States. Bishop Tikhon was canonized as St. Tikhon, Patriarch of Moscow, Enlightener of North America, in 1989. He is one of the first American saints to have served as archbishop of all Orthodox on this continent. He established his cathedral in New York and presided over a vast archdiocese, and encouraged and authorized many publications in English.

1914–18   World War I (U.S.: April 1917–November 1918).

1914   Archbishop Germanos Shehadi of Baalbek and Seleucia was allowed by Bishop Raphael to come to America to collect money for an agricultural school in his Antiochian diocese. He was well known and beloved of many Syrians in America, large numbers of whom had migrated from the area that constituted his diocese in Lebanon.

1915   Bishop Raphael Hawaweeny died. Bishop Germanos and Russian bishop Alexander (Nemolovsky) presided at the funeral services of Bishop Raphael.

Post–Bishop Hawaweeny

1917   Bolshevik revolution in Russia began in October.

1917   Archimandrite Aftimos Ofiesh was consecrated Bishop of Brooklyn and North America and assumed Bishop Raphael's position under Russy (Russian) jurisdiction, notwithstanding the Antakya (Antiochian) group.

1917   Metropolitan Germanos claimed to be acting bishop of the Syrian Antiochian Church in North America (as stated in his letter to Archbishop Evdokim of the Russian Orthodox Church, April 24). Although his patriarch (Antiochian) disavowed him, he nevertheless incorporated a separate "mission" of his own (1918) that eventually also included the Ukrainians in Canada. Germanos traveled extensively throughout the United States and Canada to perform ecclesiastical responsibilities and found churches. He consecrated the newly built St. George Syrian Orthodox Church, Tyler Street, Boston, in 1924, the church originally having been founded in 1900.

1917   About fifteen years after the death of Bishop Raphael, a schismatic movement arose in North America among the Syro-Arabs. The dichotomy was between two groups of prominent members of communities who had the same love, passion, and zeal for what they believed was best for the church. One group was faithful and loyal to the historical original church in North America under the Russy. The other group was loyal to the native church that represented their Syrian historical heritage under the Antakya patriarchate. A substantial number of Syro-Arab parishes remained faithful to Bishop Aftimos (Russy), but a majority were faithful to Bishop Germanos (Antakya).

1917   May 17. In Worcester the first meeting of the incorporators of the Syrian Antiochian St. George Orthodox Church of Worcester was held at an attorney's office. The meeting was called to order by Rev. Michael M. Husson. The bylaws of the corporation under the laws of Massachusetts were drawn in addition to other business. A second meeting on the same day at 9:00 P.M. was held at a church member's home, with Rev. Michael M. Husson as chairman. Frequently it was stated that Worcester was the first church to proclaim "Antioch in America" and was "Number One" to return to the Antioch patriarchate.

About   In Worcester Rev. Joseph Ghiz (1869–1927) was pastor of St. George
1917   Syrian Orthodox Church (Russy), and included among its other clergy were Rev. Benjamin T. Hoffiz and Rev. Paul Hicha. Liturgy was held at 88 Wall Street.

1921   Antiochian Patriarch Gregory IV sent Metropolitan Zacharia of Houran as patriarchal legate[1] together with Archimandrite Victor Aboassaly to America, and both resided in Worcester.

1922   Antony Bashir arrived in America as archdeacon to Metropolitan Gerassimos Messara of Brooklyn.

1923   Bishop Aftimos Ofeish was elevated to the status of archbishop.

1924   Finally Patriarch Gregory IV officially followed examples of other ethnic churches that established separate ethnic jurisdictions in America, allowing the consecration of an Antiochian bishop headquartered in North America who assumed jurisdiction over the Syro-Arabs who favored an Antiochian diocese.

1924   Archimandrite Victor Aboassaly was consecrated as the first Archbishop of New York and All North America under the Antiochian archdiocese at St. Mary Assumption Albanian Orthodox Church, Worcester. The consecration was held in Worcester in accordance with Aboassaly's request, and the church was chosen in order to accommodate the large number of attendees. Rev. Michael M. Husson remained as rector of the local Antakya parish. An attempt to unite the Antakya and Russy groups in North America was made by the three hierarchs serving in North America, Ofiesh of Brooklyn, Germanos of Brooklyn, and Aboassaly of New York; however, negotiations failed.

1925   Patriarch Tikhon died.

1925   With the takeover by the Communist government came the persecution of Russian Orthodox churches. The Syrians loyal to the Russian jurisdiction together with other ethnic Orthodox Catholics, primarily English-speaking people, formed an autonomous, independent American Orthodox Catholic Church. This was approved at a meeting called in 1925 by Metropolitan Platon and attended by bishops from Brooklyn, Chicago, Alaska, Winnipeg, and San Francisco. The new church was to "preserve at all times its brotherly and filial relationship to the Orthodox Church of Russia represented by the Authority of Moscow." Archbishop Aftimos Ofiesh was named primate of the American Orthodox Catholic Church. In 1927 the new church was established and Archimandrite Emmanuel Abohatab of the Russian archdiocese was consecrated as bishop of Montreal and vicar to Bishop Ofiesh. In 1928 Archimandrite Sophronios Bishara was consecrated bishop of Los Angeles. Thus the American Orthodox Catholic Church had three bishops, Ofiesh, Abohatab, and Bishara.

1928   In Worcester the Antakya group purchased the Syrian Antiochian St. George Orthodox Church of Worcester, which was consecrated in 1929.

1929   The stock market crashed and the Great Depression began.

1929   In Worcester the former Russy group (now under the jurisdiction of the American Orthodox Catholic Church) began construction of its new St. George Syrian Orthodox Church building on Plantation Street.

1930   Construction of the first floor was completed. In less than a couple years the two Worcester churches reunited as one under the Antiochian jurisdiction. The Syrian American Club moved to the one-story building that it had purchased.

1931   Bishop Emmanuel Abohatab of Montreal was appointed as bishop of Brooklyn for the Russian bishopric. Toward the end of his life he worked to secure the canonical release from the Russian hierarchy of the Russy for the Antiochian archdiocese. The release was granted after Abohatab's death on May 29, 1933.

About   The Russy and the Antakya were reunited under the Antiochian
1933   jurisdiction.

1933   Metropolitan Germanos returned to Lebanon. St. George, Boston, sponsored a going-away affair for him. Representatives from many churches, including both Worcester's Antakya church and American Orthodox Catholic Church, attended.

1934   Germanos died.

1934   Archbishop Victor Aboassaly died September 19, 1934, at age 46. At his request the hierarchical funeral and burial were in Worcester, although his cathedral was in Brooklyn.

The *Sunday Telegram,* September 23, 1934, described the funeral: "With ceremonies as ancient as the church itself, laden with its centuries-old color and tradition, the body of Archbishop Victor Aboassaly lay in state at St. George's church here last night while prelates, monsignori and hundreds of parishioners from all parts of the country took part in a four-hour Lamentations service, conducted in the ancient Syrian tongue, Arabic.

"Every new train brought in hundreds of members of the Syrian Orthodox church to pay tribute to Archbishop Aboassaly, . . . The funeral will be this afternoon at 2 o'clock, following a three-hour solemn high mass in which bishops, archbishops, 45 monsignori and clergy as well as thousands of members of the church from all parts of this country as well as Canada and Mexico will participate. . . . Thirty speakers, in English and Arabic, were heard during the four-hour service, dwelling upon his life and good works, and intoning prayers for him. . . . Outside Wall street was lined with automobiles, from Grafton to Suffolk streets, and on all nearby side streets.

"A solemn high mass of requiem will be celebrated at 9 o'clock this morning by Archbishop Benjamin of Brooklyn, N.Y. The preacher at the three-hour mass, which will include all the ancient requiem customs of the church will be Very Rev. Michael Zarbabary [Zarbatany] of Montreal. . . .

"The Archbishop will be buried, by special permit from the city, in a grave outside the St. George's parish rectory, on the church grounds."

John P. O'Keefe, *Telegram* staff reporter, wrote in the *Worcester Telegram* on Monday, September 24, 1934: "In a setting that was Worcester but could well have been the far-away and ancient city of Antioch, Archbishop Victor Aboassaly, beloved of his people, was buried in Worcester

Timeline.1. Mausoleum of Archbishop Victor Aboassaly, 1934. Photo taken winter of 1945 at church grounds location. Byzantine-style mausoleum and bronze bust of Bishop Victor with miter, a crown-like headpiece topped with a cross, his arms bent at the elbows with the right hand on top and the left hand on the bottom of an open Bible. The bust was two feet four inches high and rested on a pedestal inside the monument. *Upper left background:* Visible is three-story wood-shingled hall behind church.

yesterday. . . . The services took long hours before the archbishop's body was consigned to the earth in a vault on the church grounds. . . . The tolling of the church bell, the wailing of the women and the gruff voices of the men, the singing [chanting] by the priests, the scores of eulogies for the dead prelate brought a new realism to many of the watchers.

"There were more than a half-a-hundred speeches in the church. These were relayed to the assembled thousands in the street outside by a loud speaker. Bishops and monsignori would speak, to be followed by an [a] humble parishioner. All told the same story, a great leader was gone.

"During the afternoon service in the church hundreds donated money to be used in the erection of a memorial, over the archbishop's grave. More than $3000 was collected. [This was at the height of the Great Depression.]

"A procession was formed outside the church by parishioners and delegations. Twenty priests of varying rank carried the body down the steep stairs to the street, meanwhile intoning Gregorian prayers for the dead. Acolytes carried candles, a priest carried his picture held aloft. Rev. Michael Hussan [Husson], pastor of St. George's church, carried the archbishop's cane, and Rev. Raphael Hussan [Husson] of Charleston, W. Va., carried his crown.

"The casket was placed in the hearse and the slow, mournful procession moved through the streets of the parish. Up Chrome street to Orient to Grafton street and back to Wall street passed the procession.

"The casket was removed from the hearse and carried again by the priests and prelates to the burial vault constructed Saturday night on the church grounds. Here final prayers were sung, the bell tolled remorselessly and, according to ancient church ritual, the early career of Victor Aboassaly. . . . Hundreds stormed the grave to throw flowers on the casket. Workmen and police held them back.

"Mourners came from all parts of the country to attend the services. One man came from California by plane, another by plane from Mexico City. Hundreds came from Canada and as many more from the middle and far western states. . . .

"Attending the ceremonies was Mayor Mahoney, Governor Ely, Senator Walsh and other persons in public life."

Post–Bishop Aboassaly

1935   August 25. Archbishop Theodosios of Brooklyn, N.Y., Legate of the Apostolic Patriarchate of Antioch in America, arrived in the United States from Syria and conducted memorial services in Worcester for the late Archbishop Victor Aboassaly. "More than 2000 faithful, including groups from New York, the Middle Western states and Canada, attended memorial services."

1935   The nomination process across North America for a successor to the late Archbishop Victor Aboassaly began. The three candidates for the vacancy were Antony Bashir, Samuel David (Toledo), and Agapius Golam, with Ananias Kassab (Ottawa) withdrawing his name.

1936   February 5. Archimandrite Antony Bashir's nomination to succeed Archbishop Victor as Archbishop of New York and All North America was confirmed by the Holy Synod in Damascus. As a young clergyman he was adept at translating from English to Arabic. Although Arabic was the mother tongue of the great Lebanese poet Kahlil Gibran, he chose to entrust Archimandrite Bashir with the Arabic translation of his major English works. When Gibran saw the results, he wrote to the Archimandrite, "Only you could have tailored such a beautiful Arabic garment for my Prophet."[2]

1936   April 19. Disunity occurred when Archimandrite Samuel David was consecrated in Toledo, Ohio, as archbishop of Toledo. He was immediately suspended by the patriarch of Antioch and was restored in 1939 when the Holy Synod recognized his consecration with the understanding that he would assist and refer to Metropolitan Antony Bashir in all ecclesiastical matters.

1939–
1945   World War II (U.S.: 1941–45).

1939   Very Rev. Michael M. Husson died (1860–1939).

1955   "Four Churches United in Historic Success," *Worcester Daily Telegram,*
           Monday, April 4, 1955. Guests at the banquet included Metropolitan
           Antony Bashir, Archbishop Samuel David, City Manager McGrath, and
           Lt. Gov. Sumner G. Whittier. Now this unity has expanded to the annual
           Sunday of Orthodoxy with twelve area Eastern Orthodox parishes par-
           ticipating: Albanian, Antiochian, Bulgarian, Carpatho-Russian, Greek,
           Romanian, Russian, Serbian, and Ukrainian jurisdictions.

1958   Archbishop Samuel David died.

1966   Metropolitan Antony Bashir died (1898–1966).

1966   Metropolitan Philip Saliba was consecrated at St. Elias Monastery,
           Lebanon, as successor to Archbishop Bashir. He has continued Bashir's
           tradition of energetic leadership.

1966   Archbishop Aftimos Ofiesh died.

1970   In Worcester Bishop Victor's mausoleum and body had been in the
           courtyard at St. George Church, located at 32-34 Wall Street (1934).
           Friendly House is now at the Wall Street site. Because the new church
           building was not yet completed, nor the grounds landscaped, and the
           church grounds had been sold to Friendly House, the bishop's body
           and mausoleum were moved to Hope Cemetery on January 13, 1970.
           This was done under the protest of some parishioners who wanted the
           relocation to be on the grounds of the new church when completed.
           About a year later the bronze bust of Bishop Victor was stolen along
           with other bronze items at the cemetery. A granite trefoil cross replaced
           the bronze bust.

1970   In Worcester the newly built St. George Orthodox Church on Anna
           Street was consecrated as St. George Orthodox Cathedral. Ground-
           breaking ceremonies were held April 7, 1968.

1971   Archpriest Constantine Abou-Adal died at age 94. He was pastor at St.
           George Orthodox Church of Worcester from 1938 until his retirement
           in 1958. It was frequently said that with a gentle but firm hand he guided
           the church through its trying days until it emerged as a unified and pro-
           gressive spiritual body.

1976   Bicentennial of America. "[A]s a modest contribution to the Bicenten-
           nial of the United States of America," the Orthodox Church in America,
           Department of History and Archives, published a book, *Orthodox
           America, 1794-1976: Development of the Orthodox Church in America*
           (Syosset, N.Y.: Orthodox Church in America, 1975). It stated: "We are
           convinced that there could be no better way for us to participate in the
           national jubilee than by reminding ourselves and the American public
           of the path followed by the Orthodox Church on this continent, of its
           progressive integration into the fabric of American life."

1995   A century of the presence of the Syrian Eastern Orthodox Christian Church in North America (first under the Russian archdiocese, from 1895 to 1924, and, since 1924, ongoing under the Antiochian archdiocese). A centennial celebration was held by the Antiochian Orthodox Christian Archdiocese at its convention in Atlanta, Georgia.

1996   September 5. After more than six decades in Worcester, Bishop Victor Aboassaly's body was disinterred, the mausoleum was dismantled, and the body and the mausoleum were moved to Ligonier, Pa., for reburial alongside three other bishops at the Antiochian Village.[3] The mausoleum was listed under Points of Interest at Hope Cemetery from 1970 to 1996.

Timeline Notes

1. Consensus of opinion and several reliable sources stated that the patriarchal legate who accompanied Archimandrite Viktor (Victor) in 1921 was Metropolitan Zacharia of Houran. However, in 1922 Antony Bashir (consecrated as Metropolitan in 1936) arrived in America as Archdeacon to Metropolitan Gerassimos Messarra of Beyrouth (Beirut) and Brooklyn, later Patriarch of Antioch.

2. *Metropolitan Antony Bashir: An Appreciation, 1936-1961* (Brooklyn, N.Y.: Trustees of the Antiochian Archdiocese, Brooklyn), 13. (40 pp.) Introduction by Rt. Rev. Ellis Khouri, dean, and Rev. Fr. Paul Schneirla, executive secretary, and a patriarchal message from Theodosius, Patriarch of Antioch and All the East. Also see Jean Gibran and Kahlil Gibran, *Kahlil Gibran: His Life and World* (Brooklyn, N.Y.: Interlink Books, 1991), 381. (456 pp., 100 b&w photos)

> . . . but now he [Kahlil Gibran] turned over the task of translating his books to Antony Bashir. This brilliant young Syrian Orthodox priest, scholar, and translator was Archimandrite of North America.

3. Kathleen A. Shaw, "Orthodox Leader's Body May Be Sent to Pa.," *Telegram and Gazette,* July 9, 1996. Also see Shaw, "Reinterment Marks New Church Era," *Telegram and Gazette,* September 10, 1996; Megan Woolhouse, "Goodby to Archbishop Aboassaly," *Worcester Magazine,* September 11, 1996.

Timeline Sources

Abohatab, Georgette. *Reflections of the Syrian Orthodox Church While under the Russian Jurisdiction.* Unpublished essay, Brooklyn, N.Y., 1976.

Americans for Middle East Understanding. "Churches in the Arab East—Who's Who?" *The Link* (New York), AMEU 6, no. 5 (November/December 1973): 4–8.

Gelsinger, Mary Agnes Orr. Coauthor of *A Handbook for Orthodox Sunday Schools;* author of *Orthodox Catholic Religion Series.* Syrian Antiochian Orthodox Archdiocese of New York and All North America, 1945: 108–9.

Gelsinger, Rev. Fr. Michael G. H. *Orthodox Hymns in English.* Syrian Antiochian Orthodox Archdiocese. Brooklyn, N.Y. (now in Englewood, N.J.), 1939.

Kherbawi, Basil M. (archpriest and dean of St. Nicholas Greek Orthodox Catholic Cathedral at Brooklyn, N.Y.). *The Old Church in the New World.* Binghamton, N.Y.: Vail-Ballou Press, 1930.

McCrea, Edwin A. Information concerning newspaper articles and records at McCrea-Murphy Funeral Home, Worcester, Mass. (now defunct), regarding 1934 funeral of Bishop Victor, 1989.

Nassar, Rev. Seraphim. *Divine Prayers and Services of the Orthodox Catholic Church.* 1st ed.: Sisters of the Sisterhood of the Propagation of Divine Services and Religious Teachings in the United States, 1938. Mary, Elizabeth, and Sadie Abraham, Illinois: Spring Valley, 1123 pp. 2d ed.: Syrian Antiochian Orthodox Archdiocese of New York and All North America, 1961.

Orthodox Church in America, Department of History and Archives. *Orthodox America, 1794–1976: Development of the Orthodox Church in America.* Syosset, N.Y.: Orthodox Church in America, 1975).

Upson, Very Rev. Stephen H. R. (later Right Reverend Stephen Upson). *Orthodox Church History.* Brooklyn, N.Y.: Syrian Antiochian Orthodox Archdiocese, 1953.

Wysner, Glora M. *Near East Panorama.* New York: Friendship Press, 1950.

Suggested Reading

Gabriel, Antony, archpriest. *The Ancient Church on New Shores: Antioch in North America.* Autocephalous Orthodox Churches, no. 5. San Bernardino, Calif.: St. Willibrord's Press, 1996. 1059–1101.

Illustration

Timeline 1. Mausoleum of Archbishop Victor Aboassaly, 1934. Photo taken winter of 1945 at church grounds location.

NOTES

1. Historical Background

1. Anwar G. Chejne, *The Arabic Language: Its Role in History* (Minneapolis: University of Minnesota Press, 1969), 25. See also Roger Allen, *World Book Encyclopedia*, 2001, "Arabic language" and "Arabic literature," 583–84; Howard R. Turner, "The First Language of Islam," in *Science in Medieval Islam: An Illustrated Introduction* (Austin: University of Texas Press, 1999, paperback), 15; Bernard Comrie, ed., *The World's Major Languages* (New York: Oxford University Press, 1987), 666–73. Chejne, *The Arabic Language:*

> Arabic belongs to the Semitic group of languages. . . . The permanent home of the Semitic languages is in a contiguous area that includes the Fertile Crescent, the Arabian Peninsula, and Ethiopia. Within this area scholars have described three main geographical distributions of the Semitic languages. . . . Northwest Semitic comes from the area of Syria-Palestine where many dialects appeared . . . The Southwest Semitic group is included in the areas of Arabia and Ethiopia.

2. Regarding the early arrivals, consensus among those interviewed for this study supports the theory that Arabs settled in Worcester around 1880 and earlier. As a result of my research, I do not claim to pinpoint a specific date, name, or address of the earliest Arab who settled in Worcester as my investigation encountered many dead ends and inadequate data. There are several reasons why this information is not known.

(a) Multiple-return migration. Frequently, immigrants who migrated during the years 1880 to 1915 made a few return trips to their homelands before they decided to settle permanently in America. Most did not come because of political or religious persecution. Because of the lack of adequate data it was impossible to determine which was a first or a subsequent migration. Records neither tabulated how often any one person arrived in or departed from the United States nor did they distinguish newcomers who contemplated permanent settlement from those who were sojourners. Additionally, some lived elsewhere in America before they permanently settled in New England.

Author Thomas J. Archdeacon, as an example, stated in Table V-4, "Percentage of Males and Remigration Rates of Major Ethnic Groups," 1929, that Ethnic Group Syrian, Male was 69.5 percent and their Remigration Rate was 23.1 percent. *Becoming American: An Ethnic History* (New York: Free Press, 1983), 139. Source: Derived from data in Imre Ferenczi, *International Migrations,* vol. 1, *Statistics* (New

York: National Bureau of Economics Research, 1929), tables 10, 15, and 19 in the section on the United States.

(b) Transliteration from Arabic to English. Incorrect transliteration and anglicization of many names occurred in federal, state, and local public records. For example, Salim Rachid became "Rochette" in *Worcester House Directory, 1896* (Worcester, Mass.: Drew Allis Company), 294, and "Roshed" in Bureau of the Census, *Twelfth Census of the United States, Schedule No. 1: Population, 1900* (Washington, D.C.: Bureau of the Census), sheet 103B. Elias M. Bacela became "Pazila" in *Worcester House Directory, 1900*, 325. Badaway Abodeely appears as "Abudela" in *Grantee Index,* Worcester County Registry of Deeds, Book 1841, 1906, 569. John Kaneb is "John Kump" in *Twelfth Census of the United States, 1900*, sheet 7A. Anthony Massad is "Anton Masad" in *Worcester House Directory, 1900*, 325, and "Massatt" in *Twelfth Census of the United States, 1900*, sheet 82B.

(c) Patronymic and family name. As was the general custom worldwide, most Arab names consisted of a first name that was the child's given name and a second name that was the father's first name. Identification with patrilineality, the father's line of descent, was a basic ascribed relationship for both sons and daughters, and even though daughters might move to their husband's family when they married, they were still regarded as members of their father's line and were known by their father's name. It was common on marriage certificates that the bride's first name was followed by her father's first name. For example, Mary Asaffe was the daughter of Asaffe George from the family of Aboassaly. Some American-born children changed their second name to their family name in place of the father's first name.

(d) Naming the newborn. It was customary to name a newborn after a deceased relative or friend, regardless of geography, and that added to the confusion.

(e) Listing of early immigrants. The following listing identifies several early immigrants who may have migrated about 1880 or earlier. The names were randomly chosen based on mid-nineteenth-century birth dates that were engraved on monuments in local cemeteries. Of the thirty-three names listed, seventeen were widows or unmarried females, eight were males, and four were married couples. Among the early women immigrants were two centenarians, Adebe (Farrah) Haddad and Badaway [Haddad Abudela] Abodeely; two nonagenarians; six octogenarians; and four septuagenarians. Among the men, there was one nonagenarian; one octogenarian; and two septuagenarians.

Code: *n.d.—no date*

BORN	DIED	NAME
1831	1916	Eyde Ghiz, and her son, Sallem J. Ghiz (1874–1950)
1832	1907	Anne Abusamra, and Zahia R. Abusamra (1876–1948)
1836	1921	Worde Rose Abdow, and her son, George Abdow (1875–n.d.)
1838	1938	Adebe (Farrah) Haddad
1838	1925	Salim Azar, and his wife, Helen (Bourisk) Azar (1848–1937)
1841	1936	Budaweya Rizkalla
1845	1911	George Debs, and his wife, Soud (1856–1914) (Dibbs, as spelled in *U.S. Census, 1900*)
1845	n.d.	Mary Firsley [Forzley]

1847	n.d.	Abraham Smart, and his wife, Fedowa Smart
		(Smatt, as spelled in *U.S. Census, 1900)*
1851	1939	Gabriel J. Shakour
1857	1950	Nazha Ayik
1858	1938	Kalaick [Kaneb Abdow] Abdelmaseh
1858	1931	Bandar Ghiz
1860	n.d.	Michel Moore, and his wife, Noraline (1870–n.d.)
1863	1952	Nora Ghiz
1864	1933	Katherine Schuerie [Catherine Schwerie] (Catherine
		Shawire, as spelled in *U.S. Census, 1900*, sheet 84B)
1865	1918	Mary J. Abysalh
1865	1966	Badaway [Haddad Abudela] Abodeely
1866	n.d.	Mitchell Ghiz
1867	1915	Effie (Najemy) Halal
1867	1944	Furzleih Forzley
1868	1959	Fada Haddad
1874	1948	Helaney (Abraham) Abosaad
1874	1929	Charles Dowd

(f) Frequent references and documents suggest that one of the earlier immigrants was Simon George (1861–1959), also known as Semaan and/or Slayman (Simon) George. He was from Mahiethett, and in 1880, aged nineteen, he came to Worcester with two cousins. Later he sent for his elder brother Assafe George and his wife, Um Embass Mary (Tekla) Aboassaly-Skaff, to join him.

Simon George was naturalized on October 6, 1896, U.S. District Court, Boston. Source: *Men Voters, Register of Voters, Book 11,* Office of the Election Commission, Worcester, Mass., 1901, 59–60.

Thomas F. George, cousin of Simon and Asaffe George, wrote in his unpublished autobiography:

> George, son of John [Aboassaly], married and fathered two sons, Asaf [Asaffe] George and Simon George. These brothers were among the first people of Lebanese Orthodox descent to emigrate to the land of dreams, the United States of America, in about the year 1880.

Eli A. Busada, whose father was Simon George's peer, recalled:

> As I became old enough to know about who is who and about America, many of the Mahiethett people had left there to come to Worcester. They started to emigrate around 1880 and earlier.

Nicholas Alwon recalled another early immigrant, his uncle, George Assatly:

> George Assatly, the brother of Jamily, my mother, arrived here from Norwich, Connecticut, 1882. He [was the developer who] built the four-story building at 104 Norfolk Street in 1908 [still standing]. Later he moved to Norwich, Connecticut, where most of my family settled. Among those who arrived in Worcester about 1884 were Akil E. Haddad and his cousin Tanoos (Thomas E.) Haddad, and Mary Khoury (later Mary Khoury Esper) and her mother.

(g) Worcester link. An example of an early connection between a Worcester church and a Syrian was recorded by Beverlee Turner Mehdi, author of *The Arabs in America, 1492-1977: A Chronology and Fact Book,* Ethnic Chronology Series, no. 31 (Dobbs Ferry, N.Y.: Oceana Publications, 1978), 3-4:

> 1860s . . . of Tripoli, Syria, who was a strong supporter of the Union cause in the American Civil War, sent two boxes filled with cones of cedar, sea-shells, and other Syrian curios to the United States to benefit the Union cause. A church in Worcester, Massachusetts, sold the items and used the money to buy 720 New Testaments for the boys in blue.

Example of another link to Worcester as documented by Adele L. Younis, *The Coming of the Arabic Speaking People to the United States,* ed. Philip M. Kayal (Staten Island, N.Y.: Center for Migration Studies, 1995), 63:

> By 1866, . . . This was the Female Seminary, today the Beirut Women's College. The funding, about $11,000, came from the United States and England. . . . one of the teachers, was sure of her salary for two years when Mrs. Walter Baker of Worcester, Massachusetts, pledged the necessary money.

3. Alixa Naff, *Becoming American: The Early Arab Immigrant Experience* (Carbondale and Edwardsville: Southern Illinois University Press, 1993), 14-15, wrote:

> Those few who came from the Ottoman province of Palestine called themselves, of course, Palestinians. All, however, came from the historic region of Greater Syria [also known as geographic Syria] which, under Ottoman rule, had become, by the late nineteenth century, the provinces of Palestine and Syria.

4. Elbridge Kingsley and Frederick Knab, *Picturesque Worcester, Part I: City and Environments, Complete in Three Parts, with 2,500 Illustrations* (Springfield, Mass.: W. F. Adams Company, 1891), 63. See Board of Trade (forerunner of Worcester Chamber of Commerce), *A Tribute to the Columbian Year by the City of Worcester: Graphic Exhibit of a City of Diversified Industries with an Alphabetical Index of Its Productions* (Worcester, Mass.: F. S. Blanchard, 1893), 7; *Worcester House Directory, 1894* (Worcester, Mass.: Drew Allis Company), 48; and *Worcester House Directory, 1896,* 294.

Picturesque Worcester, supra, vividly describes early Worcester:

> There is no city in America, possibly excepting New York, that has such a cosmopolitan population as Worcester. . . . In Worcester the Armenian jostles the Kurd, Russian Poles and Finns walk side by side, Arabians and Chinamen, Turks and Yankees, Negroes . . . and many other people, all talking in their native tongues.

Board of Trade, *Columbian Year,* 1893, notes the same diversity:

> We have all varieties . . . Finns and Russian Jews crowd other localities, while Armenians, Turks, Arabs, Africans of all shades, and even Chinese children, may be found in certain schools. It is the province of Worcester

teachers to weld these heterogeneos [sic] parts into one compact, American whole.

Worcester House Directory, 1894, and *Worcester House Directory, 1896:*

"Arabian boardinghouse" located at 0 Bloomingdale Court (1894, p. 48), 98 Bloomingdale Road (now Franklin Street) (1894, p. 48) and 37 Norfolk Street (1896, p. 294).

5. The Orthodox Church in America, Department of History and Archives, *Orthodox America, 1794-1976: Development of the Orthodox Church in America* (Syosset, N.Y.: Orthodox Church in America, 1975), 92, 95. Interview recollections identified Constantine Abou-Adal as the same person who became a priest and served in Worcester.

Orthodox America:

Not only were there separate communities of Orthodox Russians, Greeks, Arabs and Serbs in the North American mission [1901], but mixed communities were also to be found. (92)

Orthodox America:

During this time [1895], the Syro-Arabic community in the United States was growing at an increasing rate . . . he [Father Raphael Hawaweeny] and two other Syro-Arabs (John Shamie . . . and Constantine Abou-Adal) came to the United States [from Imperial Russia] with Bishop Nicholas [of St. Petersburg, Russia] to serve the Syro-Arabic community.

Archimandrite Raphael was placed in charge of the entire Syrian mission. . . . Later in the same year [1898], he was to be ranking representative of the American Mission to greet Bishop Tikhon, the new diocesan bishop. . . . He [Father Raphael] spoke of Tikhon's mission in his sermon. "He has been sent here to tend the flock of Christ—Russians, Slavs, Syro-Arabs, and Greeks—which is scattered across the entire North American continent." (95)

According to interview recollections of Mrs. C. H. of New Jersey, wife of a deceased cousin of Syro-Arab Constantine Abou-Adal, and Right Reverend Stephen Upson of New York, Constantine Abou-Adal accompanied his cousin, Archimandrite Raphael, to America from Russia and was the same person who entered the priesthood in 1923; and later he was assigned to serve in several areas before his assignment to St. George Eastern Orthodox Church, Worcester (now St. George Orthodox Cathedral). He had served twenty years in Worcester at the time of his retirement in 1958. Archpriest Constantine Abou-Adal and Bishop Raphael Hawaweeny were born in Damascus, Syria.

6. Bureau of the Census, *Fifteenth Census of the United States: Population, by Subjects, 1930* (Washington, D.C.: Government Printing Office, 1933), 558-59, table 19, Year of Immigration, column "1900 or earlier," Worcester, Mass., Country of Birth, Syria. Listings of other Near East countries included Turkey.

World War I draft card registrations can be found at the General Services Administration Region 4, Federal Archives and Records Center, East Point, Georgia, for Eli Abraham Boosahda (no. 189, 1917, serial no. 1112, born Mohaitha [Mahiethett],

Syria, citizen of U.S.A.), Kalil Abraham Boosahda (no. 333, 1917, serial no. 3177, born Beyrout [Beirut], Syria, citizen of Syria), and Harold Fredrick Boosahda, (no. 154, 1918, serial no. 4350, born Turkey, citizen of Turkey).

See also Record of Marriages, City of Worcester. Many Arab grooms and brides at the turn of the century listed their place of birth as Syria.

7. Rev. Edmund G. Haddad, "Our Syrian and Lebanese Catholics Have Written a Proud Record in Diocese," *Catholic Free Press,* Roman Catholic Bishop of Worcester Diocese, February 25, 1955, 2.

According to Monsignor Haddad the Maronite mass, as celebrated by Our Lady of Mercy church,

> in keeping with the directives of several popes keeps alive amongst us the ancient Maronite Rite. Its liturgical language is Syro-Chaldean, Arabic and Aramaic, the language which our Blessed Lord . . . used. The Maronite Mass was celebrated in those languages and in English by ChorBishop Joseph Saidi, pastor, until his retirement in 1997, aged 87.

8. Hutton Webster, "The Lands and Peoples of the East," in *Early European History* (Boston: D. C. Heath, 1917), 29.

> The Phoenicians were the first Syrian people to assume importance. Their country was a narrow stretch of coast, about one hundred and twenty miles in length, seldom more than twelve miles in width, between the Lebanon Mountains and the sea. The tiny land could not support a large population. As the Phoenicians increased in numbers they were obliged to betake themselves to the sea. The Lebanon cedars furnished soft, white wood for shipbuilding, and the deeply indented coast offered excellent harbors. Thus the Phoenicians became preeminently a race of sailors. Their great cities, Sidon and Tyre, established colonies throughout the Mediterranean and had an extensive commerce with every region of the known world.

9. F. Kenneth Cox, Miriam Greenblatt, and Stanley S. Seaberg, *Human Heritage: A World History* (Columbus, Ohio: Charles E. Merrill Publishing Co., 1981), 322–23. See also Anthony Nutting, *The Arabs: A Narrative History from Mohammed to the Present* (New York: Clarkson N. Potter, 1965; New York and Toronto: New American Library, 3d printing), 126; J. M. Roberts, *History of the World* (New York: Oxford University Press, 1993), 272.

Cox et al., *Human Heritage:*

> Arab scientists called alchemists tried to turn base metals—such as tin, iron, and lead into gold and silver. Their efforts were not successful. But they led to the practice of making experiments and keeping accurate records of results. Thus, the Arabs are considered the founders of modern chemistry.
>
> Arab astronomers studied the heavens and gave many stars the names they still have today. They accurately described the eclipses of the sun and proved that the moon affects the ocean. The astronomers worked with Arab geographers to determine the size and circumference of the earth. . . . The astronomer-geographer Al-Idrisi created the first accurate map of the world.

Arab mathematicians invented algebra and introduced it to Europeans. The word algebra, in fact, comes from the Arabic word *al-jabr*. It is just one of many Arabic words that have become part of the Spanish and English languages. . . .

The Arabs excelled in medicine. Unlike doctors in most other countries, Arab doctors had to pass an exam before they could practice medicine. The Arabs established the world's first school of pharmacy and opened the world's first drugstores. . . .

Arab doctors advanced medical science by publishing their findings. Ibn Sina's *Canon of Medicine,* an encyclopedia of medicine, was used in European medical schools for 500 years.

The Arabs also made many contributions in the arts. (322–23)

Nutting, *The Arabs:*

. . . was Islam's golden age, not only of luxurious living but also of cultural achievement and predominance, in which the Moslem [Muslim] world was to establish and maintain a paramount influence upon western scientific and literary thought. For it was the philosophers, doctors, alchemists, astronomers, mathematicians, and geographers of the Abbasid east and of Arab Spain who developed the philosophic and scientific heritage of ancient Greece, Egypt, Persia and India, brought it into line with the religious precepts of a monotheistic world, and so provided the essential link between the teachings of Aristotle, Galen, Euclid and Plato and the thinking of the modern Europeans. (126)

Roberts, *History of the World:*

Arab Spain was of enormous importance to Europe, a door to the learning and science of the East, but one through which were also to pass more material goods as well: through it Christendom received knowledge of agricultural and irrigation techniques, oranges and lemons, sugar. As for Spain itself, the Arab stamp went very deep, as many students of the later Christian Spain have pointed out, and can still be observed in language, manners and art. (272)

10. President, Proclamation 6056 of October 25, 1989, "National Arab-American Day," *Federal Register* 54, no. 208 (October 30, 1989). See also U.S. House Joint Resolution 241; and a congressman's letter to a constituent. The presidential proclamation read:

For decades, Arab-Americans have made valuable contributions to virtually every aspect of American life: in science, medicine, education, business, culture and government. The works of many talented Arab-American artists and writers grace our museums and libraries throughout the United States. Since the first Arab immigrant came to these shores more than a century ago, men and women of Arab descent have shared with us the rich history and traditions of Arab culture.

With pride in their ethnic heritage and with great faith in the principles upon which this country was founded, Arab-Americans have added to the strength and diversity of American society.

Arab-Americans occupy positions of leadership and responsibility

throughout our system of government, setting a fine example of public service at the local, State, and national level.

Arab-Americans have also enriched our Nation with the quiet power of
strong families and close-knit communities. Many have come to the United
States in search of the blessings of peace and freedom. They have quickly
seized the opportunities life in this free and democratic country affords, yet
they have not forgotten their ancestral homelands. They join all Americans
in the desire to bring peace and security to that troubled region. Industrious
and determined, they have helped give us a more profound understanding of
the rights and responsibilities we have as citizens of a free and prosperous
Nation.

In recognition of the contributions of Arab-Americans, the Congress, by
House Joint Resolution 241, has designated October 25, 1989, as "National
Arab-American Day" and has authorized and requested the President to
issue a proclamation in observance of this day.

NOW, THEREFORE, I, GEORGE BUSH, President of the United States
of America, do hereby proclaim October 25, 1989, as National Arab-
American Day. I call upon the people of the United States to observe this
day with appropriate ceremonies and activities. . . . [signed by George Bush]

Congress passed Joint Resolution 241 in support of National Arab-American Day,
101st Cong., 1st sess., October 25, 1989:

Whereas the rich history and tradition of the Arab culture has contributed
to western civilization in many fields, including science, medicine, geography, and architecture;

Whereas the contributions made by Arab culture transcend geographic,
political, and religious classification;

Whereas Arab-Americans have made, and continue to make, important
contributions to the economic prosperity and cultural life of our Nation
since October 1854, when the first recorded Arab immigrant arrived in the
United States;

Whereas the term "Arab" represents a people who are followers of the
3 great monotheistic religions and are bound by the common language of
Arabic;

Whereas Arabs are of one origin, but are citizens of many countries;

Whereas Arab-Americans have worked hard since their arrival and have
been productive United States citizens; and

Whereas the people of the United States should always remember that
there are almost 3,000,000 Arab-Americans who are a part of the mosaic
of cultures of the United States: Now, therefore, be it

*Resolved by the Senate and House of Representatives of the United States
of America in Congress assembled,* That October 25, 1989, is designated
as "National Arab-American Day." The President is authorized and requested to issue a proclamation calling on the people of the United States
to recognize this day by becoming aware of the rich cultural traditions
of Arab-Americans and by participating in appropriate ceremonies and
activities. . . .

A Republican congressman and a cosponsor of the resolution wrote to a
constituent:

It can easily be argued that the history and cultures of Europe which led to the founding and creation of the United States owe much to Arab culture. Without the contributions of Arab historians, mathematicians, physicians, astronomers, poets and other craftsmen and artisans the Dark Ages would have ruled Europe for perhaps hundreds of years longer. Arab-Americans should take equal pride in their achievements and contributions to our nation and the world. House Joint Resolution 241 is a positive step in this direction.

11. Hans Leuenberger, *Turkey,* ed. Hanns Reich (U.S.A.: Hill and Wang, 1971), 18–19.

> 1923 Treaty of Lausanne. The Allies left Istanbul. The Republic of Turkey was proclaimed, with Ankara as the capital, and Kemal Pasha (Ataturk, "Father of Modern Turkey") was elected president.

12. Hassan S. Haddad and Basheer K. Nijim, eds., *The Arab World: A Handbook,* AAUG (Association of Arab-American University Graduates) Monograph Series, no. 9 (Wilmette, Ill.: Medina Press, 1978), 16.

13. Albert Hourani, *A History of the Arab Peoples* (New York: Warner Books, 1992), 215–16. See also William Yale, *The Near East* (Ann Arbor: University of Michigan Press, 1958), 19, 25. Hourani, *A History of the Arab Peoples:*

> The Ottoman Empire was one of the largest political structures that the western part of the world had known since the Roman Empire disintegrated: it ruled eastern Europe, western Asia and most of the Maghrib, and held together lands with very different political traditions, many ethnic groups—Greeks, Serbs, Bulgarians, Romanians, Armenians, Turks and Arabs—and various religious communities—Sunni and Shi'i Muslims, Christians of all the historic Churches, and Jews. It maintained its rule over most of them for 400 years or so, and over some of them for as many as 600. (215–16)

Yale, *The Near East:*

> When the Ottoman Turks became the rulers of a vast empire in Europe, Asia, and Africa, many of the older institutions were greatly modified, while some of those of the Byzantine Empire were adopted. Culturally the heritage of the Ottomans was Islamic, Persian, and Arab; politically, it was Moslem [Muslim] and Byzantine. (19)

Yale further states:

> The ruling classes in the Ottoman Empire were not exclusively Turkish by race, they included Arabs, Kurds, Egyptians, and Albanians, Bulgarians, Slavs, and other Balkan peoples who had accepted Islam. (25)

14. William Yale, *The Near East,* 19–20.

15. Adele L. Younis, "Salem and the Early Syrian Venture," *The Arab World* (January 1967): 10–12.

16. Louise Seymour Houghton, "Syrians in the United States," *The Survey: A Journal of Constructive Philanthropy* 26 (July 1, 1911): 483.

17. Younis, *Arabs in America,* ed. Kayal, 1995, 150.

18. Ibid., 152.

19. Younis, "The Arabs Who Followed Columbus," Part 2, *The Arab World* (August 1966): 15.

20. Ibid., 15.

21. Alixa Naff, *Becoming American: The Early Arab*, 86. Dominique Chevallier, *Western Development and Eastern Crises,* cited in Polk and Chambers, *Beginnings of Modernization,* 220, 29; Philip K. Hitti, *Lebanon in History* (New York: MacMillan, 1967), 447; and M. M. Maloof, "From Beersheba to Berlin, via Boston: The Little Known Zeal of New England Syrians in Flocking to the Colors," *Boston Evening Transcript* (one of the prestigious Boston newspapers during its period of 1830–1920s), August 22, 1917, pt. 2, 5.

Chevallier, *Western Development and Eastern Crises:*

> That persecution in Syria drove Christians from their homeland before World War I was a myth found mainly in the post–World War II studies on Arabs in America—a myth that tended to distort the immigration motivations as well as the social and political realities of late nineteenth century Syria. In the words of Dominique Chevallier, the noted French historian of Syria: "From 1861 to 1914 the various provinces lived through a period of relative calm which contrasted with the extreme stress of the preceding period. This fact should be brought out, for it has often been masked from foreign observers by their remembrance of the 1860 massacres, Egyptian affairs, the Balkan turmoils, the Armenian massacres, the difficulties of the Turkish government, the reinforcement of police supervision at the time of Abd Al Hamid, and the revolution of 1908."

Hitti, *Lebanon in History:*

> The people of peaceful Mount Lebanon enjoyed a period of cultural flourish and economic prosperity and achieved a state of security and stability unattained by any Ottoman province, European or Asian. . . . It came to be acknowledged as the best governed, the most prosperous, peaceful and contented country in the Near East. (447)

Maloof, "From Beersheba to Berlin, via Boston":

> The Syrian is not a conspicuous member of our body politics. Coming from a country where even the poorest man is a landowner, he is naturally conservative.

22. Board of Trade, *Worcester: The City of Varied Industries*, Blanchard Press, 1909, cover page.

23. Official embossed seal of City of Worcester.

24. *Manual for General Court, 1881, State of Massachusetts,* 181.

25. *Manual for General Court, 1923-24, State of Massachusetts,* 26.

26. Leila Meo, "Social Justice and Political Equality: Key To Lebanon's Future," *Arab World Issues* (booklet), Association of Arab-American University Graduates, 1975, 2–3.

> [I]n the 19th century, as the decline of the [Ottoman] Empire accelerated, the European powers, with Britain and France in the lead, competed for control of its Arab provinces. . . . competition for control was pursued

through the "protection" that each European power extended to a specific religious community. Thus France served its interests by assuming the role of protector of the Maronite and Catholic communities; Czarist Russia by being protector of the Greek Orthodox [Eastern Orthodox] community, and Britain the protector of the Druze community. . . .

In the wake of World War 1, Britain and France, in pursuit of their imperial ambitions divided up the Arab East into their respective spheres of influence, despite earlier promises for Arab independence and unity. And each power subdivided its own sphere into smaller entities in accordance with the principle of "divide and rule." (2–3)

Out of its share of Syria, France created Greater Lebanon by attaching to the central Lebanese mountain range the coastal plains with their cities of Tripoli, Beirut, Saida, and Tyre, the fertile and expansive plain of the Biqa [Beqaa] and Jabal Amil in the south.

To the south, Britain subdivided its share of Syria into the two separate administrative units of Palestine and Transjordan. (2–3)

27. Younis, *Arabs in America,* ed. Kayal, 218.

2. Migration

1. Philip Forzley, ed., *An Autobiography of Bashara Kalil Forzley: In Commemoration of Fifty Years of Marriage* (Worcester, Mass.: Self-published, 1958), 7.

2. Thomas J. Archdeacon, *Becoming American: An Ethnic History* (New York: Free Press, 1983), 113.

3. Ibid., 117.

4. There is another al-Muhayditha in Lebanon, located next to Bikfaya. Bikfaya is about twenty miles northeast of Beirut. This al-Muhayditha is the birthplace of Iliya Abu Madi, who is best remembered for his poems in which he celebrates life, its happiness, and his belief that faith in the brotherhood of all peoples is basic to full and abundant life. Along with Kahlil Gibran and other literati, Abu Madi founded *al-Rabita al-Qalamiyya* (The Pen Association) of New York.

5. "Ellis Island Immigration Museum Directory," *National Park Service* (Liberty Island, N.Y.: U.S. Department of the Interior, 1992).

6. *Autobiography Forzley,* 8.

7. Board of Trade, *Columbian Year,* 1893, 83.

Graton & Knight Manufacturing Co. . . . commenced the manufacture of Leather Belting upon a limited scale in 1851. In 1868, to secure better and more uniform leather, it erected one of the most thoroughly equipped tanneries in the country for the production of a purely oak tannage, from which the Belting is made suitable in quality for electric, cotton, and oil plants, and in all the diversities of the application of power through belt transmission. The company was incorporated in 1872.

8. "Ellis Island: Gateway to America" booklet, *National Park Service* (Liberty Island, N.Y.: U.S. Department of the Interior, 1992), back cover.

9. George Frisbie Hoar, "President Roosevelt and the Syrian Children," ch. 31, *Autobiography of Seventy Years,* 2 vols. (New York: C. Scribner's Sons, 1903).

10. Edward A. Steiner, *On the Trail of the Immigrant* (New York: Copyright by Fleming H. Revell Company, 1906, Arno Press and the New York Times, 1969), 82–85.

11. Ibid., 85–86.

12. Ibid., 86.

13. Edmund G. Haddad, "Our Syrian and Lebanese Catholics Have Written a Proud Record in Diocese," *Catholic Free Press* (Worcester), February 25, 1955, 2.

> The late Ernest N. [Namer] Raad came here from Beirut, Syria in 1901. A year later, his wife and two children, a boy and girl, followed with intentions of making their home here.

14. "Stay Is Short, But President Has Time to Play with the Children," *Worcester Telegram,* September 2, 1902, front, 2.

15. Edmund G. Haddad, "Our Syrian and Lebanese Catholics," 2. A letter over the signature of Senator Hoar on Senate Judiciary Committee letterhead addressed to Joseph John George acknowledged the letters of appreciation and stated:

> But I ought to say your chief debt is to President Roosevelt. When every other appeal failed, a direct statement of the case to him brought an immediate response from his clear head and kind heart, and the children in whose behalf all efforts of mine would otherwise have been futile, were released in an hour as soon as he heard of it.

16. Younis, *Arabs in America,* ed. Kayal, 181.

17. About 1885 or earlier was the consensus among those interviewed who were knowledgeable of the history and founding of the Syrian Orthodox Church of Worcester. See Alixa Naff, *Becoming American: The Early Arab Immigrant Experience,* 143–44: "The Right Reverend Raphael Hawaweeny, the first Syrian Orthodox bishop in America, counted his congregation in 1898. . . . and Worcester, Massachusetts, [ranked] third with 152."

18. *Orthodox America, 1794–1976,* 337–38. "Syro-Arabian Mission" included seven churches, one of which was "Worcester, Mass.—St. George, J. Hussan [Michael M. Husson]" as shown on the "Parish Listing of the Orthodox Diocese of North America and Aleutian Islands, 1906."

19. Ibid., 127.

20. Ibid., 85.

21. Ibid., 94.

22. Kahlil Gibran, *The Wisdom of Gibran: Aphorisms and Maxims,* ed. Joseph Sheban (New York: Philosophical Library, 1966), p. B, Brotherhood. See Kahlil Gibran, *A Second Treasury of Kahlil Gibran: The Words of the Master,* trans. Anthony R. Ferris (New York: Citadel Press Book, published by Carol Publishing Group, 1990, copyright 1962, Citadel Press), 69.

> Gibran, an immigrant boy from Bchari (Besharri), Lebanon, lived in Boston and was a major figure in both lands. One of Gibran's books, *The Prophet* (published 1923 by Knopf), has been translated into more than twenty languages, and 6,000,000 copies had been sold by 1975, according to Alice Payne Hackett and James Henry Burke, *Eighty Years of Best Sellers: 1805–1975* (New York, London: R. R. Bowker, 1977), 11, 22, 53. It continues to be a popular book.

See *Arab Digest* (January 1973): 25.

The spelling of Khalil (Arabic) Gibran was changed to "Kahlil" at the instigation of his teacher of English at the Boston high school he attended between 1895 and 1897.

23. *Our Lady of Perpetual Help Melkite Catholic Church, 1923–1988, 1963–1988,* Worcester, Mass., September 17, 1988, 11–12. (The anniversary dates represent sixty-five years since the church's founding and twenty-five years since the building and dedication of the present church building.)

> When they [Melkites] first arrived ["began coming to Worcester about 1890"], they attended the nearby Latin rite churches and St. George Orthodox Church. . . . The Syrian Orthodox Community was our constant friend. Some of the founders of the church in 1923 were Ernest Aneese Abdelnour, Max Milhem Abdelnour, Antoon Arraje, Salim Attaya, Michael Debs, Amen Esper, George Esper, George Lutfy Esper, Salem Esper, Samuel Esper, Elias F. Haddad, Max Haddad, Peter Haddad, Elias Halal, Fred Kalil, Elias Karam, Jacob T. Lian, Elias Najemy, Kamel Najemy, Charles Nejaimy, Shaker Sayegh (Syiek), Gabriel Shakour, Charles E. Shagoury, Elias Skaff, Abraham Thomas, David Thomas, Shaker N. Trabulsi.

24. "Our Greek Community," *Worcester Sunday Telegram,* March 29, 1981, section F, 10: "The first Greek arrivals held services in the Syrian Orthodox Church on Wall Street. In 1915, Greek Orthodox services were held in a hall at 69 Grafton St."

Nicholas Gage, in *A Place For Us* (Boston: Houghton Mifflin, 1989), 45, indicates that "Greeks worshiped in Eastern Orthodox Church at . . . Wall Street." Dean M. Moschos writes in "Greeks," *Worcester Massachusetts Celebration 1722–1972,* ed. James E. Mooney (Worcester, Mass: Commonwealth Press, 1972), 112–13, that "until 1914 our people [Greeks] had their baptisms, weddings, etc., performed at the sister Saint George's Syrian Orthodox Church."

25. *Orthodox America, 1794–1976,* 194.

26. Elaine C. Hagopian and Ann Paden, *The Arab-Americans: Studies in Assimilation,* AAUG (Arab-American University Graduates, Inc.) Monograph Series, no. 1 (Wilmette, Ill.: Medina University Press International, 1969), 77.

27. *Autobiography of Eli Abraham Busada, Sr., Washington, D.C.* (Washington, D.C.: Self-published, 1983), 17.

28. "Fife, Drum and Bugle Corps of Yesteryears," *Grafton News,* n.d. (about 1959).

29. Date appeared on raised seal of "The Myrra Bearing Women Society, Founded 1919, St. George Orthodox Church of Worcester."

3. Multicultural and Multireligious Neighborhoods

1. *Worcester Directory, 1907* (Worcester, Mass.: Drew Allis Company), 34. Fifteen "HILLS" listed, including Oak Hill and Chandler Hill:

> Oak Hill—Between Bloomingdale road [now Franklin Street] and Plantation street. Height 700 feet.
> Chandler Hill—South of [and included] Belmont street. Height 721 feet.

2. *Atlas, City of Worcester, 1870, Portions of Wards 3 and 4* (Springfield, Mass.: Richards Map Co., 1870), 19.

3. Albert B. Southwick, *More Once-Told Tales of Worcester County* (Worcester, Mass.: Databooks, a division of Tatnuck Bookseller and Sons, Inc., 1994), 25.

4. Board of Trade, *Columbian Year,* 1893.

5. Franklin P. Rice, *Dictionary of Worcester (Mass.) and Its Vicinity* (Worcester, Mass: F. S. Blanchard, 1893), 30, "Dungarvan or Dutch Hill is a particular locality above Bloomingdale Road long known in political circles."

6. Kingsley and Knab, *Picturesque Worcester,* 1895, 84–85.

> The earliest accurate records of Catholicity, in Worcester, tell of Roman Catholics coming to this vicinity, in 1826, when Worcester was a village with something over three thousand inhabitants. . . . This labor [for the building of the Blackstone Canal] was to be principally drawn from the many emigrants who flocked to these shores. Among them were many Irish Catholics. . . . Just when the first Catholic came to Worcester or what his name was, is not definitely known. . . . There is found in French Canadian annals, by Chandonnet, a statement that some French-Canadians located here in 1824, others came in 1825, and others in 1826. This record is found in no other place and it may be presumed to be correct. . . . When appointed pastor [Rev. Matthew W. Gibson, ordained in 1841] of St. John's, Worcester, he found a congregation of seven hundred Irish Catholics and six hundred French Canadian Catholics.

7. Rice, *Dictionary of Worcester,* 1893, 77.

8. Dr. John McCoy (pastor of Saint Ann Church, Eastern Avenue, Worcester), *History of Catholicism in the Diocese of Springfield,* 1900. Courtesy of Catholic Free Press, Worcester, Mass.

9. Compiled by Lois R. Yeulenski, *The Old Photographs Series, Worcester* (Augusta, Me.: Alan Sutton, 1994), 96. Distributed by Berwick Publishing, Inc., Dover, New Hampshire. Photograph of Saint Ann Church: brick twin-tower, Gothic structure that seated 1,150 people, built 1884–85.

10. Worcester Registry of Deeds, Book 1635, 229–31. Paul J. Henry et al. to Akil E. Haddad, deed dated July 17, 1899.

11. Worcester Registry of Deeds, Book 1705, 332. Akil E. Haddad to Shaker Saayeke and Naahim Saayeke, deed dated January 21, 1902.

12. Kingsley and Knab, *Picturesque Worcester,* 1895, 91. Illustration: "Norfolk Street." Center, *el-saha,* and left, "the flatiron" building at intersection of Wall and Norfolk Streets.

13. *Worcester House Directory, 1892,* 283.

14. *Worcester House Directory, 1902,* 57. Thomas J. Gannon Bakery, 63 Bloomingdale Road.

15. Amy Zuckerman, *Worcester Magazine,* August 21, 1991, n.p. Illustration: Center background is "the Barracks." Left foreground, Paul Aboody, proprietor of El Morocco Restaurant.

16. *Worcester Directory, 1900,* 51.

17. *Worcester House Directory, 1896,* 294.

18. *Worcester House Directory, 1894,* 48.

19. Sister Marie-Michel-Archange, p.f.m., *By This Sign You Will Live: History of the Congregation of the Little Franciscans of Mary, 1889–1955.* Translated from the French by Sister Marie-Octave, p.f.m. and Betty Dunn, Baie-Saint-Paul-Quebec,

1955 (Worcester, Mass.: Heffernan Press, 1964), 80. Courtesy of Saint Francis Home, Worcester, Mass.

In 1887 the building served as a chapel for the French Canadians of St. Joseph Church and later was purchased by the Eastern Orthodox Arab Americans. Illustration: Titled "Saint Joseph Chapel," was topped with Oriental bulbous lantern.

20. *Worcester Directory, 1900*, 232.

21. Worcester Registry of Deeds, Book 1849, 343–44. "Badaway Abodeely and Nassar Abodeely, mother and son, to Trustees for St. George, Orthodox Society (Syrian)," deed dated March 11, 1907.

22. Edmund G. Haddad, "Our Syrian and Lebanese Catholics," February 25, 1955, 22. Illustration: 57-59 Norfolk Street.

23. Ibid, 22.

24. Ibid., 22.

25. Marie-Michel-Archange, *By This Sign*, 80. Illustration: 80 Wall Street, "The Rondeau Homestead," later purchased by Hajj Boosahda.

26. *Golden Jubilee 1956 of St. George Syrian Antiochian Orthodox Church* commemorative book. Its front cover has replica of rectory and church with first- and second-floor wraparound porches, in relief on gold leaf–stamped, imitation leather–bound.

27. Elliott B. Knowlton, ed., *Worcester's Best: A Guide to the City's Architectural Heritage* (Worcester, Mass.: Commonwealth Press, 1984), 58. Copyright by Worcester Heritage Preservation Society, now Preservation Worcester.

4. Work

1. Houghton, "Syrians in the United States," *The Survey*, August 5, 1911, 647–48.

2. Adam & George Company, established 1906. Closed in 1969, by which time the business was a clothing manufacturer and general manager was Lillian G. Russell, first-American-born-generation daughter of Patrick (Bahkous) J. and Angelina (Adams) George.

3. Houghton, "Syrians in the United States," *The Survey*, August 5, 1911, 660.

4. Philip Forzley, ed., *Autobiography Forzley*, 8.

5. Thomas F. George, *Autobiography of Thomas Ferris George* (Worcester, unpublished manuscript, 1944), 10–13.

6. Salloom and Sons, Trumbull Street, established about 1912, forerunner of Eddy's, Stafford Street, clothing stores. Eddy's expanded to Eddy's of Park Avenue. According to custom, when the son Edward "Eddy" retired, his oldest child, a daughter, became the head of the successful establishment. Donna A. S. was a college graduate and a doctor of jurisprudence. The store closed in 1994.

7. *Worcester Telegram*, March 6, 1899, 1 and 5.

8. Jeff McLaughlin, "Remembering One of Labor's Finest Hours, Bread and Roses. Lawrence Festival Commemorates One of Labor's Finest Hours," *Boston Globe*, September 4, 1987, 45–46.

9. Evelyn A. Menconi, ed., "The Bread and Roses Strike: Syrian Connections," *William G. Abdalah Memorial Library Newsletter*, West Roxbury, Mass., January 1988. Materials for research provided by Eartha Dengler of the Immigrant City Archives, Lawrence, Mass.

10. *Worcester Directory, 1899,* 222.

11. *Worcester House Directory, 1900,* "Business Directory—A business directory of selected names of prominent business houses of Worcester," 551–52.

12. *Worcester Directory, 1907,* "Business Directory," 772. Following were Arab American businesses listed under "Dry Goods":

Aboudeely David, 88 Wall

Adams Peter, 80 Shrewsbury

Caneb [Kaneb] Mary N. & Son, 32½ Norfolk

Cattar Joseph M., 49 E. Worcester

Debs George D., 52 Wall

Debs S. & Bros., 37 Norfolk

George Simon & Co., 317 Grafton and 72 Wall

Haddad Akil E., 96 Wall

Trabulsy Joseph N., 62 Wall

Worcester Dry Goods & Wrapper Co., 192 Front [Aboumrad Abdelnour and Aboumrad Sahag, M. K. Maykel]

13. Ibid., 748–840. Barbers. Abraham Ilis [Elias], 51½ Norfolk, Massey [Massad] David, 82 Grafton, Rahaim Thomas, 52A Grafton Street, Mustafa Hisem, 87 Summer. Boot and Shoe Makers and Repairers. Abraham Lian, 14 Norfolk. Clergymen. Karum Maletious, (Greek Cath.) [Eastern Orthodox] r. [rear] 100 Wall. Confectionery Retail. Forzly Solomon Mrs., 86 Wall, Massad Anthony, 121 Main, Mohammed Hussan, 67 Summer. Dressmakers. Sednowa Julia S., 37 Norfolk.

Elastic Goods. Agbay, Samuel J., r. 20 Larkin.

Grocers Retail. Abousamra S. A., 32 Norfolk.

Restaurants. Saloom [Salloum] David G., 51½ Norfolk.

Suspenders Manufs. Haddad Thomas, rear 100 Wall.

Fruit Retail. Rachad [Rachid] Salim, 30 Norfolk. Before 1915, George Debs and Son moved their full line of dry goods, boots, shoes, and rubbers to 337-341 Grafton Street.

Mitchell K. Maykel, Maykel Auto Co., moved to 751-753-755 Main Street and sold Maxwell and Chrysler motor cars.

Corey's Filling Station moved to the Lincoln Park area and sold "Vicking Cords, Genuine Ford Parts, and Automobile Accessories."

S. M. Kouri and S. M. Souda, co-owners of "Economy Curtain Co., Manufacturers Of Ruffled and Flat Curtains and Novelties Wholesale and Retail," moved to 194 Front Street.

Francis Massad, 121 Main Street.

14. Salloum A. Mokarzel and H. F. Otash, *The Syrian Business Directory, 1908–1909* (New York: Al-Hoda Press, 1908), 135–37. See the section titled "Massachusetts, Worcester": Dry Goods & Notions. A. Haddad, Wall St., George Hykel, Issac & George, 40 Grafton, Moses Eid Dowaliby, 21 Hill, Peter Abdou, 32 Norfolk, Simon George.

Groceries. Alex Kalil, 1 Bernard Court, John M. Ghiz, 100 Wall, John Metri [Ghiz], Wall St., Joseph Tabet [Thabet], 96 Norfolk, M. Tabet [Thabet], 96 Norfolk, Soleem AbouRashad [Salim Rachid], 23 Norfolk.

Pool & Billiards. Elias Khoury, Norfolk St., F. Khoury, 2 Bernard Court, Shaheen D. Hussan, 62 Norfolk.

Real Estate. Abraham Sematt [Smart], 154 Bloomingdale Road, Kalil Jabour, 35 Norfolk.

Miscellaneous: Shoemaker. Abraham Lian, 57 Norfolk.

Baker. George T. Kalify, 12 Bloomingdale Court.

Drugs [Drug Store]. Joseph Rahaim, 46 Coral.

Cafe. M. Nassif, 42 Norfolk.

Confectionery. B. Forzly, Wall St.

15. John G. Moses, *The Lebanese in America* (Utica, N.Y.: Self-published, 1987), 36.

> Worcester, Massachusetts. [1908] Six of the twenty Lebanese merchants in Worcester were dry goods storekeepers while four were grocers. Three operated billiard parlors, two were in real estate and a miscellaneous group of five included a baker, a shoemaker, a confectioner, a cafe operator and a druggist.

16. Houghton, "Syrians in the United States," *The Survey*, August 5, 1911, 655.

17. Charles Nutt, *History of Worcester and Its People*, 4 vols. (New York: Lewis Historical Publishing Co., 1919), 1:370–81.

18. U.S. Patent 1,510,216, Commercial bleaching powder. C. A. Gammal. Gammal Chemical Company, Worcester, Mass., 1924. Also, he was awarded patents while working at the research laboratory of the Mathieson Alkali Works Inc., Niagara Falls, New York: U.S. Patent, Determination of free chlorine and hypochlorous acid in concentrated salt solutions, M. C. Taylor and C. A. Gammal, 1922; U.S. Patent 1,481,039, Hypochlorites, M. C. Taylor, C. A. Gammal, and R. E. Gegenheimer, 1924. During World War II American soldiers used this disinfectant product to purify water and now it is marketed worldwide as HTH, a swimming pool disinfectant. U.S. Patent, Hypochlorous acid and the alkyl hypochlorites, M. C. Taylor, R. B. MacMullin, and C. A. Gammal, 1925.

19. Swydan's multifarious career included "Swydan & Sons, Importers and Exporters, 80 Wall St., Worcester, Mass., Commission Agency, Representatives of Russian and American Firms," which ended with the collapse of the Russian government and the Bolshevik revolution. His business associate was a former secretary of the Worcester Chamber of Commerce.

Swydan led "The Syrian Group" participation at a City of Worcester–sponsored summer pageant titled "Pilgrims to America." It included "11 racial groups . . . only those races which had over 1000 representatives in the city." The theme was described by Nancy Burncoat of the *Sunday Telegram*, June 12, 1921, sec. 3. The first part of the pageant was about the pilgrim who came from England as the pioneer, and the last part was of the pilgrims of modern times who helped to make the country what it is "and how indebted we are to these more recent pilgrims. For instance the Syrians invented our alphabet, and gave us our laws of chemistry, and discovered how to make steel. One of the girls in their group brings on a sword of Damascus steel, which was the first steel ever made. Another girl bears a compass and another a clock, both Syrian inventions. The costumes of this episode are heirlooms, brought over here from the Orient." Some members of the Syrian group included Anna Dowd, Naphe David (later Bayrouty), Margaret Deeb, and Mary Dowd.

In 1933 Swydan was chairman of a Mardi Gras celebration for the benefit of the Syrian Antiochian St. George Orthodox Church of Worcester held at Birch Rest, Grafton, Massachusetts. The program booklet was in Arabic and English.

Among Swydan's collection of books was one published in 1450, and when viewed in 1935 was described by Isabel R. A. Currier in the Sunday *Worcester Telegram,* March 24, 1935, page 8, as a "compendium of Arabian poets, and it was handwritten in . . . and the vellum [pages] show little deterioration beyond a faint yellowing."

Swydan received a letter in 1942 from the Selective Service System state director headquartered in Boston. The director had accepted an appointment as colonel of infantry, Army of the United States and "[d]uring this past year and a half, I have had the pleasure and privilege of serving with you [Swydan] in the Selective Service System of Mass. and because of your efforts that System has made an excellent record. . . . I hope you will accept this letter as an expression of my sincere appreciation for the splendid cooperation which you have given me as State Director, and the excellent service you are rendering to the Selective Service System."

Swydan died the following year at age 58. Ecumenism continued at his funeral—officiating were Metropolitan Antony Bashir; Metropolitan Benjamin, head of the Russian Orthodox Church in North and South Americas and Aleutian Islands; Rev. Paul Hicha, pastor of the Russian Orthodox Church, Worcester; Rev. Constantine Abou-Adal of St. George Orthodox Church, and Rev. Charles Fischer of First Presbyterian Church.

20. In a taped oral interview by the author, Lillian George Shoucair stated:

> Said Shoucair met Najeeb Arbeely, an interpreter, at the immigration station (New York) and a son of Dr. Joseph Arbeeely, a professor, who brought his family to the U.S. in 1878. In response to Najeeb Arbeely's question as to what type work Shoucair did and what he hoped to do in America, the response was that he was a writer and wanted to continue writing. Najeeb Arbeely offered that he and his brother A. J. Arbeely could set him up in the newspaper business. The Arbeelys rented the garret at 108 Broad Street, New York City, paid for the printing press and put Shoucair in business and thereby were the proprietors (owners), and Said Shoucair was the founder, publisher, and editor. The office letterhead read: "Office of *Kawkab America,* 'Star of America.' The Only Oriental Tri-Weekly Independent Paper in America." On Shoucair's thirty-second birthday, he was presented a Waltham pocket watch engraved in Arabic which translated to: "1894 Presented in remembrance of your birthday. Ibraham [A. J. Arbeely] and Najeeb Arbeely." Archimandrite Raphael Hawaweeny at Brooklyn, N.Y., married Said J. Shoucair and Emilia A. Jabbour in 1903. Later Shoucair purchased *Kawkab America* and around 1907 sold the newspaper and moved with his family to Scranton, Pennsylvania. [See "In Celebration of the Publication of the First Issue," *al-Jamilah* (New York) vol. 5, 75–76, July 15,

1906. Article referred to Said Shoucair (al-Sharqiyah) as owner of *Kawkab America* in 1906.]

According to Michael W. Suleiman, in the November 14, 1989, issue of *K-State News,* Kansas State University, Manhattan, Kansas: The Kansas Historical Society of Topeka has the 1892–96 issues of the first U.S. newspaper printed in Arabic, *Kawcab* [also spelled Kawkab] *America,* "which began in 1892 and lasted seventeen years."

21. New England Historical Genealogical Society, Boston, *Index to the Probate Records of the County of Worcester, Mass., from July 1, 1897, to January 1, 1910.* Residence, 1908, Abufaris, Assad K., and Michael Abufaris, Rio Janeiro, Brazil. Nature: Administration/Business, Case Nos. 43180, and 107820, respectively.

22. Promissory note secured by mortgage recorded in Worcester District Registry. Bank No. 6757. Property situated at 314 Grafton Street:

$22,000. Worcester, Mass. November 19, 1925. On Demand for Value Received, We, Abraham Boosahda and Alexandra Boosahda, jointly and severally promise to pay to the Worcester County Institution for Savings, on order, at the office of said Institution in Worcester, twenty-two thousand (22,000) Dollars with interest at the rate of six (6) percent per annum, payable semi-annually.

5. Tradition, Education, and Culture

1. *Autobiography, Thomas F. George,* 14.
2. Marriage license, Bureau County, State of Illinois, Spring Valley, February 10, 1914.
3. Marriage record, Commonwealth of Massachusetts, City of Worcester, November 4, 1916.
4. Marriage record, Commonwealth of Massachusetts, City of Worcester, November 4, 1897.
5. "All the Hill at a Wedding—Dungarven Turns Out for Syrian Church Ceremony," *Worcester Daily Telegram,* September 1, 1899, n.p.
6. "Assyrian [Syrian] Wedding. . . ," *Worcester Daily Telegram,* April 16, 1901, 7.
7. Philip Forzley, ed., *Autobiography Forzley,* 1958, 13.
8. Abraham Mitrie Rihbany, *The Syrian Christ* (Boston and New York: Houghton Mifflin Company, 1916), 317–18.
9. Ibid., 323.
10. *Salah-El-Deen Yusif ibn Ayyub* program book, 1924, n.p.
11. Edmund G. Haddad, "Our Syrian and Lebanese Catholics," 22.
12. Suheil B. Bushri, "Shakespeare in the Arab World," *Middle East Forum* (Beirut: Alumni Association of the American University of Beirut, spring 1971), 55.
13. St. George Syrian Antiochian Orthodox Church, *Golden Jubilee, 1956* (Worcester, Mass.), n.p.

6. Americanization

1. Alixa Naff, *Becoming American: The Early Arab Immigrant Experience,* 253. See also Reed Ueda's "Naturalization and Citizenship," *Harvard Encyclopedia of American Ethnic Groups,* 740–41.

2. Ibid., 252, 255. See also Niles Carpenter, *Immigrants and Their Children* (New York: Arno Press and the New York Times, 1969), 263; Joseph W. Ferris, "Syrian Naturalization Question in the United States: Certain Legal Aspects of Our Naturalization Laws," pts. 1 and 2, *Syrian World* (February/March 1928).

3. Margaret Haddad George, ed., *Nabeha: Remembrances: An Autobiography* (from Nabeha's handwritten manuscript) (Worcester, Mass.: Self-published, 1993), 157–59.

4. "Archpriest Notes 90th Birthday," *Worcester Sunday Telegram*, December 25, 1966, 4A.

5. M. M. Maloof, "From Beersheba to Berlin, via Boston: The Little Known Zeal of New England Syrians in Flocking to the Colors," *Boston Evening Transcript*, August 22, 1917, pt. 2, 5.

6. *Autobiography Busada*, 24.

7. Ibid., 25.

8. Ibid., 26.

9. Ibid., 29.

10. St. George Syrian Antiochian Orthodox Church, *Golden Jubilee, 1956* (Worcester, Mass.).

> "To the men of St. George Syrian Orthodox Church who gave their lives in the service of their country." Michael Katrina's name was included on page devoted to veterans of the World Wars.

11. "Congressman Their Guest—Hon. Samuel E. Winslow Addresses 200 Members of Syrian Brotherhood Society—Gathering Planned as a Testimonial," *Worcester Daily Telegram*, October 4, 1920, n.p.

> "Loyal to America" . . . President Peters [Sroor] and Secretary Swydan [Shokri] referred to names of "Syrian-American Worcester boys who gave their lives for the country."

Mike Sednawi's name was included on the list.

12. *Autobiography, Thomas F. George*, 21.

13. *Worcester Sunday Telegram*, August 13, 1950, Obituaries.

14. Bruce Condo, *See Lebanon: Over 100 Selected Trips with History and Pictures* (Beirut: Harb Bijjani Press, 1960). Dedicated to "Colonel and Mrs. William A. Eddy of Beirut and Sidon, the most enthusiastic patrons of these trips through Lebanon, in appreciation of their assistance and encouragement, this book is respectfully dedicated."

15. *Worcester Telegram*, n.d., 1932. "Miss Lantz Going To Palestine, Will Serve as Teacher in School for Girls." Also see *Nabeha: Remembrances*, 233–34.

16. *Nabeha: Remembrances*, 173.

17. "Visit Newspapers and WTAG Station. Callers Constitute Group from Friendly House," *Worcester Telegram*, n.d., about 1940.

18. *Worcester Telegram*, n.d. 1932. "League Marks Syrian Night."

19. "Friendly House Report of Finance Committee Special Meeting, October 6, 1937," 12 pages, stated that on May 3, 1937, recognition was given Russell Talbot in appreciation of his five years of volunteer service as scoutmaster at Friendly House.

20. *Famous First Facts*, 5th ed. (New York: H. W. Wilson Co., 1997), 101.

21. Nutt, *History of Worcester and Its People*, vol. 2, 961.

22. *Cathedral News* magazine, St. George Orthodox Cathedral, June 1974, 7.

23. *Nabeha: Remembrances*, 169.

24. Franklin P. Rice, *Dictionary of Worcester (Mass.) and Its Vicinity* (Worcester, Mass.: F. S. Blanchard, 1893), 92.

25. *Some Descendants of Diggory Sargent of Boston and Worcester, Mass.* (Boston: New England Historic Genealogical Society, 1904), 378.

26. Lois R. Yeulenski, *The Old Photographs Series, Worcester* (Augusta, Me.: Alan Sutton, 1994), 79.

27. *Federation Herald*, published by Syrian and Lebanese Federation of the Eastern States, September 25, 1948, 12.

28. *Worcester Telegram*, October 7, 1945, n.p.

29. *Evening Gazette* (Worcester), November 19, 1947, n.p.

30. *Federation Herald*, September 25, 1948, 2.

31. Ibid., 1.

32. *National Herald* ("Official Organ of the National Association of Federations of Syrian and Lebanese American Clubs") 1, no. 7 (June 1956), editorial.

33. *Worcester Daily Telegram*, September 27, 1958, 1, 11.

34. *Evening Gazette*, September 27, 1958, 16.

35. *Worcester Sunday Telegram*, October 28, 1973, n.p. "Festival Casbah" party was held October 27, 1973. See *Worcester Sunday Telegram*, November 4, 1973, 1D, 8D.

36. Ralph Mitchell, Bill Ghiz, George Abodeely, Jimmy Arraj, Mitch Abraham. Others included Jimmy Esper, Fred Assad, Fred Swydan, Ed Ghiz, Ken Kaneb, George Rizkalla, Russell Samara.

37. Leo Dowd.

38. "Morris Plan Banking Co., Low Cost Financing When You Buy A Car."

39. Jimmy Esper, George Abodeely, Mitch Abraham, Bill Ghiz, or Mike Kouri.

40. George Abodeely, Ralph Mitchell, Fred Aramony.

41. Mary S., Marion B., Adele K., Adele M., Delia M., Ann F., Louise S., Sally A.

42. Raymond Morin, *The Worcester Music Festival: Its Background and History, 1858–1976* (Worcester, Mass.: Worcester County Music Association, 1976), 210. Michael C. Dowd elected vice president, 1967.

43. *The Gazette* (Worcester), May 2, 1918, n.p.

44. "Congressman Their Guest—Hon. Samuel E. Winslow . . . ," *Worcester Daily Telegram*, October 4, 1920, n.p.

45. *Sunday Telegram*, September 7, 1947, n.p.

46. "Burning of the Mortgage and Consecration of the Syrian Antiochian St. George Orthodox Church," program book, June 3, 1945. Honored guests: His Eminence Metropolitan Antony Bashir, His Grace Archbishop Samuel David, Archpriest Constantine Abou-Adal, and His Honor Mayor William A. Bennett (dual capacity as mayor and sheriff in 1945).

7. Legacy and Linkage

1. Martha Mason, photos by Mitchell C. Abou-Adal, *Sunday Telegram*, July 9, 1967, Feature Parade centerfold. Also see Dolores Courtemanche, "Worcester's

Lebanese-Syrian Community: An Ethnic Success Story," *Sunday Telegram,* September 14, 1980, Sunday Morning centerfold, 8–10.

2. "Food by Arlene," *Evening Gazette,* November 13, 1973, 20.

3. Marguerite Olmstead, "Hostess Hints—Syrians Have Unusual Desserts for Easter," *Worcester Telegram,* March 24, 1947, n.p.

4. *Arab World Studies Notebook,* ed. Audrey Shabbas (Berkeley, Calif.: A joint publication of Arab World and Islamic Resources and School Services, AWAIR, and the Middle East Policy Council, 1998), 43–44.

BIBLIOGRAPHY

Allen, Roger. "Arabic language" and "Arabic literature," *World Book Encyclopedia*. Vol. 1, 583–84. Chicago: World Book, 2001.

Antoun, Richard T. *Understanding Fundamentalism: Christian, Islamic, and Jewish Movements*. Walnut Creek, Calif.: AltaMira Press, 2001.

Arab Digest. New York: Tankian Publishing Corp., January 1973.

Arab World Studies Notebook, editor Audrey Shabbas. Berkeley, Calif.: A joint publication of Arab World and Islamic Resources and School Services (AWAIR) and the Middle East Policy Council, 1998.

Archdeacon, Thomas J. *Becoming American: An Ethnic History*. New York: Free Press, 1983.

Board of Trade. *A Tribute to the Columbian Year by the City of Worcester: Graphic Exhibit of a City of Diversified Industries with an Alphabetical Index of Its Productions*. Worcester, Mass.: F. S. Blanchard, 1893.

———. *Worcester: The City of Varied Industries*. Worcester, Mass.: Blanchard Press, 1909.

Busada, Eli Abraham, Sr., *Autobiography of Eli Abraham Busada Sr.,* Washington, D.C.: Self-published, 1983.

Bushri, Suheil B. "Shakespeare in the Arab World." In *Middle East Forum,* Beirut: Alumni Association of the American University of Beirut, spring 1971.

Chejne, Anwar G. *The Arabic Language: Its Role in History*. Minneapolis: University of Minnesota Press, 1969.

Comrie, Bernard, ed. *The World's Major Languages*. New York: Oxford University Press, 1987, 666–673.

Condo, Bruce. *See Lebanon: Over 100 Selected Trips with History and Pictures*. Beirut: Harb Bijjani Press, 1960.

Courtemanche, Dolores. "Worcester's Lebanese-Syrian Community: An Ethnic Success Story." *Sunday Telegram (Worcester),* Feature Parade section, September 14, 1980.

Cox, F. Kenneth, Miriam Greenblatt, and Stanley S. Seaberg. *Human Heritage: A World History Teacher's Annotated Edition*. Columbus, Ohio: Charles E. Merrill, 1981.

Famous First Facts. 5th ed. New York: H. W. Wilson Co., 1997.

Forzley, Philip, ed. *An Autobiography of Bashara Kalil Forzley*. Worcester, Mass.: Self-published, 1958.

Gage, Nicholas. *A Place for Us*. Boston: Houghton Mifflin, 1989.

George, Margaret Haddad, ed. *Nabeha: Remembrances: An Autobiography* (from Nabeha's handwritten manuscript). Worcester, Mass.: Self-published, 1993.

George, Thomas F. *Autobiography of Thomas F. George.* Worcester, Mass., unpublished manuscript, 1944.

Gibran, Jean, and Kahlil Gibran. *Kahlil Gibran: His Life and World.* Brooklyn, N.Y.: Interlink Books, 1991.

Gibran, Kahlil. *A Second Treasury of Kahlil Gibran: The Words of the Master.* Translated by Anthony R. Ferris. New York: Citadel Press, 1990.

———. *The Wisdom of Gibran: Aphorisms and Maxims.* Edited by Joseph Sheban. New York: Philosophical Library, 1966.

Hackett, Alice Payne, and James Henry Burke. *Eighty Years of Best Sellers: 1805–1975.* New York, London: R. R. Bowker, 1977.

Haddad, Rev. Edmund G. "Our Syrian and Lebanese Catholics Have Written a Proud Record in Diocese." *Catholic Free Press,* February 25, 1955.

Haddad, Hassan S., and Basheer K. Nijim, eds. *The Arab World: A Handbook.* AAUG (Association of Arab-American University Graduates) Monograph Series, no. 9. Wilmette, Ill.: Medina Press, 1978.

Hagopian, Elaine C., and Ann Paden. *The Arab-Americans: Studies in Assimilation.* AAUG (Arab-American University Graduates) Monograph Series, no. 1. Wilmette, Ill.: Medina University Press International, 1969.

Hitti, Philip K. *Lebanon in History.* New York: MacMillan, 1967.

Hoar, George Frisbie. *Autobiography of Seventy Years.* 2 vols. New York: C. Scribner's Sons, 1903.

Houghton, Louise Seymour. "Syrians in the United States." In *The Survey: A Journal of Constructive Philanthropy* (Chicago) 26 (July 1, August 5, September 2, 1911); 27 (October 7).

Hourani, Albert. *A History of the Arab Peoples.* New York: Warner Books, 1992.

Kingsley, Elbridge, and Frederick Knab. *Picturesque Worcester, Part I: City and Environments, Complete in Three Parts, with 2,500 Illustrations.* Springfield, Mass.: W. F. Adams Company, 1895.

Knowlton, Elliott B., ed. *Worcester's Best: A Guide to the City's Architectural Heritage.* Worcester, Mass.: Commonwealth Press, 1984. Copyright by Worcester Heritage Preservation Society.

Leuenberger, Hans. *Turkey,* ed. Hanns Reich. U.S.A.: Hill and Wang, 1971.

Maloof, M. M. "From Beersheba to Berlin, via Boston: The Little Known Zeal of New England Syrians in Flocking to the Colors." *Boston Evening Transcript,* August 22, 1917, pt. 2.

Marie-Michel-Archange, Sister, p.f.m. *By This Sign You Will Live: History of the Congregation of the Little Franciscans of Mary, 1889–1955.* Translated from the French by Sister Marie-Octave, p.f.m., and Betty Dunn, Baie-Saint-Paul-Quebec. Worcester, Mass.: Heffernan Press, 1964.

McCoy, John. *History of Catholicism in the Diocese of Springfield.* 1900. Courtesy of *Catholic Free Press,* Worcester, Mass.

McLaughlin, Jeff. "Remembering One of Labor's Finest Hours, Bread and Roses. Lawrence Festival Commemorates One of Labor's Finest Hours." *Boston Globe,* September 4, 1987.

Mehdi, Beverlee Turner. *The Arabs in America, 1492–1977: A Chronology and Fact Book*. Ethnic Chronology Series, no. 31. Dobbs Ferry, N.Y.: Oceana Publications, 1978.

Menconi, Evelyn A., ed. "The Bread and Roses Strike: Syrian Connections [1912]." *William G. Abdalah Memorial Library Newsletter*, West Roxbury, Mass., January 1988. Materials for research provided by Eartha Dengler of the Immigrant City Archives, Lawrence, Mass.

Meo, Leila. "Social Justice and Political Equality: Key to Lebanon's Future." *Arab World Issues*. Association of Arab-American University Graduates, 1975.

Mokarzel, Salloum A., and H. F. Otash. *The Syrian Business Directory, 1908–1909*. New York: Al-Hoda Press, 1908.

Morin, Raymond. *The Worcester Music Festival: Its Background and History, 1858–1976*. Worcester, Mass.: Worcester County Music Association, 1976.

Moses, John G. *The Lebanese in America*. Utica, N.Y.: Self-published, 1987.

Naff, Alixa. *Becoming American: The Early Arab Immigrant Experience*. 1985. Reprint, Carbondale and Edwardsville: Southern Illinois University Press, 1985, 1993.

Nutt, Charles. *History of Worcester and Its People*. 4 vols. New York: Lewis Historical Publishing Co., 1919.

Nutting, Anthony. *The Arabs: A Narrative History from Mohammed to the Present*. New York: Clarkson N. Potter, 1965.

Orthodox Church in America, Department of History and Archives. *Orthodox America, 1794–1976: Development of the Orthodox Church in America*. Syosset, N.Y.: Orthodox Church in America, 1975.

Rice, Franklin P. *Dictionary of Worcester (Mass.) and Its Vicinity*. Worcester, Mass.: F. S. Blanchard, 1893.

Rihbany, Abraham Mitrie. *The Syrian Christ*. Boston and New York: Houghton Mifflin, 1916.

Roberts, J. M. *History of the World*. New York: Oxford University Press, 1993.

Sargent, Diggory, of Boston and Worcester, Mass., Some Descendants of. Boston: New England Historic Genealogical Society, 1904.

Southwick, Albert B. *More Once-Told Tales of Worcester County*. Worcester, Mass.: Databooks, a division of Tatnuck Bookseller and Sons, 1994.

Steiner, Edward A. *On the Trail of the Immigrant*. Copyright by Fleming H. Revell Company, 1906. Reprint, New York: Arno Press and the New York Times, 1969.

Turner, Howard R. "The First Language of Islam." In *Science in Medieval Islam: An Illustrated Introduction*. 1995. Austin: University of Texas Press, 2d paperback printing, 1999.

Webster, Hutton. *Early European History*. Boston: D. C. Heath, 1917.

Worcester, City of, Atlas 1870, Portions of Wards 3 and 4. Springfield, Mass.: Richards Map Co.

Worcester Directory, 1907. Worcester, Mass.: Drew Allis Company.

Worcester House Directory. Worcester, Mass.: Drew Allis Company, 1892, 1894, 1896.

Yale, William. *The Near East*. Ann Arbor: University of Michigan Press, 1958.

Yeulenski, Lois R., compiler. *The Old Photographs Series, Worcester.* Augusta, Me.: Alan Sutton, 1994. Distributed by Berwick Publishing, Dover, N.H.

Younis, Adele L. "The Arabs Who Followed Columbus," pt. 2. *The Arab World* (August 1966). New York: The Arab Information Center.

———. *The Coming of the Arabic-Speaking People to the United States.* Edited by Philip M. Kayal. Staten Island, N.Y.: Center for Migration Studies, 1995.

———. "Salem and the Early Syrian Venture." *The Arab World* (January 1967). New York: The Arab Information Center.

ILLUSTRATION CREDITS

The persons interviewed loaned the majority of the pre-1920 photographs in this book. Most were taken at photographic studios that no longer exist. Most of the studios used in Worcester, for example, were located in downtown (six on Front Street and three on Main Street): C. L. Blair, 44 Front Street; J. A. Cassone, 194 Front Street; Duke's Studio, 421 Main Street; Gray, 44 Front Street; Hevy Studio, 44 Front Street (where the bulk of the photos were taken); Knight, Worcester; National Studio, 78 Front Street; Park Studio, 503 Main Street; Lee Roy, 44 Front Street.

Recent photographs were taken by the following people and one photo studio: Right Reverend Stephen Upson, Elizabeth Boosahda, Dedication.1; June Benoit of Melikian Studio, 2.4, 2.6–2.8, 2.10–2.14, 5.6, 5.16, 5.25, 7.8; Mitchell C. Abou-Adal, 6.14, 6.15, 7.3, 7.6, 7.7.

Recent photographs from collections include the following: Elizabeth (Busada) Marinaro, 3.2, from the Collection of Eli A. and Nellie (Williams) Busada; Nellie (Williams) Busada, 5.23, 6.10; *Telegram-Gazette*, 6.11, 6.18; John Souda, 6.12; Diane Shoucair Bender, 6.13; *Christian Science Monitor*, Boston, 6.17, 7.1.

ANNOTATED SUGGESTED READING

Abourezk, James G. *Advise and Dissent: Memoirs of South Dakota and the U.S. Senate*. Chicago: Lawrence Hill Books, 1989.

This is the personal odyssey of James Abourezk, son of Lebanese immigrants, from his coming of age as a farmhand, bartender, bouncer, and cook to his entrance into and voluntary exit from the U.S. Senate. He served South Dakota in the U.S. House of Representatives and Senate from 1971 to 1979. *Advise and Dissent* is the testimony of a public official who refused to compromise his beliefs in the face of opposition. In 1980 he founded the American-Arab Anti-Discrimination Committee (ADC) in Washington, D.C., with a nationwide membership, in response to stereotyping, defamation, and discrimination directed against Americans of Arab descent.

Abraham, Nabeel, and Andrew Shryock, eds. *Arab Detroit from Margin to Mainstream*. Detroit, Mich.: Wayne State University, 2000.

Metropolitan Detroit is home to one of the largest, most diverse Arab communities outside the Middle East. Yet, the complex world that the Arabic-speaking immigrants have created there is barely visible on the landscape of ethnic America. The works of twenty-five contributors create a richly detailed portrait of Detroit.

Abraham, Sameer Y., and Nabeel Abraham, eds. *Arabs in the New World: Studies on Arab-American Communities*. Detroit, Mich.: Wayne State University Center for Urban Studies, 1983.

At the national level, the articles focus on the immigration patterns, residential settlements, occupations, and religious institutions that have facilitated or hindered the acculturation and assimilation of Arab Christians and Arab Muslims. Additionally, there are case studies of communities in Detroit.

Abu-Laban, Baha, and Faith T. Zeadey, eds. *Arabs in America: Myths and Realities*. Wilmette, Ill.: Medina University Press International, 1975. Available in cooperation with Association of Arab-American University Graduates, Inc., Washington, D.C.

Akash, Munir, and Khaled Mattawa, eds. *Post Gibran: Anthology of New Arab American Writing*. West Bethesda, Md.: Kitab, a Jusoor Book, 1999. 476 pp., b&w photos of many of the featured writers. Distributed by Syracuse University Press.

This anthology reexamines the field of contemporary Arab writing in the United States and the manifold ways in which Arabness and its system of values, attitudes, and manners define the Arab American. In particular the book reveals the multi-leveled textures of the exiles of new Arab writing. It includes poetry, fiction, essays, and dramas.

Ali, Abdallah Yousuf (also called Abdullah Yusif Ali). *The Glorious Kuran: Translation and Commentary.* Benghazi and Tripoli, Libya: The Call of Islam Society in the Libyan Arab Republic, 1973. 1895 pp., 7×10 inches.

Each page of this translation and commentary contains two columns, the Arabic of the Quran and its English translation. On the full lower portion of each page is the English commentary. The Quran recounts many Christian and Judaic traditions, for example, those about Abraham, Isaac, Ishmael, Joseph, Mary, and Jesus; and declares that Christians and Jews are "People of the Book" who, as believers, hold juridical rights under Islamic law to live as protected people. Ali states that it is impossible to understand the reality of the Quran's inimitability and discover the secret of Its eloquence except in the Arabic language in which It was revealed by God through the Prophet Muhammad.

Ali, Wijdan. *Modern Islamic Art: Development and Continuity.* Gainesville: University Press of Florida, 1997. More than 150 b&w and color photos.

A beautifully illustrated book and a historical survey of the development of modern painting in the Islamic world from the nineteenth century to the present. Ali provides background on dominant artistic traditions before 1900 as well as an evaluation of the loss of traditional aesthetics under the impress of Western culture. She substantially expands the study and concept of "modern art" beyond the narrow province of American and Western European schools.

Antoun, Jane. *The Arab World: Focus on Diversity.* Inquiry into World Cultures series, ed. Jack R. Fraenkel. Englewood Cliffs, N.J.: Prentice-Hall, 1977.

The author provides a brief historical and contemporary background of the Arab world. Divergent viewpoints are presented to avoid implying in any way that there is one "right" way to view a culture or the people who live within a culture.

Aramco World (now called *Saudi Aramco World*). "American Connections." November–December 1976.

Among the stories are a celebration by Lebanese Americans in New England, a description of early Arab Muslims in America, and a profile of Farouk El-Baz, "space age immigrant." This work was published in Houston, Texas, by Aramco Services Company.

Aramco World. "The Arab Immigrants." September–October 1986.

The entire issue is devoted to Arab immigrants to the United States. To interview and photograph Arab-American immigrants and their descendants in every state in the union, *Aramco World* assigned a team with years of research on Arab Americans in the United States and years of experience in the Middle East. A section describes the Naff Arab American Collection at the Smithsonian Institution's Museum of American History.

Aramco World. "A Banquet for the Teacher." May–June 1994, 14–19.

Aileen Vincent-Barwood, author, describes a workshop for teachers conducted by educator and founder Audrey Shabbas of Arab World and Islamic Resources and School Services (AWAIR) that was one of hundreds given nationwide in the last thirty years. Recently, most of the workshops have been conducted in a joint program with the Middle East Policy Council.

Aswad, Barbara C. "Arab American Families." In *Families in Cultural Context: Strengths and Challenges in Diversity*, ed. Mary Kay DeGenova. Mountain View, Calif.: Mayfield Publishing Company, 1997.

The author provides a comparative, comprehensive view of families from eleven ethnic groups. A consistent framework between chapters is maintained to help the reader better compare and contrast each group's strengths and the challenges of families. This approach encourages the stripping away of preconceptions about superficial cultural variations to uncover similarities among groups and to bridge the mental gap between "us" and "them."

Aswad, Barbara C., ed. *Arabic Speaking Communities in American Cities*. A joint publication of the Center for Migration Studies of New York, Inc., Staten Island, N.Y., and the Association of Arab-American University Graduates, Inc., 1974.

This collection of essays depicts several Arabic-speaking communities in America, showing their similarities and varieties of adaptation according to their background in their country of origin as well as their conditions in America.

Aswad, Barbara C., and Barbara Bilgé, eds. *Family and Gender among American Muslims: Issues Facing Middle Eastern Immigrants and Their Descendants*. Philadelphia: Temple University Press, 1996.

Since the beginning of the twentieth century, Muslims have been emigrating to the United States from nations such as Lebanon, Yemen, Palestine, Turkey, Iran, Pakistan, and Bangladesh, yet their experiences have been largely unrepresented in ethnic studies literature. *Family and Gender* provides information ranging from the social and historical conditions of the Muslim migration to the issues affecting Muslim-American life and provides new and valuable information on topics such as intergenerational conflict about identity and values, gender, and family structure.

Benson, Kathleen, and Philip M. Kayal, eds. *A Community of Many Worlds: Arab Americans in New York City*. New York: Museum of the City of New York/ Syracuse University Press, 2002.

Explores the history of Arabs as part of New York, a community of diversity.

Brox, Jane. *Five Thousand Days Like This One: An American Family History*. Boston: Beacon Press, 1999.

Brox writes of farmers, mill workers, and her immigrant Lebanese grandparents, and leads to the history of a New England place, the Merrimack Valley, and the immigrant workers in the industrial textile age.

Corey, Helen. *Food from Biblical Lands: A Culinary Trip to the Land of Bible History*. Terre Haute, Ind.: Charlyn Publishing House, 1989. B&w and color photos, 8×10.

In addition to the infinite variety of recipes of Syria and Lebanon, the author takes the reader into an adventure of regional foods of Jordan, Palestine, Egypt, Morocco, and Saudi Arabia. Corey is widely known for her freelance television and cooking shows. Her previous book, *The Art of Syrian Cooking,* was on Doubleday's bestseller list for twenty-four years.

Corey, Helen. "Food from Biblical Lands: Syria and Lebanon." Videocassette in color and time-coded for easy reference. Terre Haute, Ind.: Charlyn Publishing House, 146 S. 23rd Street, 1989.

The videocassette is a presentation of health foods in Corey's cookbook *Food from Biblical Lands* that are adapted for the American kitchen with recipes written in detail along with menus for each month.

Deranian, Hagop Martin. *Worcester Is America. The Story of the Worcester Armenians: The Early Years.* Worcester, Mass.: Bennate Publishing, 1998.

This richly detailed and illustrated study of the early Armenian community is an account of the first major Armenian American settlement, a case study in immigrant adjustment, and a testament to the bravery and dedication of the Armenian newcomers in a strange land.

Desautels, Kenneth R., compiler and author, in conjunction with Saint Joseph History Committee. *History of Saint Joseph Parish, 1820-1992.* Worcester, Mass.: Kenneth R. Desautels, 1992. 538 pp., 8½×11. B&W and color photos.

This is a comprehensive story and richly illustrated celebration of the people and clergy of St. Joseph parish.

Farr, Jamie, with Robert Blair Kaiser. *Jamie Farr: Just Farr Fun.* Clearwater, Fla.: Eubanks/Donizetti, 1994.

Jamie Farr, born of Lebanese immigrant parents in Toledo, Ohio, earned a living making people laugh at the world and at themselves. When Farr hit a low point in his career, he recalled that when Danny Thomas prayed to the saint of hopeless causes, St. Jude Thaddeus, his prayer was granted, and Danny Thomas founded a hospital in St. Jude's honor. Farr said, "If St. Jude could help Danny, he could help Farr." After Farr fervently prayed to St. Jude, he got the part of an apostle in the movie *The Greatest Story Ever Told* and later was cast on the TV series *M*a*s*h.*

Fernea, Elizabeth Warnock, and Basima Qattan Berzigan, eds. *Middle Eastern Muslim Women Speak.* Austin: University of Texas Press, 1977.

For those American women who believe that their foreign counterparts share their concerns, their feminism, and their image, this collection of writings will be reassuring. The collection glides smoothly from era to era and woman to woman. In every era there are women who avoided marriage to invest their energies elsewhere and women who labored in farms and factories to educate their children. The book talks about the men behind the women. Like their wives and daughters, the men do not easily fit Western stereotypes.

Fernea, Elizabeth Warnock, ed. *Women and Family in the Middle East: New Voices of Change.* Austin: University of Texas Press, 1985.

Fernea, Elizabeth, and Robert Fernea. *The Arab World: Forty Years of Change.* New York: Anchor Doubleday, 1997.

Fernea, Elizabeth. *In Search of Islamic Feminism.* New York: Anchor Doubleday, 1998.

Fluehr-Lobban, Carolyn. *Islamic Society in Practice.* Gainesville: University Press of Florida, 1994.

The research and observations span the years 1970 to 1990. The author conveys her understanding of both Western and Islamic culture. The book focuses on Islam as practiced in everyday life and society and brings out the human dimension of a region and a cultural tradition that have been stereotyped and maligned, on the one hand, and simplified and romanticized, on the other.

Fluehr-Lobban, Carolyn, ed. *Against Islamic Extremism.* Gainesville: University Press of Florida, 1998.

This volume makes available to Western readers the writings of Muhammad Saìd al-Àshmawy, a former chief justice of the High Court of Cairo and a prominent intellectual of the modern Islamic world, and contextualizes his political and ideological position in the struggle against Islamic extremism.

Goldschmidt Jr., Arthur. *A Concise History of the Middle East.* 6th ed. Boulder, Colo.: Westview Press, 1999.

Regarding the Ottoman Empire the author states, "[R]arely in history has one state [the Ottoman Empire] enjoyed such a succession of just and brave rulers for close to 300 years. No doubt the Ottoman Empire owed some of its strength to these capable sultans who learned the principles of government and warfare from their fathers and their on-the-job training in the provinces. . . . Few of the remaining sultans would match the quality of the first ten."

Haddad, Yvonne Yazbeck, ed. *The Muslims of America.* Religion in America series. New York: Oxford University Press, 1991.

Early Muslim immigrants, arriving in small numbers around the turn of the century, are often characterized as adventurers attracted to the New World for its economic opportunities. Their intention was to make as much money as possible as quickly as possible and then return to their homeland. The author provides perspective on their history, organizations, challenges, responses, outstanding thinkers, religious activism, and intellectual contributions.

Handal, Nathalie, ed. *The Poetry of Arab Women: A Contemporary Anthology.* Northampton, Mass.: Interlink Books, 2001.

Handal has put together an outstanding collection that showcases the work of eighty-two poets. Under the rubric "Arab women poets" the collection reveals a multiplicity of imaginations, presences, roots, migrations, and artistic strategies. These are poems emerging from the ancient, rich, but exclusionary tradition of poetry in Arabic.

Hayes, John R., ed. *The Genius of Arab Civilization: Source of Renaissance.* 2d ed. Cambridge, Mass.: MIT Press, 1983.

This profusely illustrated book introduces general readers to the cultural achievements and heritage of the Arabs. Included topics are literature, philosophy, architecture, art, music, the exact sciences, life sciences, mechanical technology, trade, and commerce.

Hitti, Philip K., and Philip S. Khoury. *Arabs: A Short History.* Chicago: Regnery Publishing, 1996.

Hooglund, Eric J., ed. *Crossing the Waters: Arabic-Speaking Immigrants to the United States before 1940.* Washington, D.C.: Smithsonian Institution Press, 1987.

The story is told of more than 125,000 speakers of Arabic who came to the United States between 1890 and 1940, largely from villages in what are now Lebanon and Syria. Most of them were members of Christian denominations; others were Arab Jews and Muslims. By creating and maintaining strong communities in the United States, these immigrants were able to overcome the hardship and troubles faced in a strange, new land.

Hooglund, Eric, ed. *Taking Root, Bearing Fruit: The Arab-American Experience.* Vol. 2. Washington, D.C.: ADC Research Institute, American-Arab Anti-Discrimination Committee, 1985. (See Zogby, James, ed., vol. 1, 1984).

Hyder, L. A. "Artist, Happy." In *Food for Our Grandmothers: Writings by Arab-American and Arab-Canadian Feminists,* ed. Joanna Kadi. Boston, Mass.: South End Press, 1994.

Hyder is a self-taught/exploring artist and dancer from Worcester, Massachusetts. A third-generation Arab American, she first began using art to express her Arabness and speak to her heritage. She states that it is important for our identities to be seen clearly and that it seems images of Arabs are either romanticized or villainized. She dedicates her piece "Artist, Happy" to her mother, Minnie E. Hyder, "who always encouraged me in my artwork."

Kadi, Joanna, ed. *Food for Our Grandmothers: Writings by Arab-American and Arab-Canadian Feminists.* Boston, Mass.: South End Press, 1994.

Thoughtful and critical, this memorable collection of essays, poems, and recipes by over forty Arab women in North America honors the courage and spirit of Arab women—past, present, and future.

Kherbawi, Basil M. *The Old Church in the New World or the Mother Church.* Self-published by Archpriest Basil M. Kherbawi, dean of St. Nicholas Greek Orthodox (Eastern Orthodox) Catholic Cathedral, Brooklyn, N.Y. Binghamton, N.Y.: Vail-Ballou Press, 1930.

Rev. Kherbawi saw the need to familiarize English-speaking people—as well as young people who profess the Orthodox faith—with the principal tenets of the Holy Orthodox Catholic and Apostolic Church, "mother of all churches." Congratulatory letters on the front pages of the book are from Metropolitan Platon of the North American Diocese under the jurisdiction of the Church of Russia; Archbishop Athanassiades of Neapolis, Palestine; and Archbishop Alexander of the Greek Archdiocese of North and South America.

Lobban Jr., Richard A., ed. *Middle Eastern Women and the Invisible Economy.* Gainesville: University Press of Florida, 1998.

The essays deal with women's work in Sudan, Egypt, Tunisia, Yemen, and Lebanon, including the activity of entrepreneurs, artisans, and rural workers. The diversity of women's work patterns are described, as well as the strategies women have devised to survive and to better the economic position of themselves and their families.

Majaj, Lisa Suhair. "Boundaries: Arab/American," *Food for Our Grandmothers: Writings by Arab-American and Arab-Canadian Feminists*, ed. Joanna Kadi. Boston, Mass.: South End Press, 1994.

Majaj, Lisa Suhair. "New Directions: Arab-American Writing at Century's End" and poetry. In *Post Gibran,* eds. Akash and Khaled, 1999.

Majaj, a Palestinian American, writes on Arab-American literature and culture and on Arab women's literature.

Maloley, Laurice B. *Destiny by Default: A Memoir.* Bloomington, Ind. 1stBooks Library, 2002.

The author tells a story about her parents who emigrated from Damascus, Syria, to Boston, Massachusetts, in 1906.

Malouf, George Hanna, ed. *The Ghassani Legacy.* Hereford, Tex.: Maloofs International, 1992.

This family genealogy and history (including that of the various spellings of Maloof) appears in English in this update of the study of the Maloofs done in 1908 in Arabic by Esa Iskander Maalouf of Lebanon. It traces the history of Christianity in the Middle East and of the largest Christian tribes to rule from 27 C.E. to 626 C.E. After the advent of Islam, the Ghassani Christian Arabs scattered throughout the region. The book was presented to the Library of Congress and the Naff Arab American Collection at the Smithsonian Institution's National Museum of American History during the twenty-fourth annual convention of Maloof International at Washington, D.C., 1992. Today Maloof International perpetuates the family history and sponsors cultural programs.

Melhem, D. H., and Leila Diab, ed. *A Different Path: An Anthology of the Radius of Arab American Writers.* Roseville, Mich.: Ridgeway Press, 2000.

This cross-sectional sampling of Arab-American poetry and prose includes thirty-six writers and the diverse sensibilities and interests represented by members of the Radius of Arab American Writers, Inc. (RAWI).

Menconi, Evelyn Abdalah. *The Arab World Fun Book: Celebrating with Storytelling and Paper Theater.* West Roxbury, Mass.: Self-published, 2000. Inquiries: William G. Abdalah Memorial Library, West Roxbury, Mass.

Menconi, Evelyn Abdalah. *Eastern Mediterranean Cooking: Culinary Basics and Wholesome Ingredients and Adaptations.* Boston: Self-published, 2000. Inquiries: William G. Abdalah Memorial Library, West Roxbury, Mass.

An introduction to eastern Mediterranean cuisine and a sharing of information about the basic ingredients and cooking styles from that part of the world that has a long tradition of delightful and nutritious food. The book includes ideas for adapting the cuisine to the nutritional trends of the day as well as a busy schedule.

Menconi, Evelyn Abdalah, compiler and ed. *The Coffeehouse Wayn Ma Kan Collection: Memories of the Syrian-Lebanese Community of Boston.* West Roxbury, Mass.: William G. Abdalah Memorial Library, 1996.

A compilation of writings by historians of the early immigrant community and recollections by oral historians of succeeding generations covering such topics as the garment industry, occupations, organizations, population shifts, and textile mills. Part of the William G. Abdalah Memorial Library collection that documents the Syrian Lebanese community in New England has been given to the Boston Public Library's Special Collections.

Moses, John G. *From Mt. Lebanon to the "Sea of Darkness."* Utica, N.Y.: Self-published, 2000.

The book includes a comprehensive bibliography and an appendix that lists the names of Lebanese passengers (174 young Lebanese, including 27 families), mostly from Mt. Lebanon, who were aboard the ill-fated *Titanic* (1912) and lists names of Lebanese/Syrian passengers traveling as families.

Nader, Rose B., and Nathra Nader. *It Happened in the Kitchen: Recipes for Food and Thought.* Washington, D.C.: Center for Study of Responsive Law, 1991.

The easy-to-prepare recipes for nutritious and delicious Middle Eastern dishes as prepared in an Arab-American home are accompanied by a hearty fare of commentary on public and community affairs. Mrs. Nader wrote, "Food is more than sustenance. It is an expression of health, affection, cultural transmission, stimulation, teaching, and bonding." Author Rose B. Nader is the mother of Ralph Nader and Nathra is his sibling.

Naff, Alixa. *The Arab Americans.* The Immigrant Experience series. Philadelphia: Chelsea House Publishers, 1999.

This series celebrates shared ethnic heritage and examines a specific immigrant group's history and culture and follows the achievements of its people up to the present as they continue to enrich this continent. Juvenile literature.

Naff, Alixa. *The Arab Americans.* The Peoples of North America series. New York, New Haven, Philadelphia: Chelsea House Publishers, 1988.

Discussed are the history, culture, and religions of the Arabs, factors that encouraged their emigration, and their acceptance as an ethnic group in North America. Juvenile literature.

Nassar, Eugene Paul. *Wind of the Land.* Washington, D.C.: Association of Arab-American University Graduates, Inc., 1979.

The son of Lebanese immigrant parents talks about family and community activities in all their hilarity, irreverence, and wisdom.

Orfalea, Gregory. *Before the Flames: A Quest for the History of Arab Americans.* Austin: University of Texas Press, 1988.

Orfalea, a second-generation Arab American of Syrian-Lebanese descent, strives "to see my own people's past and not be blind in the seeing—to stand before the flames of current and historical strife and seek out their meaning." The result is a composite portrait of three waves of mostly Syrian and Lebanese immigrants, interspersed with a series of profiles of prominent Arab Americans, among them Danny Thomas, the diplomat Philip Habib, and Edward Said.

Power, Josephine Alice. "Between the Historical Lines: Oral Histories of Second-Generation Syrian-Lebanese American Women." Master's thesis, State University of New York at Buffalo, 1997.

Quataert, Donald. *The Ottoman Empire, 1700–1922*. Cambridge, U.K.: Cambridge University Press, 2000.

This book is the latest addition to a successful textbook series, New Approaches to European History, that provides concise but authoritative surveys of major themes and problems in European history since the Renaissance. The Ottoman Empire was one of the most important non-Western states to survive from medieval to modern times, and played a vital role in European and global history.

Sadd, Gladys Shibley. *The Middle East: Its Wisdoms, Wit, and Culture: My Legacy*. Santa Clarita, Calif.: Glastebar Publishers, 1989.

A first-generation American, the author was born in Boston. She describes customs in the Arabic-speaking colony of Boston in the twenties and early thirties. Part I includes the generous use of Arabic proverbs in general conversation.

Said, Edward W. *Out of Place: A Memoir*. New York: Alfred A. Knopf, 1999.

The memoir records Said's upbringing in Palestine, Egypt, Lebanon, and the United States and the saga of his family's experiences, significantly in the 1947–48 period. Said exposes a personal past, letting us observe the people who formed him and who enabled him to triumph as one of the most important intellectuals of our time.

Saliba, Najib E. *Emigration from Syria and the Syrian-Lebanese Community of Worcester, MA*. Ligonier, Pa.: Antakya Press, 1992.

The Syrian-Lebanese community in Worcester is referred to as upwardly mobile, noted for the ability of its members to acquire property and use their entrepreneurial talents. One example was "Mitchell Maykel who started out in the 1890s with a dry-goods store and eventually established the Maykel Automobile Company, one of the first car dealerships in the city."

Sells, Michael. *Approaching the Quran: The Early Revelations*. Ashland, Ore.: White Cloud Press, 1999. With compact disc.

The complexity, power, and poetry of the early *sura*s, or chapters, of the Quran and the translations of the short, hymnic *sura*s associated with the first revelations to the Prophet Muhammad contain some of the most powerful prophetic and revelatory passages in religious history. The compact disc is of the Quranic reciters who chant several of the early *sura*s, adding to the enriching spiritual experience for anyone who seeks a meaningful exposure to the scripture of Islam.

Sengstock, Mary C. *Chaldean Americans: Changing Conceptions of Ethnic Identity*. 2d ed. Staten Island, N.Y.: Center for Migration Studies, 1999.

The text probes the unique history, life, and culture of the Chaldean community in the United States and illustrates the characteristics of ethnic communities in general and their adaptation to American society and culture. The Chaldeans differ from other Iraqis both in religion—they are Roman Catholic rather than Muslim—and language—their ancestral language is Chaldean (Aramaic) rather than Arabic.

Shakir, Evelyn. *Bint Arab: Arab and Arab American Women in the United States*. Westport, Conn.: Praeger Publishers, 1997.

Weaving together a survey from the late nineteenth century to the present, Shakir focuses on each generation's negotiation between traditional Arab values and the social and sexual liberties permitted women in the West. Interspersing oral histories, Shakir challenges stereotypes and creates a unique portrait of an often-misunderstood group.

Shalhoup, George Elias, *Through the Years: A Thankful Immigrant Looks Back*. Sanford, Maine: Self-published autobiography, 1987.

Shaw, Stanford J., and Ezel Kural Shaw. *History of the Ottoman Empire and Modern Turkey*. Vol. 2, *Reform, Revolution, and Republic: The Rise of Modern Turkey, 1808–1975*. 1977. Reprint, New York: Cambridge University Press, 1987.

Excerpted from the preface, p. viii: "The story of modern Ottoman and Turkish history has been told many times, but usually on the basis of European source materials and in the context of European ambitions and prejudices. It has only been in recent years that a beginning has been made in telling the story on the basis of Turkish sources. It is the object of this work to bring together the Western and Turkish sources, adding the results of the authors' research in the Ottoman archives and libraries and presenting the story in its own context."

Shedd, Carol Johnson, editor. *Are You Listening: Voices from the Middle East*. Cambridge, Mass.: Teaching Resource Center, Center for Middle Eastern Studies, Harvard University, 1998.

This book discusses different voices, different lives, and growing pains. Includes student activities.

Shoucair, Lillian (George). *Simon AbuAssaly George: The Life Journey of a Man from Lebanon*. Orlando, Fla.: FirstPublish, 2002.

Shoucair traces her father's history, from Lebanon to the United States, and his entrepreneurship.

Simon, Linda. "Moroccan Steam." In *Food for Our Grandmothers: Writings by Arab-American and Arab-Canadian Feminists*, ed. Joanna Kadi. Boston, Mass.: South End Press, 1994.

The author tells of her experience in a *hammam* (public bath house).

Suleiman, Michael W., ed. *Arabs in America: Building a New Future*. Philadelphia: Temple University, 1999.

This volume brings together twenty-one prominent scholars from a wide range of perspectives—including anthropology, economics, history, law, literature and culture, political science, and sociology—who discuss the status of Arabs in North America in an assortment of different communities. They address both the present situation for Arab Americans and prospects for their future.

Thomas, Danny, with Bill Davidson. *Make Room for Danny*. New York: G. P. Putnam's Sons, 1991.

Through laughter and tears, Danny Thomas tells the story of his poverty-stricken childhood in Toledo, Ohio, as one of ten children born to Lebanese immigrants; his incredible rise to fame in nightclubs, and his breakthrough into movies and television, where his sitcom *Make Room for Daddy* ran for eleven years on the networks. A strong belief in God has always been a guiding force in his life and led to his personal crusade to found the world-famous St. Jude Children's Research Hospital in Memphis, Tennessee.

Tinory, Eugene. *Journey from Ammeah: The Story of a Lebanese Immigrant*. Brattleboro, Vt.: Amana Books, 1986.

The first-person narrative is the author's mother speaking. She traveled solo at the age of fourteen from her homeland to rejoin her family in America. The book was published to coincide with the centennial celebration of the erection of the Statue of Liberty in 1986.

Vecoli, Rudolph J., and Suzanne M. Sinke, eds. *A Century of European Migrations, 1830–1930*. Statue of Liberty–Ellis Island Centennial series. Urbana: University of Illinois Press, 1991. 416 pp., 23 photos.

An international roster of historians provides new analyses of causes and patterns of migration and return migration that "remove American immigrant history from its moorings in national history and effectively place it in the context of a world phenomenon" (John Bodnar). Contributors include Frank Thistlethwaite, Dirk Hoerder, Robert P. Swierenga, Hartmut Keil, and Kerby A. Miller, among others.

Williams, David. *Traveling Mercies*. Cambridge, Mass.: Alice James Books, 1993.

A poetry collection.

Williams, David. "We're History and Other Poems." In *Post Gibran: Anthology of New Arab American Writing*, eds. Munir Akash and Mattawa Khaled. Bethesda, Md.: Kitab, Jusoor, 1999.

Through poetry, a language of carefully formed intensity, Williams, a Lebanese American, takes you into the domain only poetry can really inhabit—that place in the heart and soul of things. His poems have appeared in a number of magazines, among them *The Atlantic*.

Zogby, James, ed. *Taking Root, Bearing Fruit: The Arab-American Experience*. Vol. 1. Washington, D.C.: ADC Research Institute, 1984. (See Hooglund, ed., vol. 2, 1985).

Volumes 1 and 2 provide a survey of the lifestyles, cultures, heritage, diversity, and living pulse of Arab-American communities across the country.

Zogby, John. *Arab America Today: A Demographic Profile of Arab Americans*. Washington, D.C.: Arab American Institute, 1990.

State-by-state analysis of the eleven states with the largest number of Arab Americans; demographic information on the education, economic status, settlement patterns, and occupations of Arab Americans, including family and individual characteristics; based on analysis from Immigration and Naturalization Service records and exclusive data from the U.S. Census Bureau. John Zogby is president of Zogby International, a polling firm.

ORGANIZATIONS, COLLECTIONS, AND EXHIBITS

Arab-American Focus

The following is a selected list of publications, educational resources, major national grassroots organizations, collections, and exhibits with an Arab-American focus.

aljadid. A review and record of Arab culture and arts. A quarterly publication in English that primarily covers books, films, music, fine arts, theater, and science and generally reports on the Arab world and the Middle East. Published in Los Angeles, the editor is Elie Chalala.

ALSAC, the American Lebanese Syrian Associated Charities. The fund-raising arm of St. Jude Children's Research Hospital. ALSAC raises millions of dollars annually nationwide and is known throughout the world for its fund-raising for the hospital through the efforts of more than one million volunteers of varying ethnic heritage.

ALSAC/St. Jude Children's Research Hospital. Located in Memphis, Tennessee. The world's preeminent research hospital for catastrophic childhood illnesses and the first hospital in the United States dedicated solely to children with cancer, regardless of ability to pay. Founded by Danny Thomas and opened in 1962.

St. Jude Children's Research Hospital, under the leadership of ALSAC national executive director Richard C. Shadyac Sr., has expanded its St. Jude International Outreach Program. It is now affiliated with partner sites, independent clinics, and hospitals in fourteen countries including Lebanon and Syria, the ancestral home of the founder of St. Jude. International health care professionals and researchers visit as on-site observers and receive hands-on training at St. Jude to learn from St. Jude professionals and to translate their findings to help improve the treatment outcome for children in their native lands. St. Jude by invitation and reciprocal visits is providing training and sharing knowledge and technology with local governments, health care providers, and the private sector. This program allows the world's children who are afflicted with catastrophic illnesses to receive the highest quality medical care at partner sites in their home countries. With the help of the outreach program and ALSAC, medical staff and fundraisers from abroad receive training, attend workshops at St. Jude, and learn how to organize fund-raising projects patterned after ALSAC. Each partner site is an extension of the hopes and dreams of Danny Thomas.

AMC Report. A quarterly publication of the Washington, D.C.–based American Muslim Council, with commentaries on American Muslims in politics and links to other resources. AMC aims to promote ethical values that enhance the quality of life for all Americans and to catalyze the greater presence in mainstream public life of American Muslims of all races and ethnic background.

American-Arab Anti-Discrimination Committee (ADC) and ADC Research Institute (ADCRI). A civil rights organization based in Washington, D.C., and committed to defending the rights of Arab Americans and promoting their heritage. ADC is nonpartisan and nonsectarian and serves its nationwide membership through direct advocacy in cases of defamation and through legal action in cases of discrimination. Senator James G. Abourezk founded the ADC in 1980 in response to stereotyping, defamation, and discrimination directed against Americans of Arab origin. The ADC Research Institute publishes information on issues of concern to Arab Americans and provides educational materials on Arab history and culture and on the ethnic experience of Arabs in America. It also sponsors summer internships for college students. NAAA-ADC, the government affairs affiliate of the American-Arab Anti-Discrimination Committee, serves as the lobbying arm of ADC on domestic and foreign policy issues relevant to the Arab-American community.

ADC publishes "ADC Times" and "Intern Perspectives" on a bimonthly basis, as well as other periodic special reports. Its former chairwoman and president were Naila Asali and Hala Maksoud, respectively. Its present chairman is Ahmad Sbaiti, and the president is Ziad Asali. Marvin Wingfield is director of ADC Research Institute.

American Muslim Political Coordination Council (AMPCC). Consists of the American Muslim Alliance (AMA), American Muslim Council (AMC), Council on American-Islamic Relations (CAIR), and Muslim Public Affairs Council (MPAC). The primary concern of AMPCC is to unite the American Muslim community, to mobilize grassroots social and political activism, and to have an input in government policy and public discussions dealing with the issues of domestic civil rights issues, education, and peace in the Middle East, Kashmir, and Sudan.

Americans for Middle East Understanding (AMEU). Fosters increased understanding in America of the history, goals, and values of all the peoples in the Middle East and broader understanding of their religious beliefs, economic conditions, and social customs. Located in New York, AMEU was founded in 1967 by a group of men and women whose professions brought them in contact with the Middle East and who believed that the information Americans were getting regarding the Middle East was one-sided. AMEU's bimonthly publication is *The Link.* The executive director is John F. Mahoney.

Arab-American Business. A monthly magazine published in Huntington Beach, California, focusing on business success. Editor and publisher is Nidal M. Ibrahim.

Arab American Institute (AAI) and Arab American Institute Foundation (AAIF), Washington, D.C. Engages in legislation and issues affecting Arab Americans and U.S.-Middle East policy. Publishes special reports and bulletins that communicate political developments of interest to the Arab-American community nationwide. James J. Zogby founded the AAI in 1985 and serves as its president. The AAIF was founded in 1995 and supports a broad range of public information and education programs that encourage Arab-American participation in American civic life.

"Arab Americans: A Century of Community." An exhibit and educational series presented in June 1988 by the National Conference of Christians and Jews, Worcester County Chapter, in conjunction with the Arab-American community. Included in the displays and programs were art objects, artifacts, films, lectures, and poetry reading at the Worcester Public Library. This was the sixth annual Community Heritage Program by NCCJ in collaboration with a local ethnic group.

Arab Community Center for Economic and Social Service (ACCESS). Founded in Dearborn, Michigan, in 1971, ACCESS is the largest social service agency for Arab Americans in the United States and is involved in a wide range of topics. One of its projects is the Museum of Arab Culture, established in 1987. The museum presents the historical and contemporary traditions and decorative arts of the Arab world and the Arab-American community. There are some 300,000 Arab Americans in the metropolitan Detroit area. ACCESS's executive director is Ismael Ahmed.

Arab World and Islamic Resources and School Services (AWAIR). Conducts daylong teacher workshops nationwide that provide a fact-based foundation for those who educate America's youth about the Arab world and Islam. Teachers (elementary and college levels) are exposed to a broad perspective, new material, and ways of presenting the material effectively. The program is fully funded, and any school, district office of education, or university can request workshops. AWAIR (Berkeley, California) and Middle East Policy Council (Washington, D.C.) cosponsor the workshops, led by Audrey Shabbas, founder of AWAIR in 1990. (See *Aramco World,* May–June 1994.) AWAIR and the Middle East Policy Council jointly publish *Arab World Studies Notebook,* a 540-page curriculum guide, lesson plan, and reference source in binder format, for grades seven to twelve and for college students.

The Arabic Hour. American Arab Broadcasting Network, broadcasting from West Roxbury, Massachusetts, since 1981 and staffed by volunteers. A weekly television program and extensive cable coverage provide outreach for Americans generally as well as for Arab Americans, sharing community information, cultural and political interviews, documentaries, Arabic cuisine, and music. Its goal and mission is to educate and inform the general public of the rich Arab heritage and culture, offering different and more objective views of the Arab world than the traditional media. Founder and executive producer is Mikhael Haidar.

Arabica. A bimonthly magazine published in Dearborn, Michigan. Aspires to be the magazine of choice for the Arab-American community and others who are interested in the community, its business, social affairs, and culture. *Arabica* speaks to and for the community within the broad context of contemporary American society. It addresses the community's concerns and speaks to its aspirations. Publisher is Ahmad Chebbani.

Aramco World (now called *Saudi Aramco World*). A bimonthly magazine published in Houston by Aramco Services Company. This profusely illustrated and scholarly written magazine is distributed nationwide to increase cross-cultural understanding and to broaden knowledge of the culture of the Arab and Muslim worlds and the history, geography, and economy of Saudi Arabia.

Association of Arab-American University Graduates, Inc. (AAUG), 211 East 4th Street, New York City (formerly of Washington, D.C.). An educational and cultural organization dedicated to fostering better understanding between Arab and American peoples, promoting informed discussion of critical issues concerning the Arab world and the United States, and directing its critique toward all participants in the Middle East. Publishes books, papers, and periodicals on Arab and Arab-American affairs, the Arab-Israeli conflict, and U.S. foreign policy. Founded by a group of university graduates and incorporated in 1967.

Association for Middle East Women's Studies (AMEWS). Founded in 1985 by scholars interested in promoting research in the field of Middle East women's studies. Its quarterly publication is *Middle East Women's Studies Review* (MEWS Review). AMEWS is an affiliated organization of the Middle East Studies Association of North America (MESA).

Center for Middle Eastern Studies, Teaching Resource Center, Harvard University. Offers a lending library, consulting service, and workshops. Its "Middle East Resources" newsletter provides information for teaching about the Middle East at the precollegiate level.

Gibran Park at Copley Square, opposite Boston Public Library, Boston, Massachusetts. The city of Boston honored its adopted son Kahlil Gibran by declaring the week of September 25, 1977, as "Gibran Week." A banquet sponsored by the Greater Boston Arab-American community opened festivities with the dedication of a bronze plaque placed in Gibran Park at one of Boston's most prestigious historical sites. Its dedication was an ecumenical event presided over by imams, rabbis, priests, and ministers and witnessed by hundreds of Americans representing every ethnic and religious minority. His cousin and namesake Kahlil Gibran of Boston and a distinguished and renowned sculptor designed and made the plaque. The inscription on the plaque reads: "Kahlil Gibran, a native of Becharri, Lebanon. . . . A grateful city acknowledges the greater Harmony among men and the Strengthened Universality of Spirit given by Kahlil Gibran to the people of the World in Return."

Gibran. A bronze sculpture of philosopher Kahlil Gibran given to Worcester State College by the Arab-American community of central New England. The artist is his cousin and namesake, also Kahlil Gibran. The sculpture was given in recognition of the educational opportunities afforded by the college. Unveiled at a gala event in 1987, the bust is displayed at the Learning Resource Center at the college.

Gibran Memorial Garden. The Kahlil Gibran Centennial Foundation was founded in 1983, the centennial of Gibran's birth, by a small group of dedicated Arab Americans whose projects commemorated this important artist and his message of universal brotherhood. In 1989 its chairman and president was William J. Baroody Jr. In 1991 the foundation dedicated the Gibran Memorial Garden at its U.S. National Park site in Washington, D.C., in a wooded area on Embassy Row across Massachusetts Avenue from the British Embassy, next door to the Islamic Center, and diagonally across the street from the residence of the vice president of the United States. One reason Gibran was selected by Congress for a memorial was to commemorate this versatile artist and universally loved poet who continues to have an impact worldwide. The objective of the foundation was not only to promote Gibran and his ideas of peace, love, and the common humanity of all people but also to make this gift of the Gibran Memorial Garden to America.

Institute of Near Eastern and African Studies (INEAS). An independent, nonprofit organization with the mission to educate the public and inform the media on issues related to the Arab and Islamic worlds, Africa, and the non-Arab Middle Eastern communities. Founded by Wafaa Salman in 1994 and located in Cambridge, Massachusetts.

Islamic Horizons. A bimonthly magazine published in Plainfield, Indiana, by the Islamic Society of North America (ISNA). Contains articles dealing with news about Islam in North America and the Islamic approach to contemporary issues. ISNA is an association of Muslim organizations and individuals that serves the diverse needs of Muslims in North America and through education and social services enhances Islamic identity in the society at large. Its president is Muhammad Nur Abdullah and the ex-president is Muzammil H. Siddiqi.

Kayal, Philip M., "A Guide to the Archives: The Syrian American Collection." Staten Island, N.Y.: Center for Migration Studies, 1996. The collection contains many materials on Lebanese Americans, Muslim Arab Americans, and other Middle Eastern ethnic groups. Also included are the papers of Philip M. Kayal and the original research materials of Adele L. Younis.

Mizna. Opinions, poetry, short stories, and art by and about Arab Americans. A tri-yearly journal published in Minneapolis, Minnesota. Provides a forum to promote Arab-American culture that values diversity in the Arabic community. It is committed to giving voice to Arab Americans on the local, national, and international level through literature, speakers, and community events. Executive director is Kathryn Haddad.

Moses, John G., assisted by Paul G. Nassar. "Annotated Index to the *Syrian World*, 1926–1932," ed. Judith Rosenblatt. St. Paul: Immigration History Research Center, University of Minnesota, 1994. A guide to a monthly journal in English dedicated to raising the awareness of the English-speaking Arab community in the United States and to generational and social issues of immigrants and their children. It is a treasury of literary gems by gifted writers of poems, essays, and folk tales.

Muslim Magazine (American Muslim Assistance). A quarterly publication of the Islamic Supreme Council of America (ISCA), located in Fenton, Michigan. Devoted to presenting the various perspectives of Muslims around the globe, specifically in the Western world. Promotes tolerance and understanding among different philosophies within the context of Islam. On a broader level the magazine aims to educate, inform, and entertain the entire Muslim and non-Muslim family alike. Editor-in-chief is Mateen Siddiqui.

Naff Arab American Collection. Located at the Smithsonian Institution's National Museum of American History, Washington, D.C. Alixa Naff, author and social historian, created the collection that she donated to the Smithsonian in 1984. (See *Aramco* magazine, September–October 1986.) The extensive collection includes over 2,000 photographs and over 500 artifacts and depicts the pre–World War II immigrant experience of Arabic-speaking people who migrated to the United States. It consists of two parts, archival materials and artifacts. Parts of the collection travel for exhibit to museums and universities.

Naff, Alixa. "Collection Guide and Series Description, 1995." Guide to the Naff Arab American Collection at the Smithsonian Institution's National Museum of American History.

National Association of Arab Americans (NAAA). Founded in 1972. On January 1, 2000, NAAA merged with the American-Arab Anti-Discrimination Committee (ADC). Khalil E. Jahshan was president of NAAA and is now president of NAAA-ADC, the lobbying arm of ADC.

Radius of Arab-American Writers, Inc. (RAWI). A New York organization that encourages Arab youth to write fiction and nonfiction, offers members a professional network, supports all writers and artists, and academics of Arab heritage who are beginning their careers as well as those who are established. Publishes a newsletter. Founded in 1992, its executive director is Barbara Nimri Aziz.

Saudi Aramco World. See *Aramco World*.

Teaching Resource Center, Center for Middle Eastern Studies, Harvard University, Cambridge, Mass. The outreach center serves educators, media outlets, and interested individuals across the country who would like information or material on the Middle East or Islam. The center has a lending library of videos, books, and curricula materials and a speakers bureau and holds workshops. Barbara Petzen is outreach coordinator.

Washington Report on Middle East Affairs. Published nine times yearly by the American Educational Trust (AET) in Washington, D.C. AET is a nonprofit foundation founded by retired U.S. foreign service officers to provide the American public with balanced and accurate information concerning U.S. relations with Middle Eastern states. AET's Foreign Policy Committee has included former U.S. ambassadors, government officials, and members of Congress. Publisher is Andrew I. Kilgore.

Examples of Educational Sources with Focus on American Immigration

Center for Migration Studies. An educational nonprofit institute founded in New York in 1964 to encourage and facilitate the study of sociological, demographic, economic, historical, legislative, and pastoral aspects of human migration, refugee movements, and ethnic group relations everywhere.

Immigration History Research Center (IHRC). Founded in 1965 as an international resource on American immigration and ethnic groups originating in eastern, central, and southern Europe and the Near East. It promotes the study and appreciation of ethnic pluralism by sponsoring seminars, publications, conferences, and exhibits. IHRC is housed in a new state-of-the-art archive center at the Elmer Andersen Library at the University of Minnesota. Rudolph J. Vecoli serves as its director and is a professor of history. In spring 1999 the White House Millennium Council and the National Trust for Historic Preservation honored the IHRC's "Documentation of the Immigrant Experience" as one of the initial 101 official projects of "Save America's Treasures," a public/private partnership encouraging protection of threatened U.S. cultural treasures. In 1983, Kahlil Gibran's birth centennial, IHRC sponsored the Philip K. Hitti International Symposium on Near Eastern American Studies titled "The Arabic-Speaking Immigration to North America to World War II."

AUTHOR BIOGRAPHY

Elizabeth Boosahda researches the genealogy and histories of Arab-American families who emigrated from Lebanon, Palestine, or Syria to either North America or South America and who have roots in or links to New England. The abundance of material gathered for this study was made possible by the author's personal contacts and the trust of those interviewed. She gained firsthand insight and knowledge of Arab-American customs, traditions, and values by growing up as an American and a family member of Arab-American immigrants and by her lifelong participation in many Arab-American communities.

The author was an avocational archaeologist at Native American sites in Massachusetts and has traveled extensively on an independent basis in Africa, Asia, Europe, and North America, with emphases on archaeological sites and performing arts.

Boosahda is a member of the Middle East Studies Association of North America, Inc. (MESA), Association for Middle East Women's Studies (AMEWS), American-Arab Anti-Discrimination Committee (ADC), Arab American Institute (AAI), and Association of Arab-American University Graduates, Inc. (AAUG), among others.

INDEX OF ARABIC TERMS

Note: Page reference indicates where the term is defined in the text.

Definite articles are omitted; thus *el-saha* is listed as *saha* and *al-jabr* as *jabr*. See page 2 for more information on transliterations.

adami, 109
ahlan bekum, 108
ahlan wa sahlan, 108
ahtya, 103
Allah kareem, 109
Allah yaatik elafee, 108
Allah younam aalyke, 109
amma, 84
ana mabsooton zhiddan, 109
ana tahhet amrak, 110
anta lateefon zhiddan, 110
ataba, 99

baba qhannuj, 172
baklawa, 173
batata, 172
belaad, 39
bint, 180
bism Illah, 173
bitsharrifna, 110
bitsharriftena mah shoftkoon, 109
burghul, 102
bytee kaennak fee bytak, 108

dabkah, 51
darabukkah, 51

falafel, 172
fatayer, 155
fatayer joban, 173
fatayer laham, 173–174
fatayer sabanegh, 174

fatayer simsum, 174
fatayer zahtar, 174
fellahin, 18

gharraf, 172

haflah, 112
Hajj (pilgrimage), 28
Hajj (title preceded by el-), 28
Hajji, 28
halatha barikoom, 110
hamdulillah, 109
Haq qan qaam, 156
harrate tahta, 50
hummus bi tahini, 102

ibn, 180
Iftar, 177
ihjee, 192

Jabal Lubnan, 14
jabr, 172
jebab, 34
jibneh, 103
jiddo, 94
joban. See jibneh

kaak, 155
kattar Allah kherik, 109
kattar kherkum, 110
khatirkum salama, 110
khubz Arabi, 100

khubz marquq, 100
kibbee, 192
kishk, 102
kul assena wa antum assalam, 156
kurban, 173
kushee, 65

la, istakther bekhirak, 109
laban, 102
laham ageen, 174
loobyee ahtya, 103
loola loola laysh, 98

maarmee, 106
mahallabiyeh, 54
mahleb, 173
mahrajhan, 188
mandeels, 103
mart amma, 69
Maseeh. See Masih
Masih, 172
Masih qaam, 119
matraan, 21
mazahar, 173
mezza, 109
mijwiz, 51
min fadlik, sharaftena, 109
misbaha, 110
mohajar, 40
mujaddarah, 172
Mutassarifiah, 14
myrra, 172

naasanam, 30
narghile, 110
neharkum saed wa mubarak, 108

oud. See ud

qandi, 172
qatifa, 69

sabahh el-khire, 109
sabahh el-noor, 109

sadiq, xix
saha, 51
sahra, 112
sahtain, 110
salam, 153
salam alaykum, 191
salam dayakoom, 109
sfeeha, 174
sharaftena, 109
simsum, 174
sitto, 94
suf, 172
suffa, 172

tabbuli, 102
tafoddal (male), *tafoddali* (female), 108
tahini, 102
tarif, 172
tasbeh. See misbaha
tawlah, 79
tayabe el-hamdulillah, 108
tellee, 50
tzaghreet. See zharraghat

ud, 21
um, 28
una mish naasanam, 30

wa alaykum salam wa rahmatullaha wa baraka tehi, 110
warag inab mihshee, 102
wa salam alaykum, 110
wa ukherik, 109

ya hayathi, 110
ya layli, ya layli, 98
ya Rubi, 100
ya urbi, 110
ya walidi, 110
ya youni, 110

Zahbal Libnan. *See* Jabal Lubnan
zahtar, 174
zharraghat, 98

GENERAL INDEX

Note: Page numbers in italics refer to photographs and maps.
For families, check under alternate spellings of last names.

A., Adele H. *See* Abdow, Adele Haddad
A., Albert A. *See* Abdelnour, Albert A.
A., Alice. *See* Abdow, Alice
A., Ameen. *See* Antoun, Ameen
A., Amelia G. *See* Aboud, Amelia Ghiz
A., Francis. *See* Abdow, Ferris Francis
A., Girgis (George), 104
A., Lilian Maloof, 106
A., MaryAnne L. *See* Awad, MaryAnne Lotuff
A., Michael, 181
A., Michael N., 92, 135
A., Monsour, 28
A., Moxie, 52
A., Ms., 36
A., Nicholas, 22, 30, 83, 181
A., Peter M., 135
A., Sally A., 151
A., Sam G. *See* Abdelmaseh, Samuel G.
A., Sophia (Sophie). *See* George, Sophie A.
AAUG, 204
Abbasid dynasty, 3–4
Abdallah, Hanna, 131–132
Abdelahad, Michael, *196*
Abdella, Charles A., 183
Abdella, George J., 183
Abdella, Joseph, 158
Abdella, Mabel (Paquette), *196*
Abdella, Martha, 184
Abdella, Martha M., 151
Abdella, Rita J., 140
Abdelmaseh, Henry, 157
Abdelmaseh, Kalaick (Kaneb) Abdow, 69

Abdelmaseh, Samuel G., 66–67, *126*, 135
Abdelnour, Albert A., 106, 112–116, *129*, *196*
Abdelnour, Aneese, 115, *129*, 179
Abdelnour, Milhelm, 106, *129*
Abdelnour, Underwood J., 141
Abdo, George, *168*
Abdow, Adele Haddad, 55, 81
Abdow, Alice, 67, 69, 102–103, 143–144, 149
Abdow, Ferris Francis, 19, 59, 143
Abdow, George, 53, 157
Abdow, Pete, 51
Abdow, Sooriya (Soriye) El-Hajj, 59, 143
Abdow, Worde "Rose," 53
Abdul Hamed, Sultan, 131
Abi-Saada, El-Hajj. *See* Boosahda, Abraham
Abisamra, Alexandra, *124*
Abisamra, Esther (Estelle) W., 95–96, 105, 106, *124*
Abisamra, Faries, 95–96, *124;* family of, *124*
Abisamra, Victoria, *124*
Aboassaly, Victor, 33, 35, 43, *61,* 214–218; mausoleum of, *217,* 219, 220
Abodeely, Angia Angelina Haddad, 180
Abodeely, Badaway Mary Haddad, 55–56, 87, 105, 180
Abodeely, David, 180
Abodeely, George, 55
Abodeely, Michael N., 182
Abodeely, Nassar, 87

Abohatab, Emmanuel, 215, 216
Aboody, Charles, 180
Aboody, Charles J., *195*
Aboody, Helen Kalil, 75
Aboody, Julia Thomas, 180
Aboody, Paul, 75
Abou-Adal, Constantine, 106, 135–136, *170*, 219, 226n.5, 239n.19
AbouAjaj, 52
Aboud, Amelia Ghiz, 70, 97–98, 182
Abourezk, James, 4, 249
Abraham (Ibrahim), Prophet, 178, 211
Abraham, Abdow, 141
Abraham, Farrah, *124*
Abraham, Henry, *124*
Abraham, Michael S., *166*
Abraham, Musalam Farrah (Sam), family of, *118*
Abraham, Sophia (Sophie), 93, *118*
Abraham, Sophie Khoury, *124*
Abraham, Spencer, 184
Abraham, Stephen G., 187
Abudula, Badaway Haddad. *See* Abodeely, Badaway Mary Haddad
Abufaris, Assad K., 86
Abufaris, Habooba (Rose) S., 19, 86
Abufaris, Michael K., 86
AbuHider lineage, 176
Abu Madi, Iliya, 232n.4
Abusamra, Hind-Helene (Mrs. Henry B.), *117, 154, 196*
Abusumra, Saelem, 96
ACCESS, 262
Adam & George Company, 69, 236n.2
ADC, 4, 205
Aftimos, Bishop. *See* Ofiesh, Aftimos
Agbay, Anthony J. "Tony," 186, 187
Ahmed, Ali, 36
AL=FUNOON: THE ARTS, 85
Algebra, 228n.9
Al-Hoda (newspaper), 104
Allah (God), 1, 37, 108
ALSAC, 152, 158–159, 182, 186
Alwon, Nicholas, 224
American-Arab Anti-Discrimination Committee (ADC), 4, 205
American Civil War, 8, 14, 225n.2

American Lebanese Syrian Associated Charities (ALSAC), 152, 158–159, 182, 186
American Muslim Heritage Day, 205
American Muslim Political Coordination Council (AMPCC), 261
American Palestine Committee, 204
American Red Cross, *165*
American University of Beirut (AUB), 6
Americanization. *See* Integration patterns
Americans for Peace and Justice in the Middle East, 205
Anatolia, 3, 4
Anglicized names, 29–30
Angora Orphan Aid Association, 35, 36
Ankara, Turkey, 18, 36
Ankara Aide Society, 35, 37
Antakya. *See* Antioch
Antioch, 18, 33
Antiochian Orthodox Church, 33, 211–221 passim. *See also* St. George Orthodox Church/Cathedral
Antony. *See* Bashir
Antoun, Ameen, 21, 57, 71, 80–81, 82, *169*
Antoun, Nora. *See* Hakim, Nora Antoun
Antoun, Richard T., 185
Antoun, Tufeek Taft, 40, 80–81, 82, 83, 93, 104
"Arab": definition of, 1; in U.S. Census, 132–133; use of term, 3, 225–226nn.4–5
Arab American Collection, Naff, 265
Arab-American Day, 4, 228–230n.10
Arab-American Planning Committee, 205
Arab Americans: definition of, 3; genealogy of, 175–176, 207–210; and Middle East after World War II, 204–206; pride in heritage of, 189–190; public personalities of first generation of, 182–187; public personalities of second generation of, 187
Arab Community Center for Economic and Social Services, 262
Arab contributions to civilization, 4, 227–228n.9, 229, 238–239n.19
Arab Empire, 1, 3–4, 9
Arab immigrants. *See* Immigration; Lebanese; Palestinians; Syrians
Arab World after World War II, 204–206

Arab World and Islamic Resources and
School Services (AWAIR), 262
"Arabian Boarding House," 3, 225–226n.4
Arabic language: Arabic expressions used
in English speech, 172, 191; English
words derived from, 172; and liter-
acy, 103–104; in military, 141; Modern
Standard Arabic, 2; oral and writ-
ten forms of, 1–2; oratory, 114–115;
in Ottoman Empire, 4, 5; plays, 112–
114, 129–130; poetry, 5, 114; and the
Quran, 1; schools for, 104–107; spelling
and transliterations of, 2; spread of, 1;
storytelling, 5
Arabic-language newspapers, 85–86, 104,
239–240n.20
Aramony, Fred R., 154–156
Aramony, William, 185
Arbeely, A. J., 85, 239n.20
Arbeely, Najeeb, 85, 239n.20
Archdeacon, Thomas J., 17–18
Arraj, Joseph, 166
Arraj, William J., 141
Arranged marriages, 40, 91–94
Arts: Arab contributions to, 4, 6, 228n.9;
plays, 112–114, 129–130, 156; visual
artists and art educators, 187
Ashkar, Isabella (Maryam), 96–97, 120
Assad, Frederick C., 145
Assatly, George, 224
Assimilation. See Integration patterns
Association of Arab-American University
Graduates, 204
Astronomy, 4, 227–228n.9
Aswad, Barbara C., xvi
Attella, Edwin M., 141
AUB (American University of Beirut), 6
Austria, 14
Autobiographies, 175
Awad, Blanche Barhoum, 184
Awad, Henry, 184
Awad, John F., 153, 169
Awad, MaryAnne Lotuff, 69, 168, 169
Ayik, Mary (Mrs. Salem), 174–175
Ayoub, John, 114
Azar, Helen Bourisk, 57–58
Azar, Salim, 57–58

B., El-Hajj (Abraham). See Boosahda,
Abraham
Bacela, Elias, 20
Badran, Najeeb G., 35, 38
Bakeries, 52, 54, 57, 77, 78, 173
Baldacci, John Elias, 184
Banquets and testimonials, 156–158, 170
Baptism certificate, 117
Baptists, 33, 95–96, 147
Bashir, Antony, 170, 214, 218, 219, 220,
239n.19
Basila (Bacela), Adella, 96
Batal, James, 182
Bates, Martha Abdella, 184
Bayrouty (Beyrouty), George, 134, 138,
139–140
Bayrouty, John L., 139
Bayrouty, Naphe David, 239n.19
Beirut Women's College, 7, 225n.2
Bell Hill. See Neighborhoods
Benjamin, Metropolitan, 239n.19
Bianchi, Ytalia, 58
Bianchi Macaroni factory, 58–59, 160, 194
Bible, 175
Bikar, G. Sukrey, 37
Bilingualism of immigrants, 103, 106
Bliss, Daniel, 5–6
Blizzard of 1888, 67
Bloomingdale Court, 52–53
Bollus, Shafeeka (Sophie) Trebulsi, 123
Boosahda, Abraham (Ibrahim) (1857–
1940), 28–29, 42, 57, 78, 87, 93, 103,
128, 140, 192, 207, 240n.22; genealogy
of, 207–210
Boosahda, Alexandra (Eskandara), 28, 84,
87, 93–94, 101, 128, 140, 179–181, 192,
240n.22; genealogy of, 207–210
Boosahda, Emily Swide (Mrs. Leo S.), 174,
187
Boosahda, Harold F., 28, 93, 192, 227n.6
Boosahda, Kalil A., v, 28, 42, 192, 227n.6
Boosahda, Mary (Miryam) Najjar, 93, 115,
170
Boosahda, Nazira Mishalanie, v, 19–20,
84, 93–94
Booth, George, 186
Boston, Mass., 35, 39

Bourisk, Nellie M. Haddad, 182
Boy Scouts of America, 145–146, 152
Brazil, 19, 39, 86, 104
Bread and Roses strike (1912), 76–77
Bread baking at home, 173–174
Breastfeeding, 101
Britain, 10–11, 231–232n.26
Brooke, Edward W., 183
Buildings, 6, 51–59, 60–64
Burials and cemeteries, 31, 37, 46, 139–140, 163
Busada (Boosahda), Abraham, 145
Busada (Boosahda), Asa A., 28, 84, 192
Busada (Boosahda), Eli A., 28–29, 34, 56, 66, 122, 136, 137–138, 156, 162, 175, 192, 224, 226–227n.6
Busada (Boosahda), John K., 61, 107, 126, 145, 156, 171, 175
Business networking centers, 77–79
Business ventures, 8, 52–58, 64, 69, 71, 73, 74, 77–86, 179, 186, 188, 236nn.2,6, 237–238nn.12–15. *See also* Peddlers

C., Florence H. *See* Chrzsiewski, Florence Haddad
C., Virginia H., 105
Calendar changes, 207
Campbell, Donald W., 143
Campbell, Jeanette H., 143
Casey, William, 158
Castle Garden (processing center), 23–24
Caucasian/Asian controversy, 132–133, 135
Cedars of Lebanon, 11, 35
Celebrations. *See* Public celebrations; Wedding celebrations
Cemeteries. *See* Burials and cemeteries
Census Bureau race classification system, 132–133
Chakour, Adele M. Kefruny, 106–107
Chakour, Mitchell G., 106–107, 171
Chakour, Selma A., 140
Chandler Hill. *See* Neighborhoods
Chevallier, Dominique, 231n.21
Child care, 22–23, 68, 87
Children: Arabic schools and teachers for, 104–107; Boy Scout troop, 145–146, 152; church school training for,

147–148; clothing of, *123–128;* and Friendly House, 142–145, *164;* health care for, 143, 144; parenting of, 22–23, 68, 87; play presented by, 113–114; Roosevelt's intervention on behalf of, 24–28, 233n.15; storytelling to, 111; visits by, 110–111; work by, 87. *See also* Education
Christianity: God of, 1; and Inquisition, 4; and missionaries, 5–6; in Ottoman Empire, 5; and patriarchs, 178; and prayer, 57; religious celebrations of, 177; and wedding ceremonies, 95–97. *See also* Baptists; Eastern Orthodox Church; Maronites; Melkites; Methodists; Presbyterians; Protestants; Roman Catholic Church
Chrzsiewski, Florence Haddad, 186
Churches. *See* Christianity; Protestants; Roman Catholic Church; St. George Orthodox Church/Cathedral; Syrian Orthodox Church
Citizenship, 131–133
Civil War, American, 8, 14, 225n.2
Clothing: children's clothing, *123–128;* corsets, 101, *124;* men's clothing, 52, *122–124,* 176; sewing of, 102, 176; wedding gowns, 96, 97–98, *119–121;* women's clothing, 101, *122–125,* 140
Coffeehouses/coffee parlors, 77, 79, 104
Colonialism, 10–11, 231–232n.26
Columbia Exposition (1892), 6–7
Communist Party, 135–136
Community relations: Boy Scout troop, 145–146, 152; and communal cooking, 102–103; and community gatherings, 111–116; community interaction at public celebrations, 148–154, 156–158; kinship bonds based on home towns, 107–108; support programs in community, 141–148; women's organizations, 141–142; Worcester Employment Society, 141, 142
Conflict resolution in families, 116
Cookbooks, 174
Cooking. *See* Food
Coury, Christian C., 188–189

Coury, Elias Khalil (Eli K.), *161, 189*
Cultural events. *See* Dancing; Music and Musicians; Plays; Public celebrations
Cultural traditions: arranged marriages, 40, 91–94; food and cooking, 102–103; nuptial engagements, 94–95; wedding celebrations, 91, 95–99, *119–121*; women's position in Arab culture, 99–101; *zharraghat,* 98
Cultural traits and values, 8, 11, 35–36, 39, 65–66, 70, 81, 87, 108–111, 142, 176, 205

D., Peggy. *See* Deeb, Margaret
Dabkah (dance), 51, 111–112, *168*
Daboul, Michael, 158
Dacey, Norman F., 204
Dadah, Joseph, 158
Dahrooge, Elias (Ellis) K., family of, *123,* 182
Dahrooge, Malocke George, 28, 42, 57, *123,* 182
Dancing, 5, 51, 98–99, 111–112, 152–154, *168–169*
Daniels, Mitchell, 184
Danner, Pat, 184
Darabukkah (drum), 51, 111, 112, 153, 188
Dating, 159
David, Naphe, 239n.19
David, Samuel, *43,* 92, *170,* 218, 219
David, Solomon, 38
Davis, Edward L., 151
Davis Tower, 151, *167*
Debates, 115–116
Debs, Celia, 140
Debs, Charles G., 157
Debs, Eva, 140
Debs, James, 145
Debs, Salim, 55
Deeb, Margaret, 100, 239n.19
Dehumanization of Arabs, 204–206
Denial of ethnicity, 134, 189
Denny, Walter B., xv
Deportation of immigrants, 134–135
Diab, Najeeb M., 85–86
Diaries, 175
Discrimination. *See* Prejudice
Douma Ladies Charitable Society, 35

Dowd, David C., *170*
Dowd, George C., 158–159
Dowd, Mary, *129,* 158, *170,* 239n.19
Dowd, Michael, 156
Dowd, Nita B. (Mrs. Charles), 154
Dramas. *See* Plays
Drum and Fife and Bugle Corps. *See* Syrian American Drum Corps
Druze, 1, 18, 31, 33, 34, 35, 37, 50, 91, 110
Dry goods stores, 53, 55, 71, 73, 74, 78, 79, 80, 237n.12, 238n.15

E., Alice A., 20, 71, 94–95, 107–108
E., James. *See* Esper, James
E., Mary K. *See* Esper, Mary Khoury
E., Solomon, 83
Easter, 177
Eastern Orthodox Church, 135, 157, *195,* 211–221. *See also* Antiochian Orthodox Church
Eastern Orthodox Syrian Church: timeline of, 211–221; in Worcester, Mass., 32–33, 234n.24
Eastley, John, 96
Eddy, Col. and Mrs. William A., 143, 241n.14
Eddy's clothing stores, 236n.6
Education: and Friendly House, 142–145, *164, 165;* literacy and language, 104; literacy and marriage, 104. *See also* Children
El Morocco Restaurant, 55, 74–75, *194*
Elais, Nazer H., 76
Elderly, 178–182
Elias, Rosalind, 184
Ellis Island, 24
Emigration, 7, 18–22. *See also* Immigration
Emmanuel. *See* Abohatab
Employment. *See* Work
Endogamy. *See* Marriage
Engagements, 94–95
England. *See* Britain
English language, 6, 12, 19, 30, 67, 74, 104, 106, 172
Enterprises. *See* Business ventures; Work
Ephraim, Father (Peters, Donald J.), 187
Esper, George, 89
Esper, George Lufty, 183

Esper, James, 83, *130*
Esper, Joseph, 141
Esper, Mary Khoury, 21, 224
Esper Bros. Coal, Wood and Ice Company, 83, *89*
Ethnicity and ethnic groups, 29–30, 33, 49, 51, 225–226n.4; Albanian Americans, 33, 153; Armenian Americans, 33, 82, 132, 153, 231n.21; Assyrian Americans, 33; French Canadians, 50, 51, 57, 58, 77, 95, 104, 144, 145, 150, 153, 160, 235n.6, 236n.19; Greek Americans, 33, 77, 234n.24; Irish Americans, 49–50, 51, 59, 76–77, 95, 144, 150, 160; Italian Americans, 50, 51, 58–59, 77, 104, 144, 150, 160; Romanian Americans, 33; Russian Americans, 33, 103, 144; Turkish Americans, 132
Expositions and fairs, 6–7

F., Bashara K. *See* Forzley, Bashara K.
F., Elizabeth A. *See* Forsa, Elizabeth A.
Families: budgeting of family finances, 86–87; children's share of work in, 87; conflict resolution in, 116; dual-earner families, 68–70, 73, 74; extended family, 23, 65–66, 68, 101; genealogy of and record keeping for, 175–176, 207–210; gracious living and hospitality, 108–111, 142; household tasks in, 100–102; impact of prejudice on, 133–136, 204–206; joint spouse ownership of property, 87, 240n.22; and kinship bonds based on home towns, 107–108; parenting role in, 22–23, 68; photos of, *41, 42, 118, 123, 124, 128, 192, 193;* resourcefulness of, 176; return visits to Worcester, Mass., by, 39, 66; Roosevelt's intervention on behalf of immigrant children, 24–28, 233n.15; separation of, during immigration, 21, 22–23, 28–29; women's role in, 22–23, 68–70, 86–87, 99–101. *See also* Marriage
Fasting, 177–178
Fatool, Jennie, 157
Federation Herald, 152
Ferris, Philip J., 85

Fife and Drum Corps, 34. *See also* Syrian American Drum Corps
Fischer, Charles, 239n.19
"Flatiron" building, 54, 78, 235n.12
Fluehr-Lobban, Carolyn, xvi
Food, 6, 102–103, 109–110, 111, *128,* 142, 154, 172–175, 178, 189, *192*
Forsa, Elizabeth A., 73–74
Forzley, Almaza, 180
Forzley, Ameen Antoun, 17
Forzley, Bashara K., 17, 20, 70–71, *88,* 98, 108, 175, 180
Forzley, Fida K., 17, *129,* 175
Forzley, Rose, 175
France, 10–12, 14, 231–232n.26
Francis, Aziz G., 84, *90,* 115
French language, 12, 19, 30, 67, 104, 106
Friendly House, 141, 142–145, 146, *164–165,* 186
Funerals. *See* Burials and cemeteries; Military funeral
Fur and Leather Workers' Union, 75

G., Abraham. *See* Gammal, Abraham
G., Adele K., 114
G., Ernest J., 158
G., Faris, 31
G., Frank F. *See* George, Frank F.
G., Michael F. *See* George, Michael F.
G., Rose A., 69
G., Sayood B., 31
G., Simon. *See* George, Simon
G., Tanoos (Thomas) F. *See* George, Tanoos (Thomas) F.
G & K. *See* Graton & Knight Manufacturing Co.
Gage, Nicholas, 234n.24
Gammal, Abraham, *45, 94*
Gammal, Affeza H., 94
Gammal, Albert A., 82–83, 138, *162, 163*
Gammal, Albert A., Jr., 183
Gammal, Charles A., 82, 150, *162,* 238n.18
Gaze (Ghize), Mary, 68
George, Angelina Adams, 236n.2
George, Assafe (Asaffe), 57, 73, 224; family of, *123*
George, Charles Bashara A., 51, 57–58, 78, 79, 105, *123, 196*

George, Frank F., 31, 151, *196*
George, George A., *123*
George, John A., *123*
George, Joseph, 97
George, Joseph John. *See* Namer (Nemr) family
George, Malocke. *See* Dahrooge, Malocke George
George, Margaret Haddad (Mrs. Philip F.), 174
George, Michael A., *123*
George, Michael F., 141, 186
George, Patrick J., 158, 236n.2
George, Sarah (Sooriye) Haggar, 87, 94, *119*
George, Simon, 31, 57, 58, 82, 87, 94, *119*, 224
George, Sophie A., 93, *118*
George, Tanoos (Thomas) F., 71–73, 93, 141, 175, 224
George, Um Embass Mary (Tekla) Aboassaly-Skaff, *123, 224*
George Gregory Orchestra, 187
Germanos, Bishop. *See* Shehadi, Germanos
Ghiz, Elias (Eli), 113
Ghiz, Joseph, 106, 114, 214
Ghiz, Salim, 68
Ghize, Mary. *See* Gaze (Ghize), Mary
Gibran, Kahlil (philosopher and poet), 11, 32, 185, 218, 232n.4, 233–234n.22, 264
Gibran, Kahlil (sculptor, author, and cousin of philosopher), 185, 263–264
Gibran Memorial Garden, 264
Gibran Park at Copley Square, 263–264
Girl Scouts of the USA, 145
Golam, Agapius, 218
Grafton Hill. *See* Neighborhoods
Grapevine arbor, *128*
Graton & Knight Manufacturing Co., 21–22, *60*, 74–75, 232n.7
Great Britain. *See* Britain
Greater Syria, 225n.3. *See also* Ottoman Empire
Greek Orthodox Church, 212, 234n.24
Greetings and responses, 108–109, 178
Grocery stores, 55, 56, 86, 188, 238n.15

H., Adele H. *See* Abdow, Adele Haddad
H., Affeza. *See* Gammal, Affeza H.

H., Alice S. *See* Halal, Alice S.
H., Charles, 21–22, 74–75
H., Charles C. *See* Haddad, Charles C.
H., Eli A., 105
H., Esau, 22
H., Fred. *See* Haddad, Fred
H., George A., 68
H., Hannah (John) Abou Asaly, 22
H., Khazma M. A., 74
H., Lori, 91
H., Michael E., 31
H., Musa (Moses). *See* Haddad, Moses
H., Nazira, 104
H., Nimry S. *See* Husson, Nimry Saba
H., Nora A. *See* Hakim, Nora Antoun
H., S. Paul, 107
H., Sally, 79, *130*
H., Sooriya. *See* George, Sarah (Sooriye) Haggar
H., Sylvia. *See* Husson, Sylvia H.
H., Victoria, 139
Haddad, Abraham Isa, 148
Haddad, Akil E., 52, 55, 68, 87, 105, 129, 224
Haddad, Ann, 140
Haddad, Charles C., 107, 210
Haddad, Dahar, 68
Haddad, Edmund G., *130, 170*, 227n.7
Haddad, Edward N., *196*
Haddad, Elias F., 79, 96–97, *120*
Haddad, Emil, 185, 186
Haddad, Florence Abdo (Vina), *168*
Haddad, Fred, 75, *129, 196*
Haddad, Isabella (Maryam) A., 96–97, *120*
Haddad, Kalil J., 143
Haddad, Kuson J., 183
Haddad, Mary Miryam Boosahda, 28, 42
Haddad, Max, 56
Haddad, Moses, 22, 146
Haddad, Nabeha Merhige (Mrs. Abraham I.), 115, 134–135, 143, 148, 175, 177
Haddad, Naimer, *166*
Haddad, Najla, 87
Haddad, Nicholas, *129*
Haddad, Philip G., 116
Haddad, Richard, 186
Haddad, Salem Ferris, 17

Haddad, Tanoos (Thomas E.), 224
Haddad, Thomas, 55
Haddad, Walter E., 187
Haffty, Rofan, *162*
Hagar, 178
Hagopian, Elaine C., 33, 234n.26
Hajj (pilgrimages), 28, 177, 178
Hajjar, Effie Trebulsi, *123*
Hakim, Clifford, 187
Hakim, Nora Antoun, 21, 39, 71, 184
Halal, Alice S., 139
Hamwey, Helen B., *196*
Hannah, Yusuf. *See* George, Joseph John
Hannauer, Edmund R., 205
Hargrove, Gordon P., 143
Haroun El-Rashad, 113–114
Harvard University, 105, 182
Hassan, Mohammed, 36
Hate crimes, 205–206
Hattem, Maxine George, 185–186, 194
Hawaweeny, Raphael, 21, 94, 213, 226n.5, 233n.17, 239n.20
Hayeck, Ernest S., 183
Health examinations, 24–25, 28–29, *41*
Hicha, Paul, 214, 239n.19
Hilow, Assad, 158
Hilow, Catherine Anna, 182
Hitti, Philip K., 141, 231n.21
Hoar, George Frisbie. *See* Namer (Nemr) family
Hoffiz, Benjamin T., 214
Holmes, Pehr G., 135
Homeland ties, 39–40, 56, 81, 131
Honor, 65, 68
Hoskins, Franklin E., 143
Hospitality, 39, 108–111, 142
Houghton, Louise Seymour, 6, 67–68, 70
Hourani, Albert, 5, 230n.13
Households. *See* Families
Husson, Makhool, 53, 68, 86
Husson, Michael (Archpriest), 189–190
Husson, Michael M. (1860–1939), *61*, 68, 92, 93, *117*, 140, 171, 189, 214, 215, 217, 219
Husson, Nicholas, 189
Husson, Nimry Saba, 53, 68, 86
Husson, Raphael, 113, 189, 217
Husson, Sylvia H., 150

Hyder, Edward G., 176, 188
Hyder, Joseph G., 159

Ibrahim (Abraham), Prophet, 178, 211
Ice business, 83, *89*
Id al-Adha (Eid al-Adha), 177, 178
Id al-Fitr (Eid al-Fitr), 177, 178
Immigration: adventure as reason for, 7, 20; and Anglicized names and ethnic confusion, 29–30; anti-immigration legislation, 132, 133–134; and Castle Garden, 23–24; deportation of immigrants, 134–135; in 1880s or earlier, 7–8, 18, 222–225n.2; and Ellis Island, 24; and health examinations, 24–25, 28–29, *41*; listing of early migrants, 223–224; missionaries' influence on, 5–6; and overpopulation, 17–18; peak immigration years to U.S., 18; recruitment for immigration to U.S., 7, 21–22; separation of families, 21, 22–23, 28–29
Integration patterns: church school training and other youth activities, 147–148; community interaction at public celebrations, 148–154, 156–158; community support programs, 141–148; and denial of ethnicity, 134, 189; multicultural neighborhoods, 49–50; Syrian American Club/Association, 150
Intermarriage, 159
Inventions, 82, 238n.18
Ishmael (son of Abraham), 178, 211
Islam: and Allah (God), 1, 37, 108; Hajj, 28, 177, 178; hospitality, 39, 108–111, 142; and Muhammad (the Prophet), 1, 28, 35–36, 37, 177; Quran, 1, 175, 177; religious celebrations of, 177–178; spread of, 1. *See also* Muslims
Islamic Society of Greater Worcester, 37, 50
Islamic Society of North America (ISNA), 264
Israel, 12, 204. *See also* Middle East conflict
Issa, Darrel, 184

Jabal Lubnan (Mount Lebanon), 2–3, 7, 14, 18, 231n.21

Jabara, Abdeen, 4
Jabbour, Emilia A., 239n.20
Jabour, Jabour "Joe," 74
Jahleelee, Milhem, 103
Jalboot, Alex, 129
Jalboot, Rose, 129
Jerusalem, 5, 6, 28
Jews. See Judaism
Jobs. See Work
John, Chris, 184
Joseph, Massoud, 85
Journalism. See Newspapers; Periodicals
Judaism, 1, 5, 178
Junior League of Worcester, 141–144

K., Ethel H. M., 171
K., George, 87
K., George N. (Bob). See Kalil, George N.
    (Bob)
K., Hannah. See Kaneb, Hannah John
K., Helen, 106
K., Kenneth, 81, 87, 107, 152
K., Mary, 78
K., Mike, 87
Kakaty, Edward, 195
Kalil, George N. (Bob), 23, 106–107, 144,
    196
Kalil, Irma, 145
Kalil, Issa, 74
Kalil, James, 121, 157
Kalil, Nicholas, 78
Kalil, Victoria Shakour, 121
Kaneb, Hannah John, 81, 95
Kaneb, Nerzeh Dadah, 38, 95
Karakey, Samuel, 144
Kassab, Ananias, 218
Kassab, Salem, 112–113
Katrina, Michael, 139, 241n.10
Kawkab America (newspaper), 85–86,
    239–240n.20
Kenney, Helen, 146–147
Khoury, Mary, 224
Know-Nothingism, 134
Kouri, Victoria Abisamra, 124
Kouri, William G., 141

Labor movement, 75, 76–77
LaHood, Ray, 184

Lajoie, Melanie, 153–154
Landownership, 8, 13, 14–16, 56–59, 81,
    82, 83, 143, 179. See also Work
Language: bilingualism of immigrants, 12,
    19, 103, 106; communication across
    the language barrier, 51, 74; English, 6;
    multilingualism of immigrants, 67, 106;
    trilingualism of immigrants, 12, 68, 85,
    106. See also Arabic language; Semitic
    language
Lantz, Marian G., 143
League of Nations, 10–11
Lebanese, 2–3, 7, 8, 74–75, 160
Lebanon: created about 1923, 11; geogra-
    phy of, 11; history of, 11–12; immigrants
    from, 2–3, 8, 17, 37; Israeli invasion of
    (1978), 12; mandate system in, 10–11,
    12, 232n.26; map of, 10; missionaries
    in, 5; peddlers from, 66
Lebanon, Mount (Jabal Lubnan), 2–3, 7,
    14, 18, 231n.21
Lebanon Youth Society, 35
LeBesque, Frances Boosahda Miles, 127,
    136
Leisure activities: in coffeehouses/coffee
    parlors, 79; Friendly House, 141, 142–
    145, 146, 164; musical shows, 156; plays,
    112–114, 129–130, 156; song about,
    154–156; testimonials and banquets,
    156–158, 170, 189–190
Lenorson, Samuel, Jr., 151
Leon, Judith "Judie," 205
Lian, Emeline Amelia, 56, 97
Lian, George J., 152, 183
Lian, Jacob. See Lian, Yacoub Tunous
    (Jacob Thomas)
Lian, Joseph L., Jr., 183
Lian, Nazira, 120
Lian, Yacoub Tunous (Jacob Thomas), 56,
    143, 179
Libraries, 104, 187
Lingua franca, 4, 230n.12
Literacy. See Education
Literature: Arabic, 85, 106–107, 171–
    172; influence of, on West, 4, 228n.9;
    poetry, 5, 114, 232n.4; Syrian-American
    Literary Association, Maine, 85
Lotuff, Joseph, 158

Lotuff, Robert G., 153
Lotuff, Salim "Sam," *168*

M., Evelyn A. *See* Menconi, Evelyn Abdalah
M., Frances B. *See* Lebesque, Frances Boosahda Miles
M., Mae M., 94, 100–101, 103
M., Tekla (Annie) H. A. *See* Mahassel, Tekla (Annie) H. A.
MacKoul, Raymond J., *125*
Mahassel, Tekla (Annie) H. A., 19, 22
Mahiethett Society, Young, 34–35, 44, 48, 200–203
Mahrajhans, 188
Makkah, pilgrimage to, 28, 177
Maloof, M. M., 137, 231n.21
Malooly, Nicholas, 138, 139
Mandate system, 10–11, *12*
Mansour, Farrar, 71
Mardi Gras, 239n.19
Maria, Francis "Frank," 182–183
Maronites, 3, 33, 50, 84, 157, 227n.7, 232n.26
Marriage: arranged, 40, 91–94; intermarriage, 159; and literacy, 104; and nuptial engagements, 94–95; remarriage, 19–20; and wedding celebrations, 91, 95–99, *119–121. See also* Families
Massachusetts, 30, 37, 76–77, 82, 150–151. *See also* Boston, Mass.; Worcester, Mass.
Massachusetts Institute of Technology, 83
Massad, Anthony, 158
Massad, David G. "Duddie," 186
Massad, Peter Paul, 175
Massad, Philip M., 158
Massad, Robert B., 175
Mate selection. *See* Arranged marriages
Mathematics, 4, 228n.9
Maykel, Albert E., 159, 183
Maykel, Charlie, 135
Maykel, Michael, 68
Maykel, Mitchell K., 135, 148, 237
McCoy, Dr. John, 50
Meadows, The. *See* Neighborhoods
Mecca. *See* Makkah

Mehdi, Beverlee Turner, 225n.2
Melkites, 33, 96–97, 112–113, 147, 157, *195,* 234n.23
Memorials, 35, 138–141, 151
Menconi, Evelyn Abdalah, xv, 77, 104, *169, 192*
Merchandising. *See* Peddlers
Messara, Gerasimos, 214
Methodists, 33, 147–148
Middle East conflict, 12, 182–183, 204–206
Midwives, 82
Migration. *See* Immigration
Mijwiz (musical instrument), 51
Military funeral, 139–140, *163*
Military service, *123,* 134, 136–141, 149, 151, *161–163,* 185, 187, 189, 241nn.10–11. *See also* World War I; World War II
Milk wagons, 53, 54
Millet system, 5
Missionaries, 5–6
Mitchell, Angelina R., 70
Mitchell, George, 184
Mitchell, Malvina, *127,* 184
Mitchell, Nassif (Nasif), 70, 133
Mitchell, Richard P., 185
Moffett, Toby, 184
Moossa, Anthony "Tony," 73, 180, *193*
Moossa, Michael, *193*
Moossa (Moosa), Walter J., 153, 158, 183
Moschos, Dean M., 234n.24
Moslem [Muslim] Brotherhood Association, 35, 37, 46
Mount Lebanon. *See* Jabal Lubnan
Muhammad (the Prophet), 1, 28, 35–36, 37, 177, 212
Multiculturalism, 144. *See also* Ethnicity and ethnic groups
Music and musicians, 5, 21, 34, 51, 97, 99, 103, 111, 148–150, 153–156, *162, 168–169,* 184, *185–186,* 187, 188, *194*
Music Festival, 154, 156
Musical shows, 156
Muslim/Moslem Brotherhood Association, 35, 37, 46
Muslims, 50; charitable organizations of, 35–38; definition of, 37; and Hajj, 28, 177, 178; population worldwide, 4; pri-

vate organizations, 261, 264; religious celebrations of, 177–178; in Spain, 4, 228n.9. *See also* Islam

Mustaffa, Murad, 36

Mutassarifiah, 14. *See also* Jabal Lubnan

Myrra Bearing Women Society, 38–39, *48*

N., Sadie B. *See* Namee, Sadie B.

Nader, Ralph, 185

Naff, Alixa, xv, 132, 225n.3, 265

Najemy, Bertha Peters, 184

Najemy, George R., 205

Najemy, John, 187

Najemy, Robert E., 187

Namee, Joseph, *88–89*

Namee, Sadie B., 84, 179, 190

Namer (Nemr) family, 24–28, 148, 233nn.9–16

Nasif, George, 78

Nasseem, N., 85

Nassif, Joseph G., *166*

National Association of Federations of Syrian and Lebanese American Clubs, 152

National Council of Churches, 183

National Herald, 152

Nativism, 133–134

Naturalization, 131–133

Nawfel, Rajie, 85

Nedder, J. Richard "Dick," 186

Needlework, 146

Neighborhoods: Chandler Hill (Bell Hill), 49, 59, 234n.1; communication across the language barrier in, 51; *harrate tahta* (The Meadows), 49, 50, 59, *194*; multicultural and integrated neighborhoods, 49, 59, 160; *el-saha,* 51–55, 58–59; *eltellee* (Oak Hill, Grafton Hill), 49–59, 61–64, 160, *194*, 234n.1

Nejaimey, Kamel, 54, 78

Nejaimey, Toby, 138

Nemr family. *See* Namer (Nemr) family

Networks, 30–39, 77–79

Newspapers, 84–86, 104, 152, 184, 239–240n.20

Norfolk Street, 53–55, 62, *63*

Nuptial engagements, 94–95

Nutt, Charles, 81–82

Oak Hill. *See* Neighborhoods

Oakar, Mary Rose, 184

Occupations. *See* Work

Ofiesh, Aftimos, 214, 215, 219

Oil business, 81

Omar, Osman, 36

Oratory, 114–115

Organizations: church-related, 38–39, *48*; private-sector, 33–38, 43–47, 85, 148–153, 158–159, 182, 197–203, 262; women's, 35, 38–39, 141–145, 151, 174. *See also specific organizations*

Oriental rugs, 81–82

Orthodox Brotherhood Society. *See* Syrian Brotherhood Orthodox Society

Orthodox Church in America, 33, 219, 221, 234n.25

Osman (Othman of Osmanli dynasty), 4

Ottoman Empire, 2–5, 7, 9, 18, 230–231nn.13,21

Our Lady of Perpetual Help Church, 112, 114, 147

P., Bernice E., 179–180

P., George "Bitar," 172

P., Julia A., 69

P., Louis, 55

Palestine: creation of Israel (1948), 204; mandate system in, 10–11, *12*; as national entity after World War I, 3; in Ottoman Empire, 4; schools in, 85, 143

Palestine Liberation Organization, 205

Palestine National Council, 205

Palestinians, 2–3, 7, 8, 160, 225n.3. *See also* Palestine

Parades, 105, 148, 150–151, 167

Parenting role, 22–23, 68, 87

Patents, 82, 238n.18

Patriotism. *See* Military service

Patronymic and family name, 223

Peddlers: cultural traits of, 65–66; hardships of, 66–67, 71–74; language skills of, 67, 68, 74, 104; men and women working together, 68–70, 73, 74; pack peddling, 65–73, *88*; travel of, 8, 20, 66–68, 71–73, 80–81, *88–89*; wares of, 70, 71, *89*; women, 53, 68–70, 73, 74

Peddlers, geographic areas covered by
—Canada, 19, 78, 190, 215, 216, 218
—Eastern U.S.: Connecticut, 37;
  Maine, 85, 182; Massachussetts, 5,
  7–8, 30, 36, 68, 72, 82, 83, 94, 157,
  183; New York, 2, 80, 94, 216, 218;
  Ohio, 20, 80, 216, 218; Pennsylva-
  nia, 22; Rhode Island, 37; Vermont,
  96; West Virginia, 80
—Mexico, 216
—Midwestern and southwestern U.S.:
  Illinois, 34, 73–74, 92; Iowa, 92;
  Kansas, 189, 190; Michigan, 189;
  Nebraska, 38; Oklahoma, 189;
  Texas, 38, 189
—South America, 8, 19, 22, 25, 39, 86,
  104, 190
Periodicals. *See* Newspapers
Peters, Annie Bourisk (Mrs. Joseph T.), 115
Peters, Bertha, 184
Peters, Donald J., 187
Peters, Joseph S., *161*, 187
Peters, Sroor, 157, 241n.11
Philadelphia Centennial Exposition
  (1876), 6
Philosophy, 228n.9
Phoenicians, 3, 227n.8
Photography studio, 69
Pike, Lena (Dadah), *196*
Pilgrimages, 28, 177, 178
"Pilgrims to America" pageant, 238–239n.19
Plays, 112–114, *129–130, 156*
Poetry, 5, 114, 147, 149, 187, 232n.4,
  239n.19
Political activities, 150, 183–184
Postage stamp, 178
Prayer, 57, 87, 110
Prayer beads, 110
Prejudice, 133–136, 204–206
Presbyterians, 33, 239n.19
Priest, Terri, 187
Princess Venus of England, 114, *130*
Princeton University, 141, 185
Proclamation of Arab-American Day, 4,
  228–230n.10
Prophet. *See* Muhammad
Protestants, 5–6, 33, 148. *See also* Baptists;
  Methodists; Presbyterians

Public celebrations: and private-sector
  organizations, 150–154; rededication
  of Worcester Memorial Auditorium,
  153; Roosevelt's visit to Worcester, 148;
  Syrian American Club, 150–152; Syrian
  American Drum Corps, 34, 148–150,
  156, 157; Worcester Music Festival, 154,
  156. *See also* Organizations: private-
  sector
Publishers, 84–86, *90*
Pyramid Dance Group, 153–154

Quran, 1, 175, 177

R., Miryam (Mary) Debs, 23, 84, 100
R., S., 179–180
R., Takala H. *See* Rizkalla, Takala H.
Raad, Ernest N. *See* Namer (Nemr)
  family
Race classification system, 132–133
Rachid, Salim, 55
Rahaim, Nelson T., 75
Rahall, Nick, 184
Railroad station, 8, *60*
Ramadhan, 177–178
Rami, John, 77
Rankin, Lydia Haddad, 186–187
Raphael, Bishop. *See* Hawaweeny, Raphael
Rashad, Haroun el- (Harun ar-Rashid),
  Caliph, 113–114
Raudat, Al- (magazine), 84
Real estate. *See* Landownership
Recipes. *See* Food
Red Cross, *165*
Religion. *See* Christianity; Druze; Eastern
  Orthodox Syrian Church; Islam; Juda-
  ism; Maronites; Melkites; Muslims;
  Protestants; Roman Catholic Church
Remarriage, 19–20
Resource persons for immigrants. *See*
  Networks
Resourcefulness, 176
Restaurants, *63*, 74–75, 77, 78–79, *169*,
  184–185, *194*
Rihbany, Abraham Mitrie, 99–100
Rizkalla, Salem, 86
Rizkalla, Takala H., 19, 86, 182
Rochette, Salem, 55

Roman Catholic Church, 50, 58, 95, 96–97, 147, 235n.6
Rondeau Court, 57
Roosevelt, Theodore, 24–28, 148, 233n.15
Rug makers and traders, 81–82
Russell, Lillian G., 236n.2
Russia, 14, 18, 33, 135–136, 232n.26, 238n.19
Russian Orthodox Church, 135, 212, 239n.19

S., Adele, 100
S., Doris A., 22
S., Eli. See Salloum, Eli
S., George, 52–53, 159
S., Janet H., 111, 142, 196
S., Lillian G. See Shoucair, Lillian George
S., Louise, 30–31
S., Mary. See Saba (Saber), Mary
S., Michael. See Sulvane, Michael
S., Sam, 171
S., Violet N., 171
Saayeke, Naahim, 52
Saayeke, Shaker (Syiegh, later Syiek), 52, 78, 87
Saayeke, Zamorde H., 87
Saba (Saber), Mary, 113–114, 129, 151, 184
Saidi, Joseph, 157–158, 195
St. George Orthodox Church/Cathedral: Arabic school at, 105; buildings and location of, 58, 61, 140, 236n.26; testimonials and banquets at, 157, 158, 189–190; women's societies of, 38–39, 48, 174. See also Syrian Orthodox Church
St. Jude Children's Research Hospital, 158–159, 182, 186. See also ALSAC
St. Louis Fair (1904), 7
Saladin. See Salah El-Deen
Salah El-Deen, 112–113, 129–130
Salem, Edward, 166, 175
Salesmen/saleswomen. See Peddlers
Saliba, Najib, 171
Saliba, Philip, 219
Salih, Mrs. Chikri D., 122
Salloom, Salem, 74
Salloom and Sons, 236n.6
Salloum, Eli, 20, 66, 78–79

Salloum, Thamal (David G.), 63, 78–79
Sayegh, Fayez A., 205
Scheffel, Jane Esper, 168
Scholars, 85, 105, 185, 187
Schools. See Education
Schuerie (Schwerie), C. Catherine/Katerina, 15–16
Science, 4, 82–83, 227–228n.9, 238–239nn.18–19
Search for Justice and Equality in Palestine/Israel, 204–205
Sednawi, Michael, 139, 241n.11
Selim, Nazer (Nerzeh) Dadah, 95
Semitic language, 222n.1
Sergeant, Diggory, 151
Sèvres, Treaty of (1920), 4
Shadyac, Richard C., 260
Shafeeka, Sophie Ferage, 39
Shaia, Peter A., 84, 90
Shalala, Donna, 184
Shamie, John, 226n.5
Shamon, Elias F., 158
Shannon, Eli, 158
Shannon, Malaky M. Coury, 82
Shannon, Mary C., 82, 183
Shedd, Carol Johnson, xvi
Shehadi, Germanos, 140, 213, 214, 215, 216
Sherer, C. T., 147
Shoucair, Edmund, 167
Shoucair, Lillian George, 82, 86, 94, 167, 196, 239–240n.20
Shoucair, Said, 86, 239n.20
Shweire, Afifi C., 122
Smithsonian Institution (Arab American Collection), 265
Snowstorms, 67, 73–74, 77
"Song Reminiscences of the Thirties," 154–156
Songs. See Music and musicians
Souda, Emil, 162
South American businesses, 86
Southwick, Albert B., 49
Spain, 4, 9, 21, 228n.9
Star News and Pictorial, 184
Steiner, Edward A., 24–28
Stevens, Anthony J., 186
Storytelling, 5, 111
Strikes, 76–77

Suleiman, Michael W., 240n.20
Sulvane, Leo, 181
Sulvane, Michael, 30, 79, 181, *193*
Sununu, John, 183–184
Sununu, John E., 187
Support systems: business networking, 77–79; church-related organizations and programs, 38–39, 147–148; community support programs, 141–148; kindergarten program, 146–147; kinship bonds based on home towns, 107–108; networks for immigrants, 30–39; private-sector organizations, 33–38, 43–47. *See also specific organizations and churches*
Swydan, Anne, 186
Swydan, Fred V. (Vladimir), 145–146
Swydan, Hafeeza Khoury, 106
Swydan, Herbert, 145
Swydan, Hind-Helene. *See* Abusamra, Hind-Helene
Swydan, Shokri K., 38, 85, 106, 135–136, 157, 238–239n.19, 241n.11
Syiek, Nazira Lian, *120*
Syiek family. *See* Saayeke
Syria: in Arab Empire, 4; civil war in, 14; immigrants from, 2–3, 7, 8, 18, 24–28, 70, 225n.3, 231n.21; mandate system in, 10–11, *12*, 232n.26; missionaries in, 5; as national entity after World War I, 3; peddlers in, 66; restaurants in, 78; schools in, 85. *See also* Syrians
Syrian-American Athletic Club, 34
Syrian-American Review, 85
Syrian American Club/Association, 145, 150–152
Syrian American Drum Corps, 34, 148–150, 156, 157, *166*
Syrian American Federation of New England, 150
Syrian-American Literary Association, 85
Syrian and Lebanese American Association Auxiliary, 151
Syrian and Lebanese American Federation of the Eastern States, 151–152, 182
Syrian bread bakeries, 78, 173
Syrian Brotherhood Orthodox Society, 33–34, 43–45, 197–200

Syrian Cooking, 174
Syrian Daily Eagle, 35, 38, 85
Syrian-Lebanese American Association, 151–152
Syrian Lebanese Cooking, 174
Syrian-Lebanese Folk Dance Group, 154
Syrian Orthodox Church, 32–33, 42, 55–56, 58, 92, 95, *194*, 234n.24, 236n.19. *See also* St. George Orthodox Church/Cathedral
Syrians, 2–3, 7, 8, 76–79, 137–138, 145, 160, 225nn.2–3, 226–227nn.5–6. *See also* Syria

T., Genevieve M., 23, 159
T., Margaret J., 103
Table etiquette, 109–110
Talbot, Russell P., 145, 241n.19
Teachers. *See* Education; Scholars
Tellee, el-. See Neighborhoods
Testimonials and banquets, 156–158, *170*, 189–190
Textile industry, 21, 76–77, 84
Theater. *See* Plays
Theodosios, Archbishop, 218
Thomas, Danny, 158. *See also* St. Jude Children's Research Hospital
Thomas, Helen, 184
Thomas, Tony, 184
Tikhon, Bishop, 32, 213, 215. *See also* Orthodox Church in America
Timeline of Eastern Orthodox Syrian Church, 211–221
Tony Agbay and the Continentals, 186, 187
Traditions. *See* Cultural traditions
Trebulsi, Saada (Sadie), *123*
Turkey, 3, 4, 33, 37, 133

Ud, el- (musical instrument). *See* Music and musicians
Union Railroad Station (Worcester, Mass.), 8, *60*
Unions. *See* Labor movement
United Syrian Christian Association of North America, 38
United Way of America, 185, 186
Upson, Stephen, 221, 226n.5

Victor (Viktor), Bishop. *See* Aboassaly, Victor

W., Freeda H., 94
Waked (Wakid), Esther (Estelle). *See* Abisamra, Esther (Estelle) W.
Warde, Polycarpe, 114, *130*
Watchorn, Robert, 24, 27
Wedding celebrations. *See* Marriage
Wedding gowns, 96, 97–98, *119–121*
Westernization. *See* Integration patterns
Williams, Abraham, 51
Williams, David, 187
Winslow, Samuel E., 156–157
Women, 7; breastfeeding by, 101; budgeting of family finances by, 86–87; clothing for, 101, *122–125*, 140; college education for, 183, 184; economic role of, 68–70, 86–87; elderly, 180–182, 223–224; family role of, 22–23, 68–70, 86–87, 99–101; joint ownership of property by, 87, 240n.22; military service by, 140; and needlework, 146; organizations for, 35, 38–39, *48*, 141–145, 151, 174; and parenting role, 22–23, 68; peddling by, 53, 68–70, 73, 74; position of Arab-American women in Arab culture, 99–101; wedding gowns for, 96, 97–98, *119–121*. *See also* Families; Marriage
Wood, Charles Albert, 141
Wood, James Albert, 141
Wood, Michael Albert, 141
Worcester, Mass.: Arab immigration to, 7–8; description of, 7–8, 225–226n.4; landownership in, *13*, 14–16, 56–59; network of communication in, 30–39,

77–79; return visits to, 39, 66. *See also specific churches and organizations;* Work
Worcester County Music Association, 154
Worcester Employment Society, 141, 142
Worcester Memorial Auditorium rededication, 153–154
Worcester Music Festival, 154, 156
Work: and business networking centers, 77–79; business ventures, 3, 8, 52–58, 63, 69, 71, 73, 74, 77–86, 179, 186, 188, 225–226n.4, 236nn.2,6, 237–238nn.10–15; children's share of, 87; and cultural traits, 8, 11, 39, 65–66, 81, 87; leather workers, 21–22, 74–75, 232n.7; moving to find work, 83–84; and occupational progression, 8, 80–87, 182–184; occupations of immigrants, 18–19; sacrifices and hardships for economic survival, 11; and South American businesses, 86; in textile mills, 76–77; Worcester Employment Society, 141, 142. *See also* Landownership; Peddlers
World expositions, 6–7
World War I, 3, 4, 11, 22, 134–135, 136–140, *161–163*, 181, 187, 189, 226–227n.6, 232n.26, 241nn.10–11
World War II, 37, 140–141, 149, 151, 181, 238n.18

Yale, William, 5, 230n.13
Young Mahiethett Society, 34–35, 44, *48*, 200–203
Younis, Adele L., 6–7, 11, 225n.2

Zakhem, Joseph G., 38
Zharraghat, 98